. . .

LANGUAGE, HISTORY, AND IDENTITY

LANGUAGE, HISTORY, AND IDENTITY

Ethnolinguistic Studies of the Arizona Tewa

■ ■ ■

PAUL V. KROSKRITY

■ ■ ■

THE UNIVERSITY OF ARIZONA PRESS
Tucson & London

The University of Arizona Press
Copyright © 1993
The Arizona Board of Regents
All rights reserved

This book is printed on acid-free, archival-quality paper.
Manufactured in the United States of America
98 97 96 95 94 93   6 5 4 3 2 1

Library of Congress Cataloging-in-Publication Data

Kroskrity, Paul V., 1949–
    Language, history, and identity: ethnolinguistic studies of the Arizona
Tewa / Paul V. Kroskrity.
        p.   cm.
    Includes bibliographical references and index.
    ISBN 0-8165-1427-5 (alk. paper)
    1. Tewa language—Arizona—Social aspects.   2. Tewa language.
3. Tewa Indians—Ethnic identity.   I. Title.
PM2431.K76   1993   93-7645
497'.49—dc20   CIP

British Cataloguing-in-Publication Data
A catalogue record for this book is available from the British Library.

Dedicated to all my teachers and all my students
and to the discourse that unites us,
but especially to the memories of

Dewey Healing,

Albert Yava,

Carl Voegelin,

Flo Voegelin,

and

Judith Friedman Hansen.

■ ■ ■

CONTENTS

■ ■ ■

TABLES

■   ■   ■

ACKNOWLEDGMENTS

The studies presented in this volume are based on about three and a half years of field research conducted between 1973 and 1989 on and around Tewa Village, First Mesa of the Hopi Reservation in northern Arizona. Although it is impossible to properly recognize all the people whose contributions have informed this work, I will do my best to uphold the acknowledgment tradition.

I am most indebted to the many Arizona Tewa people who provided the comradery and trust on which all intercultural understanding is based. During my research no one helped me more than Dewey Healing to understand the Tewa language and people. His efforts at translation ran in two directions as he helped make culturally distant Tewa texts more accessible to me, on the one hand, and actively interpreted and defended my own work, often the product of our collaboration, to a larger Tewa community. Other important teachers include Albert Yava, Edith Nash, Juanita Healing, and a host of other individuals who would prefer not to be singled out. These and others taught me a great deal not only about Tewa language structure and use but also provided me with many lessons of inestimable value about the importance of family, the value of traditions, and the importance of adapting to diversity. To all of you, I say *kunda*.

Although this book is about the Arizona Tewa, it is also about linguistic anthropology and the larger tradition of academic anthropology of which it is a part. I owe my induction into this community to Carl and Flo Voegelin. Their enthusiasm and guidance helped to make fieldwork and communication between native and academic communities enjoyable.

Other people who provided critical guidance, wisdom, and encouragement during my academic initiation include Charles Bird, Allen Grimshaw, Ray DeMallie, and Judith Friedman Hansen. Many people commented on papers and chapters that have become a part of this book. They include Keith Basso, Alton Becker, Robert Black, Elizabeth Brandt, Jane H. Hill, Dell H. Hymes, Wick Miller, Michael Moerman, Alfonso Ortiz, Michael Silverstein, Dennis Tedlock, and Laurel Watkins. Thanks to all.

While I find it easier to recall the individuals who assisted me in the research presented here, I would like to acknowledge the many institutions that supported my research over the past few decades. These are the Department of Anthropology, Indiana University; the Phillips Fund of the American Philosophical Society; the National Endowment for the Humanities; the Melville and Elizabeth Jacobs Fund of the Whatcom Museum of Science and Art; the Academic Senate of the University of California, Los Angeles; and the Institute of American Cultures Grant administered through the American Indian Studies Center, University of California. To all these institutions and the individuals behind their decisions to support my research, I am grateful for the sustaining support.

Also worthy of recognition for their roles in bringing this volume into print are a variety of people associated with the University of Arizona Press. Greg McNamee was responsible for securing the original contract. Christine Szuter made sure the manuscript did not fall between the cracks. Virginia Purcell carefully copyedited the manuscript and made many useful suggestions. Marie Webner ably guided the manuscript to publication. To all, thanks for your interest, expertise, and patience.

Last but certainly not least, I would like to thank the members of my family for their behind-the-scenes support of my research. Over the years, my wife Jackie has provided an unmeasurable range of supportive activities, always providing timely encouragement, insightful observations, and relief from family responsibilities during critical periods of research and writing. I would also like to thank my children, Jason, Sarah, and Eric, for their occasional interest in the peoples and cultures that have been my professional preoccupation, for their patience, and for their energizing diversion. I cannot forget also to thank my parents, Sid and Martha Kroskrity, for their steady support over the years, and to my in-laws, Max Gordon and Vira Gordon, for their confidence and support. To one and all, many thanks.

Los Angeles

October 1992

■ ■ ■

GUIDE TO THE PRONUNCIATION
OF ARIZONA TEWA TERMS

Because this book has been designed for a wider audience than professional linguists, I have opted for a slightly less technical orthography than that normally employed by those who study American Indian languages. The following table organizes information so that interested readers can better approximate the normal pronunciation of Tewa terms and linguists can relate the orthography used here to those normally employed by Americanists (such as that used in the *Handbook of North American Indians*).

SYMBOL	AMERICANIST USAGE	PRONUNCIATION
b	b	*b* as in "*b*oy"
d	d	*d* as in "*d*og"
g	g	*g* as in "*g*irl"
c	c	*ts* as in "i*ts*"
p	p	*p* as in "s*p*at"
t	t	*t* as in "s*t*op"
k	k	*k* as in "s*k*in"
kw	k^w	*qu* as in "se*qu*in"

ky	k^y	*ky* as in "bac*ky*ard"
h	h	*h* as in "*h*ot"
'	ʔ	the stop, or catch, between
c', p', t', k'		syllables of "oh-oh." When
kw'	k$^{w'}$	it occurs with any of these con-
ky'	k$^{y'}$	sonants, it adds complete glot-
		tal closure to the resulting
		sound.
ph	p^h	*p* as in "*p*art"
th	t^h	*t* as in "*t*ar"
kh	k^h	*k* as in "*k*ernel"
kyh	k^{yh}	similar to *y* in "*y*olk" if it is pre-
		ceded with a *k*
kwh	k^{wh}	*qu* as in "*qu*een"
l	l	*l* as in "*l*emon"
m	m	*m* as in "*m*ore"
n	n, ŋ	*n* as in "*n*o"
hw	h^w	similar to English "*wh*at" when
		pronounced with an initial *h*
hy	h^y	similar to English "*y*ellow" when
		pronounced with an initial *h*
w	w	*w* as in "*w*et"
y	y	*y* as in "*y*et"
a	a	*a* as in "f*a*ther"
e	e	*a* as in "t*a*ste"
ɛ	ɛ	*e* as in "r*e*d"
i	i	*ee* as in "m*ee*t"
o	o	*o* as in "t*o*ne"
u	u	*u* as in "t*u*ne"
a̧, ɛ̧, ȩ, i̧, o̧, u̧		same as above but pronounced
		with nasal resonation

á, ɛ́, é, í, ó, ú   same as above but pronounced
                         with a higher pitch or "tone"

a:, ɛ:, e:, i:,   same as above but vowel is pro-
   o:, u: nounced for a slightly longer
                         duration

Note: Arizona Tewa vowels permit various combinations of nasality, tone, and length.

. . .

LANGUAGE, HISTORY, AND IDENTITY

1

· · ·

INTRODUCTION: ARIZONA TEWA LANGUAGE,
HISTORY, AND IDENTITY

> Far far away, where shells are shaken by the waves,
> From there the Tewa People came bearing corn.
> This is what our elders have always said,
> This is what our grandmothers have always said.
>
> Heeding their words, we exchange greetings
> and kind words here.
> This is how we should live our lives!
> How far will we carry forth our Tewa Language,
> We elders, as we live our days?
>
> When I think about this,
> I look to my grandchildren and great-grandchildren,
> And I embrace them.
> May our people live on!
> (text of a Ya:niwɛ song composed by Dewey Healing[1])

For many readers, both general and academic, the terms *language, history,* and *identity* suggest three analytically distinct categories; each with its own tradition of specialized investigation. Yet for the Arizona Tewa people these notions are unified in their collective and individual experience in a manner unsurpassed by any other people. Their ancestors brought a distinctive language to the Hopi mesas almost 300 years ago. Today this language continues to be spoken by their descendants and has become the most powerful symbol of their still discrete ethnic identity, as

well as the means for transmitting their unique history to new generations of Arizona Tewa people. The purpose of this book is to examine
and explore the experienced unity of language, history, and identity for
the Arizona Tewa.

There is a very different awareness of this group of about 600 Native
Americans by the general public and by professional anthropologists. In
1980 *The Arizona Republic*, a Phoenix-based daily newspaper, printed
an informative series of feature articles on the state's sixteen Indian tribes.
Writing about the Arizona Tewa, staff writer John A. Winters opened his
feature story in the following way:

> They are the least known of Arizona's Indian peoples. Mention of the Mari-
> copa or the Chemehuevi may bring a glint of recognition to the eyes of
> some of the uninitiated. But knowledge of the Tewa is a sure sign of the
> anthropologist.
>
> No reservation bears their name. No sign identifies their village. No barrier
> delineates it. They live in a circle within a circle, surrounded by the Hopi,
> who are, in turn, surrounded by the Navajo.
>
> Only a pile of stones marks the boundary line between the Tewa Village
> of Hano at the Eastern end of the First Mesa and the Hopi Villages of Sicho-
> movi and Walpi to the west. Yet the Tewa maintain their own language and
> culture separate from those of the Hopi.

At the time this feature series originally ran, I was in my seventh con-
secutive year of research on the Arizona Tewa and their language and
was quite shocked to learn that the group which I had devoted so much
time to studying was so generally unknown. After all, among anthropologists, the Arizona Tewa enjoyed considerable renown.

This attention primarily resulted from the prodigious ethnographic
achievements of Edward P. Dozier. In an early paper and monograph
(Dozier 1951, 1954), he documented the "resistance to acculturation and
assimilation" which this tiny group displayed in its 250 years of adaptation to the Hopi after the immigration of its ancestors from their former
location in the Rio Grande River valley. His popular ethnographic text,
Hano, A Tewa Indian Community in Arizona (Dozier 1966a) provided
many anthropology students with vivid descriptions of the daily lives of
this transplanted Pueblo group. What made, and continues to make,
these works even more remarkable was the fact that Dozier himself was
Tewa, though hailing not from the Arizona pueblo but from the New

Mexican pueblo of Santa Clara. In their introduction to his ethnographic text, George and Louise Spindler remark on this special attribute:

> He is accepted as a friend, as an insider, and speaks the language fluently. He never violates this friendship and acceptance in what he writes about the Tewa, and yet the reader achieves a feeling of directness and intimacy that is often lacking in descriptions of Pueblo life. This is also an unusual case study because the adaptation and assimilation of one way of life and one people to another non-Western society as well as to Western culture is described. This is indeed rare in anthropological literature. (Dozier 1966a, v–vi)

In addition to noting the insider status of Edward P. Dozier—a point which I will discuss later—the Spindlers highlight the general ethnographic importance of Dozier's contribution as a study of culture contact between two Native American groups. For North American Indians, as for most of the world's native cultures, culture contact is all too often limited to a study of the disruptive influence of contact with a politically superordinate non-native cultural group.

In addition to this generally useful and important study of inter-Indian contact, Dozier's work is especially relevant for students of the Pueblo Southwest since it is the only detailed study of such inter-Pueblo culture contact resulting after the disruptive Spanish colonial program and the Pueblo revolts of 1680 and 1696 that it engendered. Historians of the period affirm that migration, both forced and voluntary, occurred frequently in Pueblo groups, sending many of them to live among other Pueblo Indian groups as well as among Apacheans. Yet none of these other immigrant groups still retains the distinctive language and culture of their ancestors. Why?

This question returns us to a focus on the role of language in Arizona Tewa history—a concern which was relatively undeveloped in Dozier's ethnographic treatments. Though he used the Tewa language as a means of collecting ethnographic data, he wrote at a time when the study of language and communication were not viewed as cultural systems worthy of the same attention as kinship, social organization, religion, and traditional economy. While anthropologists were exhorted to study beliefs about religion, they were not similarly encouraged to study native beliefs regarding language. While the instrumental role of language in conveying cultural information, both between members and from members to anthropologists, was conventionally acknowledged, the affective significance of language was often ignored. That the Tewa language was used to teach children how to plant and how to pray was never doubted. That this same language might also be used to convey ethnic and other social identities was never explored.

In the pages that follow I explore the intimate association of Tewa language, history, and identity. Special attention is directed to such questions as, What are Tewa cultural beliefs about their language and about language in general? How does the Arizona Tewa language reveal the history of its people? How does the speech of individual Arizona Tewa people reveal their biographies? How are social identities conveyed by language and ways of speaking? How does the use of the different languages available—Tewa, Hopi, and English—display a strategy of selection from among a repertoire of culturally available identities?

This book is about the Arizona Tewa and one of their most distinctive possessions—their language. Who are the Arizona Tewa? This question cannot be answered completely without reference to the Arizona Tewa language.

Who Are the Arizona Tewa?[2]

We can begin this task of identification by describing the Arizona Tewa as they exist today, as a Pueblo Indian group of approximately 625 members, most of whom reside on and around First Mesa of the Hopi Indian Reservation in Navajo County of northeastern Arizona (Stanislawski 1979, 587). About 200 Arizona Tewa currently reside in the easternmost of the three villages nestled atop First Mesa. Though they call it "Tewa Village," only the Hopi name "Hano" appears on a sign at the intersection of the road which begins the serpentine ascent to the Mesa.[3] Some 300 other Arizona Tewa people live in Polacca, a newer community consisting of dispersed single-family houses, which sits before the steep slopes of First Mesa. Most of the remaining Arizona Tewa live elsewhere. They inhabit Keams Canyon—a small trading-post town about a dozen miles to the east—or the larger, more remote cities of northern Arizona such as Flagstaff (eighty miles to the southwest) and Winslow (fifty-five miles to the south).

While such demographic and geographical details do serve to locate the Arizona Tewa in the contemporary world, they fail to adequately distinguish them from their more numerous Hopi neighbors. Such a distinction proves elusive for a variety of reasons. For purposes of federal accounting and administration, the Arizona Tewa are regarded as members of the Hopi Tribe and included in their population of between 7,000 and 8,000 individuals. The Arizona Tewa attend the same Bureau of Indian Affairs (BIA) schools, use the same Public Health Service hospitals, and generally share the same rights and obligations as Hopi members of the Hopi Tribe.

This confusion exists if we limit our study of the Arizona Tewa to the investigation of their demography, geography, and federal administration. A more ethnographic focus hardly dispels this confusion. Travelers through the area—tourists, journalists, even many anthropologically trained observers (Eggan 1950, 140)—will find little if anything that distinguishes the Tewa from the Hopi. The clothes they wear, the food they eat, the houses they live in, and the fields they tend are not significantly different. No abrupt change strikes the stranger who walks the few paces from the Hopi village of Sichomovi into Tewa Village and its central plaza. In fact few strangers, including myself on my initial visit, realize that they have even crossed the boundary between the two contiguous villages.

As observation of the Arizona Tewa is supplemented by conversations with them, we could reasonably expect to learn of the elusive differences that distinguish the Arizona Tewa from the Hopi. Yet even discussions with the Arizona Tewa can, at first blush, appear both unhelpful and quite confusing. Albert Yava, a prominent Arizona Tewa elder and formerly the official interpreter of the Hopi Tribe, once offered the following insights:

> We are interrelated with Hopi families in all the villages. Many of us have become members of the various Hopi Kiva Societies. We share dances and festival days with the Hopis. We belong to the same clans. We are usually represented on the Hopi Tribal Council. In many ways we are indistinguishable from them, and often you hear us say in conversation, "We Hopis," not because we have forgotten that we are Tewas but because we identify with the Hopi in facing the outside world. (Yava 1979, 129–30.)

But, as Yava maintains, though there are times when the Arizona Tewa regard themselves as Hopis, they reserve an identity for themselves which is unavailable to the Hopi and uniquely their own.

The most important symbolic vehicle of this identity is the Arizona Tewa language—a language brought by their ancestors from the Rio Grande Pueblos almost 300 years ago and a language still spoken today. Arizona Tewa and Hopi, while very distantly related, are very different languages which are mutually unintelligible. Arizona Tewa is a dialect of Tewa, a Kiowa-Tanoan language spoken in such New Mexican pueblos as San Juan, San Ildefonso, Santa Clara, Nambe, Pojoaque, and Tesuque (Ortiz 1979; Edelman 1979; Arnon and Hill 1979; Speirs 1979; Lambert 1979; Edelman and Ortiz 1979). As a member of the Kiowa-Tanoan family of languages, Tewa is related to Tiwa (spoken in the New Mexican pueblos of Taos, Picuris, Sandia, and Isleta), Jemez (spoken in the New Mexican pueblo by the same name), and Kiowa (spoken today in western Oklahoma).

Hopi, on the other hand, is a member of the Uto-Aztecan family—a linguistically diverse and geographically dispersed family which includes such languages as Mono, Comanche, Ute, Yaqui, Huichol, and Nahuatl. While all adult Arizona Tewa know both Hopi and Tewa, few Hopis even have a passive knowledge of Arizona Tewa.

The history of the Arizona Tewa and the Arizona Tewa language seem to merge on many important occasions of use. Arizona Tewa folk history is conveyed from generation to generation through means of the Tewa language. This account details and explains existing linguistic differences between the Hopi and the Tewa (e.g., the linguistic curse on the Hopi). It nearly equates cultural perseverance and linguistic persistence, while simultaneously chronicling such persistence and encouraging its continuation as an alternative to Hopi assimilation.

Tewa History and Folk-History

The ancestors of the present-day Arizona Tewa were the Tano, or Southern Tewa, who occupied the pueblos of San Marcos, San Lazaro, San Cristobal, and Galisteo in the eastern pueblo frontier, in what is now New Mexico, at the inception of Spanish colonization around the turn of the seventeenth century (Dozier 1954, 273; Reed 1943, 74). Reed (1943, 254) claims that these people as early as 1583 were designated as *Tano* by the Spanish who regarded their pueblos as forming a discrete administrative unit. Reed infers from this that these people "constituted a distinct entity, or tribal group, not only as a Spanish colonial administrative unit, but essentially in their own estimation." To what extent the label *Tano*, in contradistinction to *Tewa*, was based on observable cultural or linguistic differences between the two groups (at that point in time) remains an unresolved ethnohistorical problem.[4]

Because of their proximity to Sante Fe—the colonial base of the Spanish—both the Tano and the Tewa were especially subject to the Spanish colonial program. They supplied more than their share of tribute and services and "probably suffered most severely from disciplinary measures" (Dozier 1951, 271). But rather than enforcing allegiance to the foreign regime, the military oppression and religious intolerance of the Spanish eventually precipitated the Pueblo Revolt of 1680 (Simmons 1979, 184). In this revolt both the Tewa and the Tano played an active role. Planned by a Tewa religious leader from San Juan Pueblo, the revolt was initiated by the Tano. They sieged Sante Fe, holding the Spanish there under military pressure for five days until northern Tanoan reinforcements arrived.

Though the revolt was temporarily successful in repelling the Spanish, their retreat was soon followed by an increased wave of Apache attacks on the outlying pueblos during a renewed period of inter-Pueblo dissension that undermined a cooperative defensive effort. In response to these attacks the Tano abandoned the Galisteo Basin. The Tano of Galisteo and San Marcos remained in the captive settlement at Sante Fe; those of San Lazaro and San Cristobal moved to the Northern Tewa country in the vicinity of what is now Santa Cruz. When Don Diego de Vargas reconquered the Pueblo area in 1693, the Tano occupying Sante Fe were forced to surrender and were later relocated (Simmons 1979, 187). The remaining Tano refused to submit for nearly a year but were finally forced to sue for peace. These Tano (those from San Lazaro and San Cristobal) were resettled together further north from the site of their former villages in order to make room for the Spanish settlement at Santa Cruz. This newly created community of dispossessed Tano Indians was named San Cristobal. Both the Arizona and Rio Grande Tewa recognize the ruined remains of this site as *c'εwaréh* (Dozier 1954, 273)—the place from which the Tano ancestors of the present-day Arizona Tewa migrated to First Mesa.[5] This migration occurred in 1696, when many Pueblos rose again in revolt against the Spanish. After the revolt the Tano at San Cristobal marched west to Zuni, where they were given temporary food and shelter (Bailey 1940, 226–28), and from there to First Mesa.

Strangely enough, however, no mention of any of these events occurs in the Arizona Tewa folk-historical account of the migration. According to their view, their forefathers were invited by First Mesa chiefs to protect the Hopi from the onslaughts of Ute invaders. At that time, according to Tewa accounts, the First Mesa Hopi living at Walpi Village had been reduced to only seven families. Leaders from the Bear and Snake clans set out on a long journey to enlist the protection of some eastern Pueblo warriors who had been recently tested in the Pueblo Revolt of 1696. Three times they tried unsuccessfully to persuade the Southern Tewa from *c'ę́-wa:de*. Albert Yava continues the account:

> So the delegation went to Tsewageh for the fourth time. They brought a bundle of prayer feathers, pahos, for the Tsewageh leaders. There were three feather sticks—we call them uudopehs [u:tophé] in Tewa—and they represented three things. One was a male paho and one was a female paho. . . . The male and female pahos together meant people, you might say population. The third paho was plain, not painted, and it represented land. These pahos were a pledge to the Tewas. They meant that if the Tewas would come to help Walpi they would be given land and they would be allowed to take Walpi's sons and daughters as husbands and wives. Land and people, that was the pledge. This time the Tsewagehs accepted. They received the pahos as a sacred promise. They said, "Go home, tell your people we are coming." . . . The compact that the Hopis and Tewas made at Tsewageh is still memorialized in Tewa Village. When we carry out certain rituals one of our masked figures carries a tall stick with cotton strings and feathers attached, representing land and people. They recall the sacred promise made by the Hopis to the Tewas. (Yava 1979, 27–28)

The Arizona Tewa account goes on to document Hopi ingratitude after the Tewa had fulfilled their mission. Dozier quotes one of his Arizona Tewa consultants:

> When our ancestors had defeated the Utes and made life safe for the Hopi, they asked for land, women, and food which had been promised to them. But the Hopi refused to give them these things. Then it was that our poor ancestors had to live like beasts, foraging on the wild plants and barely subsisting on the meager supply of food. Our ancestors lived miserably, beset by disease and starvation. The Hopi, well-fed and healthy, laughed and made fun of our ancestors. (Dozier 1954, 292)

This account, replete with more graphic instances of cruel ingratitude, such as the pouring of boiling gruel on the outstretched hands of the starving Tewa, is still told today in the kivas—semisubterranean religious buildings—and constitutes an obligatory part of all Arizona Tewa initiation rites. That the Tewa were less than appreciated by their Hopi hosts is clear from Spanish accounts by Gov. Felix Martinez, who as late as 1716 was still set on punishing the Tano refugees and returning them to New Mexico. When he asked permission of the Walpi chiefs to ascend First Mesa, it was granted immediately (Bloom 1931, 192). An indecisive skirmish ensued and the Spanish, thinking they had punished the Tano enough, returned to New Mexico.

The Linguistic Curse

Dozier offers a plausible explanation for the omission of all detail regarding the Spanish in the Arizona Tewa accounts:

> Apparently the oppressive treatment suffered by the original migrants became less important and eventually forgotten by succeeding generations of the Tewa at Hano who had not actually experienced Spanish rule. Later generations found the injustices and ill-treatment directed at them by their Hopi hosts more important to record in their traditional history. (Dozier 1966a, 18)

The Hopis, on the other hand, regarded the Tewa not as invited protectors but as potentially dangerous refugees—aggressive intruders who demanded land. Traditional Hopi disdain for warfare further fueled animosity toward the more warlike Tewa. Rio Grande Tewa traditions tend to confirm the Hopi version (Dozier 1951, 58). In any event the Arizona Tewa found themselves proscribed by the Hopi. Mindeleff (1891, 37) reports, "The Walpi for a long time frowned down upon all attempts on the part of the Hano to fraternize; they prohibited intermarriages and in general tabued the Hano."

According to Arizona Tewa folk history, the inhabitants of Hano responded by placing a linguistic curse on the Hopi:

> Because you have behaved in a manner unbecoming to human beings, we have sealed knowledge of our language and our way of life from you. You and your descendants will never learn our language and our ceremonies, but we will learn yours. We will ridicule you in both your language and our own. (Dozier 1954, 292)

The folk history of the Arizona Tewa, then, can be viewed as an attempt to manipulate historical events by redefining them in ways that could sustain a favorable self-image, instill pride, and provide a basis for the maintenance of cultural distinctiveness for a persecuted minority. The migration account served to explain the Tanoan exodus, not as escape from Spanish oppression, but as a noble gesture on the part of Tewa warriors on behalf of the helpless Hopi—a gesture repaid by ingratitude. The linguistic curse rationalized Tewa isolation not as Hopi stigmatization but rather as voluntary removal—a cultural revenge consisting of the denial, to the Hopi, of the benefits of a culture perceived by the Arizona Tewa as superior.

In a sense, the potency of the *linguistic curse* manifests itself in the contemporary fact that while almost all Arizona Tewa speak Hopi, no Hopi—even those who have married into Tewa Village—commands Arizona Tewa. Though this kind of asymmetry between the linguistic knowledge of minority and majority speakers is quite common (Barth, 1972) and probably represents the ethnographic rule rather than the exception, the Arizona Tewa, via their folk history, are able to view it as a product of their cultural revenge on the Hopi rather than as a mere reflection of their minority status. The real potency of the linguistic curse resides not in its capacity to cause the probable but rather in its function as a self-gratifying account of the present linguistic asymmetry.

An Ethnographic Sketch of the Arizona Tewa

For readers who are unfamiliar with the Arizona Tewa, or with Pueblo Indians in general, it may be useful here to sketch some of the details of their traditional culture and social organization as relevant background.[6] Like most Pueblo Indian groups, the Arizona Tewa inhabit a high desert environment. Perched atop the flat, windswept sandstone of First Mesa, Tewa Village occupies the easternmost tip about 600 feet from the ground below. Unlike the eastern pueblos of New Mexico, which are situated in and near the Rio Grande River Valley, the Arizona Tewa and the Hopi did not have a stable source of flowing water suitable for irrigation. Instead they traditionally relied on dry-farming—the practice of planting in washes and sand dunes which retain water through most of the growing season from runoff produced by winter rain and snow. Several permanent springs situated below the mesa provided the Hopi of First Mesa and the Arizona Tewa with their only source of drinking water.

Despite the great variability in annual precipitation, ranging from five to twenty inches, and the risk associated with dry farming in high desert environments, the Hopi and the Arizona Tewa were primarily agriculturalists. In early spring, fields would be prepared by clearing, terracing, and erecting windbreaks to protect young plants from damage by wind-driven sand. Green corn, onions, chili, beans, and squash were among the first crops planted, followed by watermelons and corn, the main crop. An early harvest occurred in midsummer, followed by harvests from late summer through late fall.

Winter provided a respite from agricultural work and permitted First Mesa villagers to devote themselves to hunting, sheep breeding, and the manufacture of leather goods, pottery, ceremonial items, and jewelry. Temporarily freed from the long hours of painstaking labor associated with agriculture, Arizona Tewa and Hopi people reserved winter as a special time for telling traditional stories; preparing for seasonal ceremonies; playing games of chance; and conversing near the warmth of a stove with household members, clan relatives, and friends.

Kinship and social organization were shaped to the demands of agricultural subsistence in a difficult and often unpredictable environment. Though the traditional household, consisting of a married couple, their children, and the wife's parents, was the primary unit of production and consumption, it was complemented by the matrilineal clan in many important economic and ceremonial activities. These clans typically consisted of several lineages whose members traced themselves through maternal lines of descent to a common female ancestor. These clans greatly enlarged the support group an individual could rely on in times of economic, psychological, or spiritual need. Clan members were localized in adjoining houses, providing ready access to many kinsmen from the mother's clan. According to the traditional pattern, a maternal uncle would teach his nephew important economic skills and dispense any necessary discipline. Though he was still an authoritarian figure to his nieces, they would learn their gender-appropriate economic skills from their mother and her sisters. From the maternal uncle as well as the maternal grandparents came knowledge of the clan's history and traditional stories. In addition to membership in the matrilineal clan, children were also considered to be relatives of the father and his clan. Relatives from this side, especially the father, his parents, and his sisters, would emphasize the lighter side of Arizona Tewa life and engage in a wide variety of pranks and joking behaviors. Fathers would typically show great affection and generosity to their children, who would find a relatively unrestrained openness in their relationship with him and the members of his mother's household.

In addition to being related to both the mother's and father's clans—as well as the clans of their associated kiva groups—each boy is given a ceremonial father, each girl a ceremonial mother. This parent instructs and guides him or her through a tribal initiation ceremony, which is normally undertaken when the child is between eight and ten years old (Dozier 1954, 326). As with the Hopi, Arizona Tewa parents often select an individual who is not a member of either of their clans to become the ceremonial parent of one of their children. This relationship further expands the child's kinship network since he or she is also viewed as related to the clansmen of that ceremonial sponsor. In this manner, most Arizona Tewa people will be regarded as closely related to a large number of people in both Tewa Village and the other First Mesa villages and will exchange kinship terms as address forms with the majority of village neighbors whom they habitually encounter.

Each clan has its own history and ceremonial rights and duties. All land was owned by particular clans whose members had specific use rights. Given the importance of clans in so many areas of cultural life for the Arizona Tewa, one might assume that they have long been a part of their social organization. But comparative evidence from the New Mexican Tewa pueblos, where such clans are not present, clearly indicates that Arizona Tewa matrilineal clans must have emerged as an adaptation to their new Hopi neighbors sometime in the eighteenth or early nineteenth centuries.

Each Arizona Tewa clan is grouped in one of two mutually exclusive kiva groups based on their use and association with either the Plaza Kiva (*mune te'e*) or the Outside Kiva (*p'endi te'e*)—the two kivas located in Tewa Village.[7] This organization of clans is similar to both Hopi and Rio Grande Tewa patterns of social organization. Linked clans, two or more clans which claim a special affinity and display unusual interclan cooperation for either ceremonial or economic purposes, also exist among the Hopi. But the pattern of assigning all clans into one of two mutually exclusive kiva groups—not a Hopi practice—appears to be a vestige of the moiety systems common among the New Mexican Tewa and described best by Alfonso Ortiz (1972) for his native pueblo of San Juan.

There, as in other Rio Grande Tewa pueblos, each person belongs to either the Summer People or the Winter People. Each moiety has its own hierarchy of religious positions and its leaders rule for approximately half the year.

Further proof that the Arizona Tewa have evolved from a moiety system toward a clan system and currently show some features of both is the term for village chief—*p'o-'ǵ'-t'ǫyon*. This term, which has the literal meaning of "water-release/come-chief," is identical with that used for the Summer Chief in Rio Grande Tewa pueblos. But for the Arizona Tewa the term is now applied to a hereditary village chief from the Bear Clan, in accord with the dominant Hopi pattern, and this person does not alternate his leadership with any other clan or kiva group leader. Since the Bear Clan is part of the Central Plaza Kiva, it could be said that this kiva group is clearly the more politically powerful of the two. But Outside Kiva also performs many important functions. Its members perform the *sumako:le* (curing ceremony), performed each August, and host the important initiation ceremony that occurs during the winter solstice ceremony (*than-tháy*). The war chief, a member of the Cottonwood/Kachina Clan, which was part of the Outside Kiva Group, was traditionally equal to the hereditary village chief in power and possessed special responsibility for preserving law and order within the village, maintaining military preparedness for possible confrontations with invaders, and praying for the general health and well-being of the village.

Like the larger units of kinship and social organization, the native religious beliefs and practices also show patterns of cultural continuity with their Rio Grande Tewa ancestors as well as patterns of accommodation to their Hopi neighbors. Though all Pueblo Indians share a world view which emphasizes the intricate order of the cosmos and the need to maintain this order through the precise performance of an annual cycle of elaborate and collective rituals, certain regional and local differences can be detected in the emphasis on specific religious themes. For example, curing societies, which treat individual health and illness, are more common among the New Mexican pueblos than they are among the Hopi. The maintenance of the *sumako:le* ceremony, mentioned above, and the continued practice of healing through the use of ritual performance and native medicinal plants provides a strong link to the ancestral past of the Arizona Tewa. Hopi influence on their religion is most apparent in the relative elaboration of the kachina cult. The kachinas are nature spirits who are impersonated by ritual dancers wearing elaborate costumes during a number of sacred ceremonies on the annual ritual calendar. Though the kachinas represent supernatural beings who can be influenced to provide general health and well-being, they are especially important for the Hopi as a religious means of ensuring the success of their agricultural efforts. Kachinas make the fields fertile, nurture the sprouting plants, and provide the winter snow and the summer rain. This weather-control emphasis is a Western Pueblo elaboration which correlates with the practice of dry-farming. Unlike with irrigation, in this precarious type of farming the farmer is limited in what he can do to ensure the success of the crop and is especially dependent on timely rainfalls, seasonal temperatures, and few sandstorms when the plants are young and vulnerable.

A third emphasis of Arizona Tewa religion is in an area which has generally not been well documented or well understood in the study of Pueblo culture (Ellis 1951)—warfare. While vestiges of a war cult persisted in most pueblos into the late nineteenth and early twentieth centuries, this area of ceremonial life seemed to undergo the most attrition. Though the reasons for this attrition are not well known, it can be plausibly accounted for in terms of both culture contact and internal culture change. As the frequency of inter-Indian conflict was diminished by the influences of the Spanish colonial program and later the military presence of the United States, the functional role of native war societies was reduced. Religious preparation for battle and its aftermath—caring for the dead, purifying and reintegrating the returning warriors—became increasingly superfluous. Since participation in such ceremonies often was both arduous and painful, recruitment of participants in view of the diminished utility of the society would also have been increasingly difficult.

While this is true for the Pueblos in general, the unique historical association of the Arizona Tewa and their ancestors with warfare may account for the relative endurance of war ceremonies and the relative prominence of a military emphasis in their culture. Their *Thanu* ancestors once occupied the eastern frontier of the Pueblos—a position which placed them in contact with Plains Indian groups. They were leaders in the Pueblo revolts of 1680 and 1696. As has been recounted above, Tewa folk history tells that Tewa military prowess earned them an invitation to First Mesa, where they fought valiantly against the enemies of the Hopi. Given this history, there is no wonder that warfare would assume a symbolic prominence in Arizona Tewa culture. In older sources, such as

Fewkes (1900, 623) and Parsons (1926, 209–10), the traditional ceremonial cycle displayed a strong military emphasis especially in its winter
schedule. During this period the war ceremony (*kabe:na*) and the ground
freezing ceremony (*hyuhyukhí*) would be performed. In addition the
winter solstice ceremony (*than-tháy*), which includes kiva group initiation, also gives military emphasis. In short, although religious practices
concerning warfare have diminished in importance, the military emphasis
persists and joins curing and weather control as major thematic concerns
of the Arizona Tewa.

It is instructive, also, to examine the traditional life cycle of an individual Arizona Tewa. Mothers would give birth at home in a darkened
room in which they would be accompanied by their sisters and aunts and,
if childbirth was especially problematic, a native shaman. The father's
mother would also be present to serve as a cord-cutter, cutting it with a
gender-appropriate implement—an arrow shaft for boys, a corn-stirring
stick for girls. Other women from the father's clan will be called in to
assist with the baby. After the umbilical cord is cut, the baby's face and
body are ritually washed in cornmeal. After nineteen days of caring for
the baby, they will propose a number of clan-related names as part of a
naming ceremony. Selecting the name they like best, the parents will hold
the child up to the sun—its first exposure to the sun's rays—and utter
the chosen name. This pattern closely resembles Hopi naming practices
(Dozier 1954, 325; Eggan 1950).

After the ceremony, the child returns to the home of its mother and is
cared for primarily by the members of her household. Grandparents and
siblings typically played a major role in the child's early socialization. As
the child grew, it would play with siblings and cousins and begin to perform minor tasks as a service to adult kinsmen or to assist them in their
routine activities.

Between eight and ten, both boys and girls are initiated into the kachina cult and assisted by a ceremonial mother or father during the ceremony. During the initiation, which takes place four days before the Hopi
Powamu ceremony, whipper kachinas who strike each of the boys four
times with their whips, confront the children who are assembled just
outside the Plaza Kiva. The children, who experience considerable fear
and anxiety during the ritual, are comforted by their ceremonial sponsors
who ritually protect the children from additional blows and instruct their
ceremonial children about food taboos involving abstinence from meat

and salt for the four days preceding Powamu. The initiation ceremony often leaves a powerful lasting impression on the children. Many closely bond to their ceremonial parents because of their assistance during this stressful period. Some, such as the man quoted by Dozier, experience disorientation and distrust:

> After the whipping a small sacred feather was tied to our hair and we were told not to eat meat or salt. Four days later we went to see the Powamu ceremony in the kiva. As babies, our mother had taken us to see this event; but as soon as we began to talk they stopped taking us. I could not remember what had happened on Powamu night and I was afraid that another frightening ordeal awaited us. Those of us who were whipped went with our ceremonial parents. In this dance we saw that the Kachina were really our own fathers, uncles, and brothers. This made me feel strange. I felt somehow that all my relatives were responsible for the whipping we received. My ceremonial father was kind and gentle during this time and I felt very warm toward him, but I also wondered if he was to blame for our treatment. I felt deceived and ill-treated. After the Powamu ceremony my head was washed and I received a new name. At this time, too, the small feather was removed from my hair and the food restrictions were lifted. (Dozier 1954, 327)

Just as the Powamu, which represents the return of the kachina spirits to the Hopi and Tewa villages, provides a transition into the agricultural emphasis of the ritual calendar, the initiation provides an individual rite of passage that marks initiates as occupying an intermediate developmental stage between childhood and adulthood. Initiated boys may now impersonate kachinas at future ceremonies, and all children will begin to take on more of the adult responsibilities involving such tasks as household duties, farming, and participation in village activities dictated by the village chief. These village projects might include replastering the kiva and cleaning out springs that have been clogged by shifting sands.

At about age fourteen boys receive an additional ceremonial father—one selected from their own kiva group—to guide them through an initiation into that group. This occurs in conjunction with the Tewa winter solstice ceremony (*than-tháy*). This initiation is a prerequisite for participation in ceremonial societies (other than the general kachina cult) and political activities. Girls experience a comparable initiation at the time of their first menstruation. During this time, they are secluded and engage in corn-grinding activities that take four days. These initiations mark the transition into adulthood.

Courtship is primarily an individual matter. There are no prescribed or prearranged marriages. Marriageable partners cannot be selected from one's own clan or one's father's clan. Weddings most often occur while both the groom and bride are in their early twenties. The families of the couple are involved in a ceremonial exchange during both the inception and the culmination of the marriage ceremony. The process begins when the bride presents her future in-laws with a gift of *piki* bread—folded paper-thin sheets of cornmeal associated with festive occasions. In return she receives a quantity of meat. Then, usually for several weeks, the bride's relatives prepare for the wedding by grinding corn. The groom's male relatives use the time to complete the bride's wedding garments—a belt, robe, dress, and moccasins. When these garments are prepared and after the bride has spent three days grinding corn in her in-laws' house and received a ceremonial washing of the hair, she dresses in her wedding costume. Then she and her husband are taken by his mother to the bride's mother's house—their new home as husband and wife. Later, the husband's family will receive a much larger quantity of food as a "payment for depriving the family of a worker" (Dozier 1954, 330).

Adulthood will be preoccupied by economic efforts to support one's family and participation in family and village life. Individuals who inherit certain ceremonial responsibilities or those who are recruited because of special skills may continue to gain esoteric knowledge restricted to members of particular religious societies and gradually assume positions of leadership after a lengthy apprenticeship to an elder ceremonial leader.

Death by natural causes in old age is viewed as yet another transition. As in all ceremonies involving rites of passage, the hair of the deceased person is ceremonially washed. The face and body of the individual are ritually washed with cornmeal, as in the treatment of newborns. Since the deceased is now regarded as a baby in another world, a prayer stick will be made and a new name will be given. Four days after burial, the dead person has finally completed the journey to the next life. The quality of this afterlife is viewed by many as depending upon the ceremonial station that one has attained in previous life. Ordinary people are thought to experience an afterlife that is similar to the world in which they lived. Deceased members of a ceremonial elite are thought to become kachinas who may drift, in the form of clouds, above the village, observing the behavior of their descendants.

The preceding sketch of traditional Arizona Tewa culture, like the genre of the ethnography from which it derives, displays such narrative conventions as the ethnographic present, the well-bounded ethnic group, the homogeneous cultural unit, and the omniscient narrator. We should be aware that such conventions necessarily distort any descriptive effort by minimizing historical change and culture contact, ignoring the intra-cultural variation in belief and behavior, and claiming an objective status for what is necessarily an interpretive account. Rather than convey an unwarranted image of the Arizona Tewa—unchanging, isolated, homo-geneous—that magnifies their exotic attributes, it is appropriate to add some observations that might balance this view. For while it is impossible to understand the Arizona Tewa of today without knowing about their traditional past, it is equally impossible to do so without recognizing significant cultural changes in their adaptation to the present.

Certainly the most visible changes appear at the level of economic ac-tivities and material culture. Once subsistence farmers, today the Arizona Tewa and the Hopi are participants in a cash economy. While much farming is still done, it merely supplements the efforts of wage earners in providing support for their families. Formerly every Arizona Tewa man was primarily an agriculturalist, but today men and women are employed by the federal or tribal bureaucracies as hospital workers, school admin-istrators, and tribal police or by the tourist industry as silversmiths, ka-china carvers, potters, or salespeople. For most men, even though agri-cultural pursuits are no longer the mainstay of their economic activity, they will maintain fields as an avocation, in addition to their primary jobs.

While unemployment and underemployment are common on the Hopi Reservation—a factor that prompts many young people to move to neighboring towns—participation in a cash economy has brought to many people increasingly high levels of material comfort and ownership of automobiles, small appliances, television sets, and many other prod-ucts. Certainly insofar as material culture is concerned, the Arizona Tewa experience and display great variation. Some of the houses in Tewa Vil-lage are still not connected to electrical lines. Village residents use out-houses situated on the northern rim of the mesa. They must carry water from the holding tank at the edge of the village to their homes in large containers since they do not have running water. Meanwhile many Ari-zona Tewa people living in recently constructed single family ranch homes situated below the mesa in Polacca, enjoy all the modern amenities such as electricity, indoor plumbing, forced air heating, and the like.

Removal from the constraints of a subsistence economy has also had some impact on kinship behavior. In the past a newly married couple usually lived with the bride's parents. While this is still an option, some couples can earn a sufficient income so as to enable them to buy or rent a new home for themselves. Though such practices certainly enhance the autonomy of the young couple and may seem to diminish the influence of grandparents who may not be living under the same roof as their grandchildren, this slight shift away from a formerly strict observance of matrilocal residence represents only a minor permutation rather than a radical change in kinship behavior. In general economic change has altered the form of economic reciprocity between kinsmen rather than having restructured the kinship system itself. Today, for example, assistance to kinsmen not only takes the traditional form of harvested crops, prepared foods, and collected firewood but may also assume the form of purchased canned goods, needed supplies like Coleman lanterns and automobile batteries, and even cash gifts.

Increasing contact with American society has occurred both through the increasing penetration of the mass media and through such representative institutions as Public Health Service hospitals, Bureau of Indian Affairs schools, and resident missionaries. Televisions and radios regularly supply news and entertainment programming from stations in Flagstaff and Window Rock, Arizona. Many Arizona Tewa people own cassette recorders, and these can often be heard playing either American popular music, in English, or recordings of the music performed at Tewa Village's most recent social dance, in Tewa.

While the mass media serve to transmit information and images from the outside world, they are not as influential as the mediating institutions which Tewa people know from their own experience as participants. Government-provided medical care in hospitals, such as those at Keams Canyon or Tuba City, has had a considerable impact on general health care. Most Tewa babies are now born in hospitals rather than at home. Many of the traditional birth and naming practices are thus delayed until mother and child return home from the hospital. Some illnesses and ailments that would previously have been treated by a village shaman are now routinely referred to the doctors at the local hospital.

Schools and missionaries have also had considerable impact on the Arizona Tewa. Despite their apparently distinct domains—education and religion, respectively—they often seem focused on eradicating native culture. Historically the schools that served the Arizona Tewa and Hopi have hardly sought to maximize continuity with the child's early family and community experience. Rather than building on such experiences in an additive manner by designing culturally sensitive curricula or teaching strategies (Kroskrity 1986), Tewa people have usually been taught in these institutions by people who are completely ignorant of Tewa culture yet are convinced that it represents an obstacle to the education they have to offer. Teaching practices in Indian schools earlier in this century included washing out a child's mouth if he or she spoke the native language. While such practices have waned, the antagonism between the culture of the classroom and the native culture of the students has remained. Only in recent decades have changes in Indian community participation, including community control, joined with changing educational theory and practice to begin to reduce this antagonism. Other changes regarding schooling have also served to make schooling less stressful. At the turn of the century all schools were boarding schools, which necessarily removed children from their homes and families at young ages. Later day schools were instituted, permitting children to attend local schools for the duration of their primary education. Finally, within the past decade an on-reservation high school has been operating, thus making high school education locally available and eliminating the need for students to attend distant boarding schools for any part of their primary or secondary education.

Missionary groups, both resident and itinerant, have exposed local Tewa and Hopi Indians to a broad spectrum of Euro-American religions. While some Arizona Tewa people have converted to one or more of these religions and renounced native religious practices, a more common adaptation for many is to practice both Christian and native religion or to embrace only the latter. Those who do practice a Euro-American religion will celebrate a Christian ritual calendar, attend Sunday church services, contribute to the maintenance of their church, and possibly elect to be buried in accord with its practices when they die.

While the preceding paragraphs suggest some of the recent changes which Arizona Tewa people have interwoven into the traditional fabric of their cultural and personal lives, it is useful to turn to a discussion of how these and other recent changes have effected change in their relationship with the Hopi majority of the First Mesa area.

Adaptation to the Hopi

As Dozier (1951; 1954) has documented, a number of factors—both traditional and modern—have contributed to the normalization of Hopi-Arizona Tewa relations, including the present integration of First Mesa society. Before the Hopi and the Arizona Tewa experienced the wave of social change initiated by increased contact with Euro-Americans and the United States government (late nineteenth century to the present), the Arizona Tewa had already proven themselves as defenders of First Mesa and become famous, among both Hopi and Navajo, for their curing prowess and native medicinal knowledge. In the modern period, the Arizona Tewa served as intermediaries between the Hopi and the increasingly influential Euro-Americans, and as interpreters—both literally and figuratively—of the social changes which were gradually reshaping considerable portions of reservation life. In a literal sense the Arizona Tewa, most notably Albert Yava who was cited above, functioned as interpreters for the Hopi in their meetings with federal government representatives. Even before English had become the second language of many Hopi after the turn of the present century, the Arizona Tewa, who enjoyed a reputation for commanding multiple languages, already exhibited considerable fluency in English. More figuratively, the Arizona Tewa served as interpreters of modernity by providing the Hopi with a model of adaptation to social change. In a political manifestation of this, the Arizona Tewa played an important role in establishing the Hopi Tribal Council.

> The council had received support primarily from the people of First Mesa. The Hano Tewa enthusiastically supported the work of government specialists who were helping to draft the Hopi constitution and were largely instrumental in "selling" the idea to the Hopi. The Tewa's friendly and cooperative attitude toward the government and toward the whites in general and their traditional role as go-betweens have helped to unite the villages of First Mesa and to convince them of the benefits that tribal unity will bring. The assumption of secular roles is traditionally correct for the Hano Tewa, and the First Mesa Hopi in recent years have generally let the Tewa lead in matters dealing with the external affairs of the group. (Dozier 1966a, 70)

Since the founding of the tribal council, several Arizona Tewa have served as Hopi Tribal Council chairmen. Tewa participation has also resulted in a high degree of political unification on First Mesa. Whereas other villages on the Hopi Reservation are represented by village-specific leaders, elected and traditional, First Mesa sends a unified delegation rather than a set of village-specific leaders from its villages of Walpi, Sichomovi, Polacca, and Tewa. This political integration is not the only evidence of Tewa participation in reservation politics. During the 1960s and 1970s, Tewa political influence also helped to fashion a more aggressive policy toward the Navajo, aimed at halting Navajo growth and expansion in territory that was exclusively reserved for the Hopi Tribe.[8] Thus the Arizona Tewa continue to wield a political influence that is disproportionately great for their small number.

In other ways the Arizona Tewa have also provided examples, usually soon followed by the Hopi, in their role as culture brokers.[9] The Arizona Tewa have been economically instrumental in effecting a change from sheepherding to more profitable cattle grazing (Mason 1965). Arizona Tewa potters like the famed Nampeyo were also influential in reviving the Hopi craft of pottery-making—an industry which contributes significantly to the income of many Hopi and Arizona Tewa families today. In addition, the Arizona Tewa were also the first to permit their children to attend the reservation school when it was founded in 1887.

Despite the Hopi characterization of them as "neighbors without manners," the undeniable fact that the Tewa did provide many valuable services to the Hopi—in both traditional and modern times—ultimately led to improved Tewa-Hopi relations. The long period of coresidence on First Mesa manifested itself in considerable accommodation to and borrowing from the Hopi. As Barth observes:

> Entailed in ethnic boundary maintenance are also situations of social contact between persons of different cultures: ethnic groups only persist as significant units if they imply marked differences in behavior, i.e. persisting cultural differences. Yet where persons of different cultures interact, one would expect these differences to be reduced, since interaction both requires and generates a congruence of codes and values. . . . (Barth 1969, 15–16)

Though Barth's characterization of interethnic interaction should be viewed as more a tendency than a social law, increased interaction between the Hopi and the Tewa did generate a discernible congruence of codes and values in the areas of kinship, and social and ceremonial organization. While the terminology of the kinship system closely resembles that of the Rio Grande Tewa, the kinship system itself is structurally akin to the Hopi system, featuring matrilineal descent and strict matrilocal residence (Eggan 1950, 41; Dozier 1955). These features represent a marked departure from the more patrilineal emphasis and patrilocal residence patterns that typified Rio Grande kinship structure.

Clans were also borrowed from the Hopi and equated with Hopi clans either nominally or mythologically. Changes in kinship structure enabled intermarriage between members of the two groups to take place without disrupting social relations. The establishment of clans facilitated the legitimization of Tewa landholdings since all properties are viewed as belonging to the clan. Both these developments may be construed as attempts by both Hopi and Tewa to enlarge kinship networks and to ensure economic security and stability.

Dozier summarizes these changes in the following manner: "It is interesting that when elements could be incorporated within the Tewa pattern without endangering cultural aloofness, borrowing was in order" (Dozier 1951, 61). Dozier's statement may seem somewhat paradoxical: despite extensive borrowing from the Hopi, the Arizona Tewa still retain a distinct culture and a discrete status as a separate ethnic group. Yet how is this accomplished?

The answer to this problem is at least partially a symbolic one. As interethnic interaction over a long period of time has reduced the total inventory of sociocultural differences that formerly characterized the two groups, the persisting differences assume a new symbolic function as badges of identity or, in Barth's terminology, *diacritica of ethnicity* (Barth 1969; Jackson 1974). For the Arizona Tewa, two of the most significant diacritica are the Arizona Tewa language and an abiding, albeit a transformed, military emphasis (see chapter 7). As exclusive "possessions" of the Arizona Tewa, they continue to serve as tangible evidence of persisting differences between them and their Hopi neighbors—differences which attest to the penetration of the present by the past.

But the careful reader may have detected an apparent contradiction between the imagery of ethnic boundaries and the data that seem to attest to the habitual indistinguishability of Hopi and Arizona Tewa. Intermarriage between the two groups has certainly mixed them in a biological sense (Eggan 1950, 140). Surely the quote from Yava, presented in the initial section of this chapter, suggests the possibility that the Barthian imagery may be too brittle. Still I would maintain that we are confronted here not by a true contradiction but rather by a paradox.

The Arizona Tewa as "Text"

This paradox is reflected in the ethnographic contributions of Edward P. Dozier, particularly in a remarkable turnabout in his own estimation of the cultural persistence of the Arizona Tewa. In his initial publication, "Resistance to Acculturation and Assimilation in an Indian Pueblo" (Dozier 1951) based on his first four months of a year-long period of field work, he presented the Arizona Tewa as paragons of cultural persistence: "The most pronounced feature . . . is their persistence in maintaining cultural, linguistic, and personality distinction from a numerically larger group, the Hopi" (Dozier 1951, 56). Yet in the monograph that he published at the conclusion of his dissertation research, *The Hopi-Tewa of Arizona,* he states, "At the present time it appears that the two groups are actually merging and that the antagonisms have for the most part subsided" (Dozier 1954, 259–60).

This paradox—the claims that the Arizona Tewa are retaining their distinctiveness and merging with the Hopi—like all anthropological statements is a professionally manufactured one. In other words, it rests not in the experience of Arizona Tewa people but rather in the anthropological scholarship that has attempted to describe and understand them. Recent scholarship in an area that has come to be known as critical anthropology (e.g., Clifford 1983; Clifford and Marcus 1986; Marcus and Fischer 1986), has usefully examined ethnographic writing as determined by several behind-the-scenes factors, many of which are backgrounded or ignored altogether in conventional anthropological representation of the cultural *other.* Rather than uncritically viewing ethnographic statements as definitive or authoritative, this approach views them as indexical of literary conventions (e.g., the genre of ethnography and its rhetorical devices), current theoretical debates and issues, political constraints, and general historical circumstances (Clifford 1986a, 6).[10] Simply stated, ethnographies necessarily reflect both the culture under investigation and the culture of the ethnographer. Dozier's claims, then, can be profitably viewed as reflections both of Tewa cultural behavior and of his own theoretical concerns.

It should be emphasized that though Dozier is by far the most comprehensive of all ethnographers of the Arizona Tewa, he is neither the first nor the only source of our images of Arizona Tewa people. Earlier publications by Victor Mindeleff (1891), Jesse Walter Fewkes (1894, 1899,

1900), Barbara Freire-Marreco (1914), and Elsie Clews Parsons (1926) were among the earliest sources. These early works are remarkably similar in their tone and manner of presentation. Each was produced using only one or two key consultants whose interviews become the sole basis for descriptive claims. One notable exception is Fewkes' study of altars, which is based on first-hand viewing of constructed altars in various kivas on First Mesa. The tone of these works seems a mixture of natural history and antiquarianism. The authors catalog and arrange data from specific domains of Arizona Tewa culture: their clans, their kinship terms, their ritual calendar. Even in these early works there is an orientation to a more traditional past rather than a focus on the existing situation. Thus Fewkes lists extinct clans and Parsons catalogs defunct ceremonies that were remembered by consultants although no longer part of Tewa cultural life. The tendency in these works is to present a uniform and discrete description of Arizona Tewa people and their culture in an *analogical* mode (Tedlock 1983)—one which replaces dialogue with natives and between natives with the authoritative presentation of the collector, the anthropological expert. Native discourse is reduced to the occasional appearance of native terms—a referential vocabulary for the cultural inventory collected and displayed in the article, a means for authenticating the cultural provenience of a particular attribute.

The lack of attention, in these early works, to a native perspective, to a native voice was apparent to at least one of these ethnographers—Elsie Clews Parsons. She viewed the collective documentation on the Hopis and the Arizona Tewa as extensive but deficient: "In all this volume of record, for all the towns, there is one striking gap: there is little or no record of the life of the people from within, so to speak" (Parsons 1925, 6). As an attempt to address this lack, she collaborated in the production of *A Pueblo Indian Journal, 1920–1921* (Parsons 1925)—a journal written in English by an Arizona Tewa man identified as Crow-wing and annotated and introduced by Parsons. Crow-wing had learned English in the boarding school at Keams Canyon, lived briefly off of the reservation, and later returned, marrying into the neighboring Hopi village of Sichomovi. In the journal, Crow-wing notes significant events on First Mesa from December 19, 1920, until the same day in the following year. It is a remarkable document, more like a newspaper than a personal diary, which provides valuable information about kinship behavior, the ritual calendar, and the life cycle. While Crow-wing's terse descriptions do provide a native voice—a view "from within," they are clearly the comments of a guide, addressing an audience who is unfamiliar with his culture, and display no self-revelation or reflection. It is also useful to emphasize that this native *voice* is encoded in written English and that the 123 pages of the journal contain 187 explicative footnotes by Parsons. Views from within, in Parsons' practice, appear to require abundant commentary from the authoritative perspective of the anthropologist.

When Dozier began writing about the Arizona Tewa, he inherited an ethnographic tradition of describing them as a discrete cultural group despite the facts that many changes had occurred in Tewa kinship and social organization which were clearly borrowed from the Hopi, inter-marriage with the Hopi was common, and there were relatively few differences between the Arizona Tewa and the Hopi that distinguished the two groups. Language was also an important factor. Just as previous ethnographers had viewed the persistence of the Tewa language as a validation of their discrete cultural status, so Dozier was, no doubt, initially impressed by the persistence of a language so like his own. Being greeted and hosted by the Arizona Tewa shortly after his arrival, Dozier's early exposure to their hospitality probably postponed his full confrontation with aspects of Arizona Tewa life that were most influenced by the Hopi. During this early period it would have been quite normal for the Arizona Tewa to maximize the continuity between their culture and his. Dozier himself, as the following passage demonstrates, was also preoccupied with solidifying relations between himself and his Arizona Tewa consultants.

> Once I brought back [to Tewa Village] a family of Santa Clara Tewa to par-
> ticipate in the *Yandewa* ceremony which has been borrowed from Santa
> Clara Pueblo. This provided an opportunity for observing the differences in
> general behavior between the two groups and the relation between them; for
> example, the deep respect the Hopi-Tewa have for their linguistic kinsfolk.
> The visit was useful in cementing my own relations with the Hopi-Tewa, for
> I came to be regarded as a very close friend, and everyone began to exchange
> clan relationship terms with me. (Dozier 1954, 261)

Thus Dozier's early emphasis on Arizona Tewa cultural persistence appears to reflect both his reading of prior scholarship and the early, somewhat limited, adaptive experience of his early field work. Additional field-work provided new evidence that seemed to undermine his claim about Arizona Tewa resistance to Hopi culture. Ceremonies performed in

Crow-wing's days were no longer a part of the annual ceremonial cycle observed by Dozier. Very little evidence of antagonism toward the Hopi—a phenomenon recorded in older sources, a phenomenon that he might have expected paralleling Santa Clara's relationship to neighboring Hispano towns in New Mexico—seemed to exist. Instead he found an unexpected amount of political and ceremonial cooperation and a high frequency of intermarriage between the two groups. This evidence of on-going cultural accommodation and unprecedented integration of the Arizona Tewa with the First Mesa Hopi did not seem to support his claim of Tewa resistance. In fact it argued for reinterpretation that the two groups were merging.

This finding is at least as much a product of Dozier's theories as of his observations. Though the Tewa provided ambiguous data containing evidence of both persistence and assimilation, acculturation theory tended to view culture change through culture contact as a unilineal process leading to complete assimilation (Jorgenson 1971, 67–8). Viewed from the vantage point of this theory, widespread change on the Hopi model implied eventual complete absorption into Hopi culture. Available theories of ethnic identity complemented acculturation theory in viewing ethnic identity as singular and uniform. Were Dozier to make sense of the Arizona Tewa data today, more recent theory would have provided potentially useful notions like the multiethnic society, situated ethnicity, and ethnic boundary maintenance. But the impoverished anthropological theory of the day regarding culture contact and ethnic identity, perhaps paralleling a culturally intolerant national policy, gave Dozier relatively few options.[11]

Despite these theoretical constraints, Dozier's ethnographic skills did permit him to capture considerable intracultural diversity. He accomplished this primarily by including many lengthy and eloquent passages from Arizona Tewa consultants reflecting on their own cultural experience. As a native ethnographer, Dozier rarely departed from those descriptive conventions that were tied to the perceived need for objective exposition and analysis. But in his occasional inclusion of native voices, Dozier defies what Dennis Tedlock has described as "the law of analogical anthropology that the ethnographer and the native must never be articulate between the same two covers" (Tedlock, 1983, 324).

Native voices, unnamed in Dozier's work to preserve their anonymity, can be classified both according to their rhetorical function and the social categories represented. I have distinguished three types of rhetorical function. The first is the *native expert,* a knowledgeable native practitioner who describes a cultural practice at length. An example of this from the monograph is the Arizona Tewa mother, who outlines and explains the procedures associated with birth ritual. Dozier's citation of natives, like his extensive citation of scholarly sources, both displays appropriate deference for and enhances the image of the ethnographer. A second species of native voice is the *rhetorical figment,* the native who validates the ethnographer's analytical claims. When a Bear Clan man discusses his clan, its organization, its ceremonial fetish, and the rights and duties of membership (Dozier 1954, 333), he exemplifies cultural patterns that Dozier wants to convey to the reader. In such cases the native voice provides a validating specimen. In the final type, the native voice conveys *individual affect*—strong emotions generated by cultural practices or their disruption. A mother laments how boarding schools have changed her daughter's attitude to her culture (Dozier 1954, 301). A "middle aged, acculturated" Tewa man expresses resentment of the Hopi from having heard as a boy his grandfather's many renditions of the Tewa migration legend, detailing Hopi mistreatment of the ancestral Tewa (Dozier 1954, 323). (The man's father was Hopi.) A Hopi-Tewa man said to be highly acculturated expresses distaste for the popular use of gossip and witchcraft-accusations as a means of enforcing conformity and cooperation.

Many examples in this last category, including the one cited above in which a man talks frankly about feeling abused by his kinsmen during the initiation ceremony, provide examples of discord with tradition. They are the utterances of individuals identified by Dozier as "acculturated" and "highly acculturated." While such voices are seldom heard in traditional ethnographies, Dozier's own status as a man of two cultural worlds may have prompted him to attend to their criticism of their own culture and to include them in his monograph.[12]

In addition to Dozier's language of representation, it is useful to attend to his language of data collection. As a native ethnographer, Dozier emphasizes his intimate relationships with community members: "I came to be regarded as a very close friend, and everyone began to exchange clan relationship terms with me" (Dozier 1954, 261). He presents his native status as a means of quickly establishing rapport within a notoriously closed Pueblo community. Regarding the Tewa language, he wrote, "A great deal of the information was obtained through conversations in the

Tewa language; the use of this language put my informants at ease, and thus the atmosphere was rarely artificial."

Certainly the practice of using native languages has a long history of professional endorsement in anthropology. In Dozier's case, his fluency in Santa Clara Tewa is rightfully regarded as an important preadaptation for fieldwork. As a tonal language with a large consonant inventory and complex verb morphology, Tewa is a forbidding language for anyone who is not either a native speaker or a dedicated linguist. But there is some evidence for doubting the ease of communication in Tewa between Dozier and his Arizona Tewa consultants. Even though Arizona and Santa Clara Tewa closely approximate one another, most Arizona Tewa people regard Santa Clara Tewa as especially exotic because it contains many phonological units that are quite alien to Arizona Tewa pronunciation. Even though sounds such as [f], [r], [sh], and [x] have regular phonological correspondences to familiar Arizona Tewa units such as [ph], [d], [kyh], and [kh], respectively, most Arizona Tewa are so startled by such pronunciation differences that they do not recognize further linguistic similarities. Though some Arizona Tewa individuals may have been able to accommodate their ears to Dozier's Santa Clara Tewa, his use of this language would continuously mark him as an outsider.[13]

Despite such linguistic obstacles—minor in comparison to those routinely faced by many cultural anthropologists, Dozier certainly deserves much credit for his rather comprehensive ethnographic description and nonuniformist representations of the Arizona Tewa. The publication of Albert Yava's life history, *Big Falling Snow* (1979), significantly adds to the Arizona Tewa voices on record and complements Dozier's work (Kroskrity 1983b). The present book contributes the perspective of linguistic anthropology—a dimension "locally" warranted by the special role of the Arizona Tewa language in the cultural persistence of the Arizona Tewa people and their extraordinary appreciation of it as a cultural resource. In the words of the *Ya:niwɛ* song that began this chapter, I seek to understand why and how far the Tewa have carried their language.

2

. . .

ETHNOLINGUISTIC FRAMES FOR TEWA SPEECH

For the Arizona Tewa, as for any people, speech is embedded in a body of often tacit knowledge that structures their expectations and makes the interpretation of speech possible. In anthropology and interpretive sociology, scholars such as Gregory Bateson (1972), Erving Goffman (1974), and Dell Hymes (1974) have referred to such culturally and contextually conditioned expectations as *frames*. Jane H. and Kenneth C. Hill (Hill and Hill 1986, 90; J. Hill 1988, 24–32) have argued for the special importance of attending to these frames in multilingual speech communities. Under these conditions, framing practices assume a cultural salience usually denied them in speech communities where sociolinguistic diversity is less pronounced and less pervasive. These understandings about the nature of language, appropriate verbal behavior, and attitudes toward Tewa and the other languages in their linguistic repertoire underlie Tewa linguistic choices; the examination of these choices is a prerequisite for the studies of speech variation and situated use that follow in later chapters.

Arizona Tewa *TΨ, Hi:li:* Toward a Tewa Ethnolinguistics

Is there some relationship between the Arizona Tewa understanding of their language and the fact that it has endured for hundreds of years despite intermarriage and sociocultural accommodation with the Hopi, despite their minority status, and despite more than two centuries of multilingualism in Hopi? In the present section I will discuss various aspects of what might be termed the Arizona Tewa folk linguistic theory. Certainly this theory of language is not available in the consistent and condensed form of a written document or a set of oral instructions from a recognized leader. Any attempt to identify, let alone analyze, such folk linguistic knowledge therefore represents an interpretation based on a variety of evidence, including statements made about the language and the way it is actually used by native speakers.

A useful starting point in the partial explication of Arizona Tewa folk linguistics is a consideration of Arizona Tewa metalinguistic terms. Like Witherspoon's (1977) account of the Navajo philosophy of language, my corresponding effort looks first at native terms for *"language"* and *"speech."* But unlike Witherspoon's treatment, mine focuses not so much on how native philosophers understand such terms, but rather on understandings that seem to be more generally shared by members of the Arizona Tewa speech community.

Though the Arizona Tewa possess a metalinguistic vocabulary that distinguishes a variety of speech acts, for example -*cikáy* (to inquire), -*yon* (to command), and -*túkyɛnu* (to put a curse on someone); verbal genres, for example *pę́:yu'u* (stories), *wo:waci*, ([life] histories), *khaw* (songs); and speech levels, for example *te'e hi:li* (kiva talk) and *t'owa-bí hi:li* (mundane talk), there are only two primary, or basic, terms that approximate English language concepts like "speech" and "language." Rather than examine this more precise terminology, as Hymes (1983, 347) has encouraged, I will instead focus on these more encompassing and multivocal terms, exploring their semantic properties and their cultural associations. This is entirely appropriate since the terms *tú* and *hi:li* are often morphologically compounded to other terms to form more precise but derivative concepts, and their very multivocality may be interpreted as a significant manifestation about folk beliefs concerning the Arizona Tewa language.[1]

Both terms, *tú* (word) and *hi:li* (language), are multifunctional (i.e., they function as more than one part of speech—here as both nouns and verbs) and polysemous (i.e., possessing multiple but related meanings). *Tú*, as a noun, may be translated as (a) "word," "phrase," "idiom," or "prior verbal interaction," and (b) "voice" or "cry." In the first of these meanings, *tú* designates some unit of a more encompassing whole that is *hi:li*. In this sense, and as its range of possible translations might suggest, it is not used to analytically distinguish different levels of linguistic organization but rather to designate some aspect of actual speech. In the latter sense, *tú* labels what makes speakers verbally distinctive: the individual voice of the person or the distinguishing cry of a particular nonhuman animal species. As an inflected verb, *-tú* may be translated as "to say" when occurring with stative pronominal prefixes, or "to tell" when occurring with active, passive, and inverse prefixes.[2]

The Arizona Tewa word *hi:li*, as a noun, may be translated as (a) "language" and (b) "discourse," "(dialogic) talk," "conversation." *Hi:li*, in the first of these senses, may be used to distinguish one language from another (e.g., *Khoson hi:li*, "Hopi language," from *Tewa hi:li*, "Tewa language"). In this meaning it includes *tú*, which is a performed instance of *hi:li*. But this inclusion should not be viewed as strictly analogous to the linguistic contrast of "language" and "speech" in modern linguistic discourse. *Hi:li* is more inclusive than "language" since it includes not only a linguistic system but also an associated body of communicative or discourse norms (Scollon and Scollon 1981). An example may be instructive here. On one occasion in the summer of 1976, I witnessed Dewey Healing, a valued friend and Tewa consultant, bargaining with Navajos who had driven up onto First Mesa in order to sell mutton. He seemed remarkably skilled in Navajo: he was able to greet them, converse freely, bargain down to what he considered a satisfactory price, and even sell some buckskin that he had long wanted to dispose of. After the encounter, I remarked on his apparent command of Navajo but he qualified his self-estimation of this apparent fluency in the following way:

> This was a good deal for me but I don't really know their Navajo language (*hi:li*). I know the greetings, the right words/phrases (*tú*) but I seem to talk too much for them. And I keep on staring at them. I know the words (*tú*) but their language (*hi:li*)—I don't know it.

In his own estimation *hi:li* includes more than the rules of pronunciation and grammar, more than the lexical items; it included other norms regarding conversational turn-taking behavior and accompanying non-verbal communication as well.

This inclusion is also reflected in the second sense of *hi:li* as 'discourse' or talk between people. In this meaning, *hi:li* can be modified to indicate a particular type of discourse such as *te'e hi:li* (kiva talk), which implies both linguistic constraints like the avoidance of non-native terms and the prescribed use of esoteric vocabulary items, as well as the regulation of talk in the form of prescribed statements and responses by kiva chiefs and other kiva members, respectively. One aspect of this sense is its appeal to a tradition of usage, an appeal that approximates what Becker (1979) has described as "speaking the past"—speaking in accord with precedent and convention.

Kiva Talk and Tewa Speech Aesthetics

Though ceremonial speech is not the focus of any chapter in the present work, no discussion of Tewa speech values can ignore the role of this most esteemed speech variety in providing native models of linguistic prestige which also influence the evaluation of everyday speech. Even though the Hopi typically view the Tewa as "neighbors without manners" and the Tewa often see themselves as more practical than the Hopi, the Tewa clearly conform to a pan-Pueblo pattern in which ceremonial speech is elevated to a linguistic ideal through its association with the highly valued cultural domain of religion.

As a key symbol of Tewa linguistic values, kiva talk embodies three closely related cultural preferences: regulation by convention, indigenous purism, and strict compartmentalization.[3] In the kiva, ritual performers rely on fixed prayer and song texts. Innovation is neither desired nor tolerated. Proper ritual performance should replicate past conventions and if such replication is impossible the ritual should not be performed at all. Thus in instances where ceremonial knowledge has not been effectively transmitted from one priest to his apprentice, the ceremony becomes defunct. This concern with regulation by convention is manifested in everyday speech preferences by adherence to greeting formulas, to the extended use of kinship terms in address forms, to rules of hospitality involving kinsmen and visitors, and to avoidance of direct confrontation in interaction with fellow villagers. Culturally valued narrative genres, involving either histories or traditional stories, must carefully conform to the traditional formal precedents associated with those genres.

If innovation is to be culturally sanctioned it must be cloaked in traditional garb. I encountered an interesting and creative use of traditional linguistic form one summer when I heard what sounded like a traditional

Tewa chant (tú-khe). The chanter was clearly using the dramatic rising and falling intonations associated with the "public address" style reserved for chiefs to call for volunteers for village projects like cleaning out a spring, replastering the kiva, or for individuals to offer birth announcements or stylized grievance chants (Black 1967). But while the form was traditional, its content was not. The chanter was issuing a call for a yard sale and inviting all within earshot to examine items of used clothing and some small appliances that she hoped to sell. Though the commercial message was hardly traditional, the chanter won general village approval by conforming to the expected intonational patterns and verbal formulas associated with the genre. The issue of convention and permissible innovation, as they pertain to traditional narratives, will be further explored in chapter 6.

Closely related to the regulation of innovation in kiva talk are the values of indigenous purism and strict compartmentalization. Stanley Newman, in his discussion of vocabulary levels of the Zuni, another western Pueblo cultural group, appears to dismiss purism:

> Likewise obviously borrowed words, such as *melika* "Anglo-American" cannot be used in the kiva. This prohibition against loanwords is obviously not to be equated with traditions of linguistic purism, whereby organizations in many modern national states legislate against foreignisms that threaten to adulterate the native language. It stems rather from the general Zuni injunction against bringing unregulated innovation into ceremonial situations. Using a word like *melika*, as one informant expressed it, would be like bringing a radio into the kiva. (Newman 1955, 349)

But in the context of Newman's discussion it is clear that he is dismissing a particular type of purism and identifying "regulation by convention" as having greater explanatory power. How else can we account for the fact that indigenous slang—popular expressions that are recently coined and lacking in prestige—is also inappropriate in kiva ceremonies? The kind of purism that Newman is dismissing amounts to an official proscription of linguistic diffusion (e.g., loanwords, grammatical interference), not only in ceremonial speech but in everyday speech as well. But Tewa ceremonial leaders, like those of other Pueblos, are not waging a campaign to dictate everyday speech norms. Their concern is with maintaining and delimiting a distinctive and appropriate linguistic variety, or vocabulary level, for religious expression and not primarily with minimizing foreign linguistic influence. The strong sanctions against foreign expressions in ceremonial speech—violations of which are physically punished—are motivated not by the linguistic expression of xenophobia or extreme ethnocentrism but by the need for stylistic consistency in a highly conventionalized liturgical speech level. Similarly, the negative evaluation of code-mixing in everyday speech by members of the Arizona Tewa speech community does not reflect attitudes about these other languages but rather the functioning of ceremonial speech as a local model of linguistic prestige. This role should not be too surprising when we observe that the prestige which accrues to standard languages in modern nation states emanates, in part, from the support of and use by national governments and by their association with formal education. Since Pueblo societies are traditionally theocratic, fusing political power and religious authority, and since ceremonial leaders must acquire appropriate knowledge through rigorous verbal instruction, the role of ceremonial speech is actually quite analogous to that of standard languages.

In addition to lacking the self-consciousness and institutional enforcement often associated with *purist* movements, Arizona Tewa indigenous purism also lacks other attributes that language planning theorists associate with linguistic purism. Scholars such as Jernudd and Shapiro (1989), for example, view such movements in modern nation-states as consisting of a bidirectional process involving the simultaneous opening of native resources and the closing of non-native ones for linguistic change. Manfred Henningsen (1989, 31–32) expands on this latter aspect when he says, "the politics of purity . . . originates in a quest for identity and authenticity of a cultural Self that feels threatened by the hegemonic pressure of another culture." Annamalai (1989, 225), too, observes that purism is "manifest when there is social change affecting the structure of social control." But while resistance to hegemony and rapid sociocultural change may be the prerequisite of linguistic purism in modern nation-states, these conditions have not continuously prevailed for the Arizona Tewa and their ancestors. What *has* been continuous is the prestigious position of the traditional religious leaders and the speech norms associated with them.

The third value, strict compartmentalization, is also of great importance to the understanding of Tewa language attitudes. Essential to *te'e hi:li* is the maintenance of a distinctive linguistic variety which is dedicated to a well-demarcated arena of use. Kiva talk would lose its integrity if it admitted expressions from other languages or from other linguistic levels. Likewise, if *te'e hi:li* were to be spoken outside of ceremonial contexts it would profane this liturgical variety and constitute a flagrant violation. This strict compartmentalization of language form and use has often been recognized as a conspicuous aspect of the notorious *linguistic conservatism* of Pueblo cultures (Dozier 1956; Sherzer 1976, 244)—a characterization that would be better reanalyzed as Pueblo *linguistic ideology* (Kroskrity 1992).[4]

What is novel in my present treatment is simply the recognition that strict compartmentalization, like regulation by convention and indigenous purism, is traceable to the adoption of *te'e hi:li* as the local model of linguistic prestige. Just as ceremonial practitioners can neither mix linguistic codes or levels nor use them outside of their circumscribed contexts, Tewa people should observe comparable compartmentalization of their various languages and linguistic levels in their everyday speech. The mixing of Tewa with either English or Hopi is devalued by members of the Tewa speech community, though in unguarded speech some mixing does occur. It is interesting that in the Tewa folk account of speech variation, social categories are ranked in respect to the perceived avoidance of language mixing. Older speakers, for example, are said to approximate the ideal more than younger. Men avoid language mixing more than women. This ranking can be readily interpreted as a reflection of the differential participation of men and women in ceremonial activities, of their differential proximity to the realm of kiva talk. In addition, it would be useful to note a parallel suggestion about the importance of ceremonial behavior as a model for other aspects of pueblo social life. In his study of Hopi personality, A. W. Geertz concluded that local models of personality were derived from ceremonial activity: "the model personality is identical to the ideal ritual person" (Geertz 1990, 329). This statement can be readily extended to the Arizona Tewa, who participate in many Hopi ceremonies and share similar cultural ideals concerning ritual preparation and practice.

The Arizona Tewa as a Speech Community

Gumperz has defined a linguistic, or speech, community as "a social group which may be either monolingual or multilingual, held together by frequency of social interaction patterns and set off from the surrounding areas by weaknesses in the lines of communication" (1962, 29). If strictly applied to the Arizona Tewa situation the criterion of frequency becomes problematic. A preliminary analysis of the personal networks of a small sample of Arizona Tewa speakers indicates that despite widespread inter-penetration with the Hopi in the eastern portion of the Hopi Reservation, the Arizona Tewa constitute a distinguishable speech community on the basis of relatively higher frequencies of intragroup social interaction. Pending a more exhaustive analysis, I will therefore view the Arizona Tewa as a speech community within a more inclusive speech commu-nity—that of greater First Mesa society (Walpi, Sichomovi, Tewa Village, and Polacca).

But while this definition adds important social criteria (e.g., interaction and social networks), it fails to specify what, apart from the knowledge of one or more languages, is shared by members of a common speech community. A later definition by Gumperz (1968, 381) attempts to ad-dress this issue. He defines a speech community as "any human aggregate characterized by regular and frequent interaction by means of a shared body of verbal signs and set off from similar aggregates by significant differences in language use."

As applied to the Arizona Tewa case, what are the differences in lan-guage use that distinguish them from the surrounding Hopi? What are the similarities that unite the Arizona Tewa? Clearly the most significant differences involve the Tewa language and its affective significance. Not spoken by the Hopi, Arizona Tewa becomes not simply a vehicle for com-munication but a symbol of Tewa ethnic identity. While they speak Hopi, the Arizona Tewa do not and cannot invest in it the same affective signifi-cance that they reserve for their ethnic language. These critical differences indicate the necessity of interpreting "language use" in the preceding defi-nition to include not merely speech performance but the norms and val-ues which guide such behavior (as in Labov 1972a, 120).

The Linguistic Repertoire

Having outlined the symbolic significance of Arizona Tewa to its speak-ers, it seems appropriate to briefly view the language in its position within the *linguistic repertoire* (Gumperz 1968) of members of the Arizona Tewa speech community. Though a more comprehensive treatment of the interactional aspects of code-switching is in progress, here I simply want to indicate in a preliminary fashion the constituency and symbolic significance of each of the codes that comprises the code matrix, or linguistic repertoire (Gumperz 1971, 102). Such information is especially significant in a speech community such as that of the Arizona Tewa since most of its members, with the exception of some of the younger children, are multilingual. Arizona Tewa thus represents only one of multiple linguistic codes available to members of the speech community.

The linguistic repertoire of the Arizona Tewa speech community consists of at least three languages: Arizona Tewa, Hopi, and English. With few exceptions all members of the Arizona Tewa speech community exhibit a knowledge of each of these languages, though this knowledge is socially distributed within the community (see chapters 4 and 5). As in other Tanoan-speaking communities such as Sandia (Brandt 1970b) and Taos (Bodine 1968) English has become the language of extra-pueblo communication. English is the language of instruction in the public schools and the language employed in interaction with both tourists and government representatives (including Bureau of Indian Affairs schools and Indian Health Service personnel). It is also the language of all published communication from the Hopi Tribal Council and the language in which *Qua' Töqti*, a now defunct weekly reservation-based newspaper, was written. English is also the language of Mormon and other Christian missionaries, both visiting and resident, as well as the religions they have imported.

In its most novel and perhaps most controversial usage, English has become the preferred language of intergroup interaction of a sizable minority of young Hopis and Arizona Tewa who have attended boarding schools in such off-reservation cities as Phoenix, Albuquerque, Denver, and Salt Lake City. While for most older speakers a knowledge of English is viewed as a practical necessity, for a significant minority of younger speakers English has been reevaluated as a prestige language—one that symbolizes their modern tastes in popular music and television, and their eclectic stance toward Euro-American culture in general. Older people blame the boarding schools and even the reservation schools for their role in creating what they perceive as a generation gap. One of the linguistic consequences of this gap is that many younger speakers will respond in English when addressed in either Tewa or Hopi by their parents. Some of the oldest speakers of Arizona Tewa adopt a fatalistic perspective, interpreting this type of behavior as evidence of the incipient demise of the language and of the cultural heritage it represents.

This attitude of concern on the part of some older Tewa finds expression in an increased willingness to cooperate with linguists to preserve the language in writing before it ceases to exist. When John Yegerlehner began his doctoral research in the mid-fifties, he attempted to find cooperative individuals in Tewa Village who would be willing to assist him in a description of Arizona Tewa. He was denied the cooperation he sought and ultimately had to perform much of his research with the assistance of off-reservation native speakers. Twenty years later, with the impact of the boarding schools now manifest, I found a comparative abundance of people who were willing to devote their time and energy to my descriptive efforts. For many Arizona Tewa individuals this first evidence of social discontinuity provided an unprecedented concern for the fate of their previously unthreatened language.

In sum, English, like the Euro-Americans who introduced it, is viewed somewhat ambivalently by adult members of the Arizona Tewa speech community; it is an important tool, the mastery of which facilitated the rise of the Arizona Tewa to a position of esteem on the Hopi Reservation. Yet it also represents the disruptive vehicle with which many younger Tewa are departing from more traditional cultural practices.

Hopi represents a symbolic compromise between Arizona Tewa and English. It is the language of nonofficial intervillage communication. Since almost all Arizona Tewa have some Hopi relatives it provides an important resource for communication with such kinsmen. It is the language of tribal solidarity and consequently conversations regarding tribal council policy-making and the status of the reservation as a whole are typically conducted in Hopi. For those Arizona Tewa who have been inducted into a Hopi ceremonial society (e.g., the One Horn Society) the Hopi language, especially its ceremonial register, assumes another role—that of a sacred, ritual language. Clearly then, though Hopi represents neither the paramount language of ethnicity and solidarity nor the primary language of reservation politics and federal administration, it is an important language in the Arizona Tewa linguistic repertoire. While it performs some functions that are analogous to those of both English and Tewa, Hopi would have to be positioned closer to Tewa if we were to locate these languages on a continuum of sociolinguistic values and functions ranging from *power*, on one end, to *solidarity* on the other (as in Ferguson's [1959] discussion of diglossia, or stable bilingualism).[5] This conclusion, established by both observational and interview data, obviously refutes the status of Hopi as a neutral, *unmarked*, or even truly intermediate language. This is a significant observation since Denison's (1971) description of Friulian—an intermediate language (between Italian and German) in the trilingual Sauris speech community of Alpine northeast Italy—does reveal such functions. Thus the position of Hopi proves potentially instructive in adding to case studies of the role that so-called *Mid* languages—languages between the *High* languages of political power and the *Low* languages of local solidarity—assume in the ethnological record.

Arizona Tewa is, of course, the language of ethnicity. It is the preferred language of communication in Tewa households and the ceremonial language spoken in the kiva. At least two levels, or registers, can be distinguished that correspond to its casual and religious functions. In its religious function numerous archaic forms appear that are not present in everyday casual speech. Few speakers under fifty years of age are conversant with the ceremonial register, though they may memorize the narratives and songs so encoded for the purpose of a religious dance or other ceremony. The casual speech of routine interaction exhibits considerable age-specific variation within the speech community. But much of this variation is beyond the stylistic control of speakers—i.e., it occurs in the form of *indicators* rather than *markers* (Labov 1972b). I will defer further discussion of this variation until chapters 4 and 5.

Most members of the Arizona Tewa speech community regard their language as their unique and self-defining possession. Many older speakers claim that the language cannot be learned by non-Tewas and cite as evidence for this claim the fact that no Hopi, their neighbors for almost 300 years, speaks fluent Tewa. The Tewa help perpetuate this situation by ridiculing any Hopi who attempts to utter even an isolated word or phrase of Arizona Tewa. On several occasions while working with native speakers of Tewa, my Tewa coworkers refused to answer my questions when Hopis were present because they did not want the curious Hopis to "catch on" to any details of the language. The efficacy of the linguistic curse is thus, in part, socially reinforced.

Two other languages are represented in the speech community, though they are spoken by comparatively few speakers. The first of these is

Navajo. Older speakers who, as children, tended flocks of sheep in graz-ing land away from the First Mesa villages acquired some facility in Navajo from nearby Navajo pastoralists. Navajo was also important as one of the first languages used by Euro-American traders (such as Tom Keam). Though their command of the language is now limited, some individuals still employ their knowledge of Navajo in intergroup trade. Today, however, intergroup hostilities have minimized this form of inter-action considerably.

Some individuals—those who have resided in one of the eastern pueb-los for an extended period of time—speak Spanish. But this group in-cludes only a handful of people and not, as Stanislawski (1979, 587) seems to suggest, a numerically significant minority. Though Spanish once served as the medium of communication for trade with non-Tewa-speaking eastern Pueblo people, these interactions are typically per-formed in English today.

This initial look at the linguistic repertoire of the Arizona Tewa merely provides a normative schematic of some of the more important institu-tional associations of the various languages present in their community. A fully adequate description of the Arizona Tewa speech community would further detail the internal variation within each of these languages and how these different speech levels are used by various members. Though this type of comprehensive synchronic analysis is beyond the scope of the present work, I go beyond this normative characterization in later chapters by examining traditional narratives and code-switching.

"Our Language Is Our Life"

Given the prominence of social and cultural factors in the Tewa under-standing of their language and the importance of Tewa as an emblem of ethnic identification, it should not be surprising to find a saying which summarizes the centrality of language. I have heard the following expres-sion on many occasions: "*Na:-'im-bí hi:li na:-'im-bí wo:waci na-mu*" (Our language is our history). This saying reflects an awareness on the part of Tewa people that their language is an emblem of historical choices they and their ancestors have made. The very fact that they speak a dif-ferent language than their Hopi neighbors is an ongoing reminder of their Rio Grande origins, their migration to First Mesa, and the efficacy of the linguistic curse. But they also view the language itself—particularly its lexicon and phonology—as shaped by historical choices. Albert Yava (1979, 1) invokes such considerations when he compares Arizona to Rio Grande Tewa:

> We First Mesa Tewas are the only ones who came and remained without losing our own culture and our own traditions. We still speak the Tewa language, and we speak it in a more pure form than the Rio Grande Tewas do. Over there in New Mexico the Tewa language has been corrupted by the other Pueblo languages and Spanish. We also speak Hopi fluently, though there are very few Hopis who can converse in Tewa.

Yava uses the imagery of general linguistic purity in this passage. He and other Tewa elders, along with many Tewa, could easily identify Spanish loanwords in Rio Grande Tewa that have no counterpart in their language. Similarly their stereotype of Rio Grande Tewa pronunciation underscores the abundance of [f] sounds which are conspicuously absent in Arizona Tewa. Where the Arizona Tewa refer to a wooden stick as *phé,* the Rio Grande Tewa say *fé.* Actually this is one instance of a tendency by Rio Grande Tewa speakers to replace the aspirated stops of Arizona Tewa with fricatives—a phonological change that is attributable to Spanish influence. Thus the linguistic form of Tewa is a reflection of historical choices, such as the evasion of Spanish influence, made by their ancestors.

Another version of the saying occurs in the singular, "My language is my (life) history," which expresses the Tewa conviction that an individual's speech reflects his or her biographical experience. Just as the Tewa language represents a linguistic recapitulation of critical historical choices made by the Tewa people, so the speech of the individual Tewa person recapitulates relevant biographical choices and patterns. Related to this is a comment by Albert Yava: "I only have to hear someone talk for a short while before I know who they are and where they have been." Many Tewa pride themselves on their ability to infer which village a relatively anonymous speaker grew up in, how much time they have spent either on or off the reservation, and who his or her significant others are solely on the basis of their linguistic performance in either Tewa or Hopi. In my experience I found many older Tewa to be astonishingly accurate in being able to distinguish Second Mesa from Third Mesa Hopi speakers even to the point of locating the specific village of the speaker after a brief five or ten minute verbal exchange with him or her. Clearly they have a knowledge of Hopi dialect geography which professional linguists, particularly those concerned with Hopi lexicography, have yet to fully explicate. But more relevant here is the observation that for the Tewa, speech is not only a *noticing* (Moerman 1988) about some circumstances in the world which occasion talk but also an act of self-expression.

Tewa *Khą́wé* "Names": Cultural Selves

In the interest of approximating a more complete account of Tewa ethnolinguistic understandings it is appropriate to briefly note the cultural recognition of variation not only between individuals but within them as well. As Levy (1983, 133) has observed, many non-Western cultures do not share the western conception of the single, unified self but rather promote a recognition of the multiplicity of selves that provide individuals with a number of discrete identities. Autobiographical narratives that were told to me often mentioned the collection of names (*khą́wé*) garnered and discarded throughout the life cycle. Names are acquired at birth, tribal initiation, clan initiation, girls' puberty ceremonies, and society inductions (Dozier 1954, 325–31). Enrollment in the Polacca Day School presupposes a first and last name in accord with the norms of the majority culture. Artists and artisans often adopt a new name. Nicknames rise and fall with participation in more informal *we-groups*, or *personal networks*. Most Tewa people have between four and seven names that are used with considerable regularity. Most of these names are context-bound, tied to specific settings (e.g., the kiva, the school, the studio), to participation in various groups (e.g., kin, religious, voluntary), and to norms that vary accordingly. As for the Cibecue Apache (Basso 1979), these names are the personal property of the individual and any abuse of names such as by using them in the wrong context or by individuals who are not part of the relevant group is regarded as offensive. The names, and their associated identities are so compartmentalized that kinsmen may not know the majority of each other's names. One man who was especially eloquent on the subject likened the use of names to the ritual impersonation of the kachinas:

> According to my thinking when I am using a particular name, I become that person. It is almost like when we dance the mixed kachina dance. Each man

is wearing a different mask, shaped and painted like that kachina. But that's just the OUTSIDE. INSIDE we must each prepare ourselves to become that specific kachina and to avoid the distractions that would block it from happening.

A Note on Tewa Attitudes Toward Literacy and Recording

In an important article on resistance to literacy among southwestern Indian groups, Elizabeth Brandt (1981, 185) has noted a "historical and contemporary aversion to writing and other relatively permanent means of data storage." She explores this aversion by examining native attitudes and institutions as cultural forces that promote opposition to literacy and recording. Brandt discusses the high regard for speech and its valued association with the primary experience of participants. She contrasts this with the disembodied texts produced by literacy, which promote a less valued, more vicarious type of participation. In addition she describes the role of speech as the "outer expression of thought" in accord with the folk idealist philosophies of language common to many southwestern Indian cultures. Underlying many of her observations about the high value of speech seems to be a *performative* view of ritual speech as a means of making and refashioning the world through situated and appropriate speech. This may be contrasted with the Euro-American *reflectionist* view, in which language merely provides a referential tool for labeling a preexisting and language-independent world. In such a view, talk can be readily divorced from worldly action, as in the American saying "actions speak louder than words." But in ritual speech, which appears to be the prototype for language use by many Southwestern Indians, words *are* actions, actions of potentially great personal and cosmic significance.

In addition to locating such attitudinal sources of resistance to literacy and recording, Brandt also notes social and institutional sources as well. She finds these chiefly in the use of oral tradition as a means of controlling access to ritual information, which is privileged knowledge available only to members of specific clans, religious societies, and other intracultural social groups. The guarding of this knowledge from ineligible members of the culture, an activity that Brandt terms *internal secrecy* (Brandt 1980, 123), makes perfect sense in stratified, theocratic Pueblo societies, where specialized ritual knowledge defines an elite and justifies their leadership. In such a system, literacy and recording are viewed as threats to traditional gatekeeping, which can be enforced by strict reliance on face-to-face oral communication. Written and recorded information, in contrast, might enable the transmission of esoteric knowledge to "unauthorized" individuals. Since many prayers and other forms of ritual speech are believed to lose their efficacy through excessive use and abuse (Tedlock 1983, 184), such "leaks" pose significant threats not only to the political control of leaders but to the continued potency of ceremonial performances as well.

As Brandt observes (1980, 130), ceremonial leaders necessarily have more control over village members than over outsiders thus "the focus for secrecy is internal, not external." While such leaders can only attempt to regulate or impede outsiders, they can wield a full range of sanctions, including ostracism, on offending insiders. These observations about both Pueblo linguistic ideology and its interaction with theocratic social control clearly support Brandt's (1981, 193) conclusion that "attitudes toward literacy and other forms of external data storage are rooted first in religious experience and knowledge." This conclusion about the centrality of ceremonial speech both converges with and complements my own observation that kiva speech serves as a folk model for evaluating speech outside of strictly ceremonial contexts. In the Arizona Tewa case, the close association of language with historical and biographical meaning further adds to the saturation of political and religious significance which makes the Tewa language so precious to its speakers.

When I began fieldwork in Tewa Village in 1973, I was unaware of this locally defined symbolic significance of the Tewa language. My training in linguistics reflected the formalist preoccupations of Noam Chomsky's (1965) transformational-generative grammar. As part of this professional socialization, I learned that languages were properly studied as objects set apart from their speakers and the sociocultural tasks which they performed. I was taught that the most important objective of linguistic analysis was the revelation of *formal* linguistic universals—structural principles, common to all languages, which were understood to be innate. My goal was to analyze the data of an exotic and relatively undescribed American Indian language for light that it might shed on these general structural principles.

This training did not prepare me to regard my research as controversial in any way. I had been warned not to attempt to collect sensitive cultural information, most notably esoteric ceremonial knowledge, by my academic advisors. Signs posted on the ascent to First Mesa clearly stated a prohibition against photographing the village or recording ceremonies in any form. When I attempted to enlist the cooperation of Tewa individuals who were regarded as fluent speakers, I carefully qualified my interests in studying just the language itself. But these attempts to assure my potential consultants of my innocent intent were unintelligible to many people. These phrases presupposed a familiarity with a tradition of divorcing language from social life that was quite alien to my prospective consultants. And, as I later discovered, even those who agreed to work with me had an understanding of language far different from the one I had transported to their village.

In Tewa Village, as in most Pueblo communities, even mundane linguistic research may be viewed as controversial precisely because of the cultural significance of the native language. When I first began research, neither the Hopi Tribal Council nor local First Mesa village leaders attempted to exercise any control on research. This contrasted sharply with practices in all eastern pueblos, which typically require official permission and routinely deny it.

In part because my consultants included Tewa individuals who were influential members of Tewa society, I was granted access to persons who became locally responsible for gatekeeping. Though I was consistently denied permission to record situated performances of stories and songs, I was permitted to record information of a public domain nature as well as demonstrations of various mundane genres of speech and song after many years of research partnership. Individuals who claimed to forget their clan histories would find it appropriate to recount their own life history or to sing a song which they had composed. Occasionally, as my command of Arizona Tewa increased, I was chided for needing recordings and transcribed notes to assist my understanding. But most, if not all, of my consultants were quite impressed by the utility of these new technologies in preserving knowledge for future generations—especially their own. They were clearly concerned with achieving this end in a manner consistent with traditionally imposed cultural constraints. As a researcher who gradually became aware of these difficult choices made by my consultants, I was content to witness more than I could record and thankful for the many opportunities to record which were ultimately granted.

Tewa and Western Ethnolinguistics Compared

To summarize this brief exploration of Arizona Tewa folk linguistics, we can meaningfully compare some of its main propositions to those of modern theoretical linguistics, which as Michael Silverstein (1977) has suggested reflects a western folk theory of language.[6] Though the Arizona Tewa folk theory of language explored here, like its somewhat more fully articulated Euro-American academic counterpart, represents a constellation of interrelated assumptions, concepts, and values, at least five significant contrasts between these two views of language may be analytically distinguished.

1. In contrast to what Elinor Ochs (1979b) describes as the *cognitive bias* of our own linguistic science, the Arizona Tewa regard language as an inherently sociocultural phenomenon. Rather than emphasizing language as a vehicle of thought, they stress its role in communicative behavior and emphasize language as an ongoing process of group history and individual biography. Although more idealist in nature, the Arizona Tewa folk view thus better approximates the position of Vološinov when he proposes that "language is a continuous generative process implemented in the social-verbal interaction of speakers" (1973, 98). These views represent a far cry from the well-entrenched position of contemporary formal linguistics under Chomsky who views language as more fruitfully understood by shifting "the main burden of explanation from the structure of the world to the structure of the mind" (Chomsky 1972, 6). Opposing this preoccupation with mentalism which dominates current linguistic theory, is the alternative focus on human communicative activity (Ochs 1990, 14) as a mediator of linguistic and sociocultural knowledge, as a force in either reproducing or changing those knowledge systems. Since according to such a view, knowledge and praxis create each other (e.g., Giddens 1979; 1984), linguistic behavior as social action can be theoretically rescued from its subordination to linguistic knowledge in contemporary formal linguistics.

2. In contrast to what Paul Friedrich (1975) has described as the formalism and atomism that have dominated modern linguistic theory, the Arizona Tewa maintain a user-oriented view of language, viewing it as inseparable from its speakers and as a part of larger communicative contexts. The autonomy that contemporary linguistics ascribes to lan-

guage—an autonomy that promotes the analysis of language apart from its speakers and encourages the study of its presumably self-contained forms—reflects the quest for purely linguistic generalizations. In this view, language—like the biblical *Word* (Tedlock 1983, 269–71)—precedes the sociocultural worlds that speakers inhabit. For the Arizona Tewa, this abstraction of language from social life is meaningless. They do, however, speak of *pure* language, but only in discussions of *te'e hi:li*—a level of speech associated with ceremonial usage and characterized by context-specific sociolinguistic constraints mentioned above. This purer level of speech thus displays even more of a pervasion of sociocultural patterning than does everyday speech.

3. In contrast to the Chomskyan interest in the homogeneity of language—best evidenced in his appeal to ideal speakers in homogeneous speech communities, who speak a single style (Chomsky 1965)—and the prescriptivism implicit in most grammatical models (Hymes 1974), the Arizona Tewa emphasize linguistic variation, viewing it as an inherent aspect of the language and its associated speech community. While theoretical linguistics brackets such variation in order to focus on shared *innate* knowledge, the Arizona Tewa incorporate this variation in their focus on language as socially learned knowledge. Since speakers' biographical experience of language differs, these differences are necessarily viewed as the basis of a social distribution of linguistic knowledge. Though the Arizona Tewa expect significant individual variation, this does not mean that they are without prescriptive designs of their own. Correct speech is speech that may be regarded as appropriate to the situation in accord with preexisting norms, or ways of speaking, that have cultural precedents.

4. In contrast to the *achronic,* or *ahistorical,* focus of contemporary linguistic typology and its associated interest in the systematic potential of linguistic rules, the Arizona Tewa view their language as an ongoing historical achievement which consists of the maintenance of both linguistic elements (e.g., words as well as morphological and syntactic patterns) and cultural conventions for using them (e.g., genres, norms of appropriate speech). While Chomsky equates linguistic creativity with the productivity of syntactic rules—the *sayable*—the Arizona Tewa are far more concerned with evaluating speech against the measure of what has been previously said. This value on "speaking the past" (Becker 1979) once again unites what has been academically segregated in our own treat-

ments of language as the linguist's grammar with the culturally available "ways of speaking" of ethnographers of communication (e.g., Hymes 1974; Sherzer 1983).

5. Related to this contrast between the achronic view of most grammarians and the historical emphasis on language in the Arizona Tewa account are the mutually exclusive preoccupations with linguistic universals on the part of contemporary linguists, and an Arizona Tewa emphasis on viewing speech as contexted action, as a resource for dealing with the here and now. Though linguistic anthropologists have vilified the extreme formalism, atomism, and preoccupation with meaning as limited to reference of conventional linguistic analysis (e.g., Friedrich 1975; Silverstein 1979; Tyler 1978) that have typified linguistic work in these traditions, it would be wrong to construe these criticisms as some attempt to utterly invalidate the approaches to phonology and syntax and the refinements in typological understanding of language structure that they have produced. Languages do have structures and many linguistic regularities can be discovered by analyzing only sayable words and sentences. It would be foolish to contend that such practices have not served to illuminate the linguistic structures of the world's languages. The frustration of ethnolinguists with such work is rather with the narrowing of interests that it represents, with the implicit reduction of a language to its grammatical rules.[7]

This reduction can be meaningfully understood in relationship to the consuming preoccupation of linguists with *language universals* (Comrie 1981). In contrast to the concern with cultural and intracultural diversity that characterizes anthropology, most linguists—except for sociolinguists—proceed from the study of *homogenized* languages to the uniformity of language universals.[8] Within theoretical linguistics, the study of particular languages is primarily valued insofar as they provide a testing ground for language universals (Cole 1976, 563).

This academic penchant for explanation in autonomous and general principles, conflicts with the Arizona Tewa insistence in understanding their language as the outcome of the unique history of a particular ethnic group and, at the individual level, as the product of an individual's biography. Concern for the particular is also an important part of the narrative competence of traditional storytellers who tell a given story quite differently depending upon the constituency of the audience, the circumstances of the telling, and the rhetorical effect desired. Thus, rather than emphasizing what is autonomous and universal about language, the Arizona Tewa highlight their language as a social institution, asserting the importance of context and culturally available prior text.

In light of the fact that such folk linguistic observations are not only rarely studied but also often systematically ignored, the reader may perhaps question their relevance. Two observations are worthy of consideration in this regard—one linguistic, the other social. As Michael Silverstein (1979, 233–34) has noted regarding such folk linguistic ideologies and their potential for contributing to an understanding of the historical dialectic between language structure and language use: "to rationalize, to 'understand' one's own linguistic usage is potentially to change it." In the case of the Arizona Tewa and other Pueblo linguistic groups, I have argued that such folk understandings have influenced the form and extent of linguistic diffusion between neighboring groups (Kroskrity 1982, 1985b). And especially in the case of the Arizona Tewa, we can reasonably assume that their attitudes toward language have contributed to the remarkable persistence of the Arizona Tewa language.

This leads to the more encompassing social relevance of these language attitudes. If, as symbolic interactionists have maintained (e.g., Blumer 1969), people act toward objects in accord with the meanings they attribute to them in social interaction, then surely observations about the meanings that speakers attach to a language cannot be irrelevant to students of linguistic behavior. This is especially true in the case of the multilingual Arizona Tewa. Since use of the Arizona Tewa language represents a selection from among three habitually used languages, *when* they use this language and *why* they find it appropriate for various instrumental and expressive communicative tasks also represent important manifestations of its meaning for them.

3

■ ■ ■

LANGUAGE AS HISTORY: LANGUAGE CONTACT IN THE LINGUISTIC HISTORY OF THE ARIZONA TEWA

For anthropologists, the publication of Edward Sapir's (1916) "Time Perspective in Aboriginal American Culture, a Study in Method" provided a convincing demonstration of the many ways that comparative linguistics can contribute to the reconstruction of culture history. Since then, the belief that languages can provide data that yield historical insights has become an important part of the conventional wisdom of anthropology. The Arizona Tewa have long been culturally endowed with the belief that their language embodies their history. In this chapter historical-comparative linguistic analysis permits us a glimpse of the past seldom considered by those who only utilize conventional historical documents in their attempts to reconstruct it. Though native speakers of Arizona Tewa find little that is familiar about the actual techniques of comparative analysis, they are more than prepared for the idea that their language can itself speak eloquently about their history as a people.

Arizona Tewa and the Kiowa-Tanoan Languages

One very significant achievement of the collective research on the Kiowa-Tanoan family of languages is the now definitive classification of the existing languages into four nearly coordinate language groups: Kiowa, Tiwa, Tewa, Jemez (Harrington 1910; Miller 1959; Trager and Trager

1959). Approximately 2,000–3,000 years ago, the ancestors of speakers of these present day languages were beginning to form discrete groups, disrupting the unity of this relatively undifferentiated speech community (Trager 1967). Lexical evidence, including glottochronological studies by Davis (1959) and Hale and Harris (1979, 171), suggests a more remote internal relationship for Kiowa and a relatively close relationship between Tewa and Tiwa.[1] But grammatical evidence disclosed over the past decade or so at the Annual Kiowa-Tanoan Language Conference does not parallel the subgrouping suggested by the analysis of basic vocabulary.

Ever since Kiowa has been demonstrated to be related to Tanoan there has been a tendency to view this most recently detected Kiowa-Tanoan language as also the most divergent. Trager (1967, 340), for example, incorporates this view into an otherwise very acceptable chronology.

DATE	INTERNAL DIFFERENTIATION OF KIOWA-TANOAN
1–500 A.D.	Kiowa diverges from Tanoan
500–750	Towa diverges from Tanoan
1050–1150	Tewa and Tiwa split

But, perhaps much to the delight of those who search for archaeological correlates of the linguistic division of Kiowa (e.g., Ford et al. 1972, 33–34), recent linguistic evidence now supports the hypothesis that a radical adaptive shift toward a Plains orientation on the part of the Kiowa might have produced linguistic consequences which give an unwarranted impression of great divergence from the other Kiowa-Tanoan languages. Laurel Watkins's (1984) grammar of Kiowa has provided an excellent opportunity for the reevaluation of Kiowa-Tanoan internal relationships.

At the phonological level, Kiowa displays many similarities to the other Kiowa-Tanoan languages: a four-way stop contrast (plain, aspirated, voiced, glottalized), symmetrical vocalic inventory, phonemic length and nasality for vowels, and intricate tone correspondences including even processes of tone sandhi. Harrington (1928, 11) and Hale (1967, 113) have also noted that Kiowa shares with the other Kiowa-Tanoan languages a morphophonemic ablauting of certain verb stem-initial consonants. Davis (1979, 401) agrees that such parallel kinds of morphophonemic alternations provide "an especially convincing type of evidence for a relatively close relationship."

At the level of morphology, Kiowa displays striking similarities in the complex noun classification, the *inverse number* phenomenon, and the elaborate series of pronominal prefixes that appear to be rather uniquely Tanoan. Such facts have led Watkins, on purely linguistic grounds, to conclude that "it is difficult to point to any constellation of features that might indicate a particularly long period of separation from Tanoan before the Tanoan languages split from each other" (Watkins 1984, 2). Even at the level of grammar only two differences distinguish Kiowa from the Tanoan languages: its innovation of *switch-reference* anaphors (Watkins 1984, 292) and its lack of any formal affinity between subordination and negation (Kroskrity 1984; Watkins 1984, 265).

While the definitive comparative work remains to be done, all available evidence now strongly suggests that we abandon the notion of Kiowa divergence. This conclusion clearly has implications for Trager's (1967, 348) hypothesis about a northern Plains origin for the Kiowa-Tanoans. For, as Hale and Harris (1979, 174) have observed, if Kiowa divergence is spurious then the north is no more likely than the south as a directional source. Future comparative work may ultimately yield appropriate evidence to help illuminate this early history of the ancestors of the Arizona Tewa and other Kiowa-Tanoan speech communities.

The issue of Tewa linguistic divergence in the more proximate proto-historical period has also attracted scholarly attention. Arizona Tewa, or Hopi-Tewa, has variously been described as a separate language (Speirs 1966, 4) or the most divergent dialect of Tewa (Kroskrity 1978a, 24; Hale and Harris 1979, 171). George Trager expressed this problem in its most cogent form: "The Hano, or Hopi-Tewa, speak a language that is mutually intelligible with those of the Rio Grande Tewa, but is possibly 'Tano,' and therefore a separate language" (Trager 1967, 337). While linguists possess no definitive criteria for distinguishing the distance that separates dialects of the same language from the distance between discrete languages, the task of assessing the linguistic distance between Arizona and the Rio Grande Tewa dialects is important and instructive as more than a case study in *splitting* versus *lumping*. Since the Arizona Tewa are commonly regarded as the descendants of the Tano, or Southern Tewa of the Galisteo Basin (Dozier 1954, 275–77), their language provides the best available access to that spoken by the Tano before their abandonment and/or removal from their pueblos in historic times (Schroeder 1979, 247–48).

To shed light on how different the Southern Tewa were from their more northern Rio Grande Tewa neighbors, we can measure their linguistic distance in both the lexicon and the grammar. Appendix 1 provides Arizona (AT) and Rio Grande Tewa (RGT) words for approximately 200 terms—a standard lexicostatistical word list modified slightly by Samarin (1967, 270). Of the 215 terms for which data was available in both languages, 201 appear to be shared, or cognate, vocabulary. Only about fourteen appear to be unshared (e.g., words 2, 7, 23, 27, 30, 42, 64, 88, 111, 124, 151, 173, 201, and 216) when one compares the words taking into consideration such regular correspondences as RGT/θ/ = AT/th/, RGT/ɸ/ = AT/ph/, RGT/x/ = AT/kh/, RGT/ñ/ = AT/y/, and so on. Since such correspondences are exhibited in both inter-Tewa Pueblo and intra-Tewa Pueblo variation (Speirs 1966), the practice of equating these phonemes can hardly be viewed as extraordinary. There is 94 percent overlap in this basic vocabulary, which represents the same linguistic distance as that between Santo Domingo and Cochiti—two Keresan New Mexico Pueblo languages usually regarded as relatively close stations on a dialect continuum that stretches westward to include more distant western Keresan Pueblo languages like Acoma and Laguna.

Though lexical measures are the most frequently used means of assessing the linguistic distance between languages and dialects, grammatical measures should also be used as a complementary check. For the Tewa data, the determination of a close relationship between Arizona and Rio Grande Tewa, on the basis of lexical comparison, is reaffirmed by my grammatical findings, clearly refuting any interpretation of these languages as highly divergent. In their morphology and syntax, Arizona Tewa and Rio Grande Tewa display almost identical rules and regularities. What few differences exist usually take the form of minor differences within a shared grammatical pattern. While both languages, for example, have an associational postposition that marks oblique, or nonsubject, case, Rio Grande Tewa has innovated an agentive use of this postposition in active transitive sentences in which the agent is a speech act participant (i.e., "I" or "you"). This is exemplified in the following Rio Grande Tewa sentence:

1. 'u-ri 'i sen nâ:-mû'.
    you-A the man 2sg/3.ACT-see
    You saw the man. (Speirs and Speirs, 1981)

Similarly, while both languages basically share an elaborate set of pronominal prefixes that attach to the verb and inflect for person, number
(singular, dual, and plural), and prefix type (e.g., dative-possessive, stative, active, inverse, and reflexive-reciprocal), they do not share a common prefix for third person, singular, active prefixes. Arizona Tewa uses
mán-, whereas Rio Grande Tewa uses the same prefix it employs for third
person, singular, reflexive *i-*.[2]

These findings raise several questions regarding the Tano and the ancestors of the Arizona Tewa. If Arizona and Rio Grande Tewa are still so
close after 300 years of geographical isolation then they must have been
even more similar at the time of Spanish contact. Given this linguistic
proximity to the Tewa, why were the Tano distinguished from the Tewa
by the Spanish, and on what basis? Clearly the distinction rests in part
on strictly geographic observation. As previously mentioned, the name
Tano is abbreviated from *thanuge'in t'owa*, literally "southern people."
The Spanish established their colonial capital among the Northern Tewa
Pueblos and from that perspective viewed these "southern" Tewa as occupying the more remote southeastern frontier. But another motivation
for the Spanish distinction between the two groups was the relative hospitality of the two groups toward the foreign regime. Though both
groups would surely have preferred that the Spanish had never entered
their world in search of the seven cities of gold, the Northern Tewa were
comparatively tolerant of them whereas the Tano displayed greater hostility and resistance (Schroeder 1979, 247).

While Trager's remarks have so far spurred genetic-historical investigation, his words have been equally provocative in regard to areal linguistics. In an unusual claim, he attributed much of Tewa divergence from
Tiwa to the supposed creolization of the former with Keresan (Trager
1967, 342). I have no evidence, however, of grammatical convergence
between Tewa and Keresan from the many Keresan language conferences
I have attended over the past ten years. While the remarks that follow,
therefore, say little of any such Keresan influence, they do proceed from
Trager's view that language contact played a significant role in the historical development of Tewa. Though Trager's motivation for examining
such areal influence was the search for the source of Tewa divergence
from Tiwa—a language, or subfamily of languages, which he erroneously
assumed to be the oldest stratum of the Tanoan language family—my

own is founded on a more general and irrefutable set of assumptions. Like the Arizona Tewa, I believe that since language is the embodiment of social life, evidence of contact with other languages can be made to speak eloquently about the nature and history of that culture contact.

Evidence of Early Contact with Apachean

Though the ethnographic literature often paints a picture of Pueblo-Apachean relations, especially Pueblo-Navajo relations, which foregrounds intergroup conflict and warfare, there is linguistic evidence that suggests that such a view is excessively "presentist," colored by the more recent history of intergroup relations rather than informed by a more accurate historical construction of such relations in the more remote past. This characterization as traditional enemies ignores the disruptive impact of the Spanish in severing productive inter-Indian trade between these groups as they attempted to encapsulate Pueblo village economies. Linguistic evidence permits a glimpse of Tewa-Apachean relations prior to Spanish domination and disruption. The most notable example of this evidence occurs in an instance of grammatical diffusion from Apachean sources which has resulted in the Arizona Tewa possessive morpheme /-bí/. This is especially appropriate since it is this very morpheme which occurs twice in the Arizona Tewa saying, *Na:-'im-bí hi:li na:-'im-bí wo:waci na-mu* (Our language is our history). Here this morpheme, used as a suffix, changes the independent first person non-singular pronoun *na:-'in* (we) into (our). Given its grammatical role in this Tewa expression, it is only fitting to explore the history of /-bí/ and what it reveals about the Southern Tewa ancestors of the Arizona Tewa.

An important scholar in comparative linguistics, Eric Hamp has long encouraged us to view genetic-historical and areal linguistics as "twin faces of diachronic linguistics," maintaining that neither of these two can be properly pursued without the complementary evidence provided by the other (e.g., Hamp 1977, 279). Guided by this vision of the interrelationship of genetic- and areal-historical research, the present study examines the history of the Tewa possessive morpheme *-bí* in an attempt to establish its diffusional source in Apachean languages—the first evidence of grammatical diffusion between Tanoan and Apachean languages in the Pueblo Southwest.

In both Arizona Tewa (AT) and Rio Grande Tewa (RGT) possession is grammaticalized in two distinct forms. In the first of these, a noun or pronoun can be suffixed by an allomorph of *-bí*—a possessive morpheme—so as to modify the following noun. The following examples illustrate this productive process: (AT) *na:-bí 'é:nu* [I-POS boy] (my boy [or son]) and *sen-bí khaw'* [man-POS song] ([a] man's song); (RGT) *na'in-bí ce* [we-POS dog] (our dog) and *te-ví tesupen* [wagon-POS wheel] (the wagon's wheel).[3] In addition to this pattern for producing possessed nouns, the Tewa languages also share sentential means of indicating possession. Examples 2 and 3 illustrate these constructions:

2. *'é:nu dín-mu:* (AT)
   boy 1sgPOS-be
   I have a boy (or son).

3. *dín-nava-ná* (RGT)
   1sgPOS-field-be
   I have a field.

In each of these examples, possessive predicates are formed by selecting an appropriately inflected pronominal prefix from a dative-like possessive prefix series. This prefix attached to certain stative or existential verb stems selected according to the number and shape of the possessed object results in a possessive predication. Incorporation of the possessed object within the verb, as in 3 is optional in Tewa.

This pattern of possessive predicates, as examples 4 through 7 attest, is shared by Isletan Tiwa, Taos Tiwa, Jemez (Towa), and Kiowa—representatives of all other existing and known branches of the Kiowa-Tanoan family.

4. *in-u-theu-m* (Isletan Tiwa)
   1sgPOS-son-live-PRESENT
   I have a son.

5. *'ôn-'u-wa-mo* (Taos Tiwa)
   1sgPOS-child-be-STATIVE
   I have a son.

6. *'ɨ-kɨ-k'á* (Jemez)
   1sgPOS-child-have/lie
   I have a child.

7. *phą:o: ioy nɔ́-dɔ́:* (Kiowa)
   three sons 1sgPATIENT-be
   I have three sons.

In each of these examples the verbal morphology consists of a dative-like prefix attached to a stative or existential verb. Thus, although the languages may differ regarding the incorporation of the possessed noun, they display shared family attributes in the expression of possessive predicates.

But this pattern of sharing does not extend to the realization of possessed nouns which was described above for Tewa. Though both Rio Grande Tewa and Arizona Tewa display structures of the type [N-*bí* N$_{NP}$], no other Kiowa-Tanoan language shares this pattern. They lack a morpheme that is either analogous or homologous to Tewa -*bí*. In the majority of Kiowa-Tanoan languages, relativized possessive predicates provide the only grammatical means of realizing possessed nouns. This is true of both Northern and Southern Tiwa as well as Jemez (Towa): (Taos Tiwa) *'an-'u-k'o-'i* [1sgPOS-son-have/lie-REL] (my son) (Trager 1946, 207); (Isletan Tiwa) *in-musa-we-'i* [1sgPOS-cat-be-REL] (my cat); and (Jemez) *ɨ-kị-k'a-'e* [1sgPOS-child-have/lie-REL] (my child). Other than Tewa, only Kiowa deviates from this pattern, permitting a simple compounding of independent pronouns and nouns with the nouns they possess, for example *nɔ́:-ì* [I-son] (my son) and *cegun-to:* [dog-house] (the dog's house). While Kiowa approximates the Tewa pattern in its lack of reliance on verbal morphology to express possessed nouns, it still lacks any constituent like Tewa -*bí* in possessive constructions of any type. Since it is not an inherited attribute of the family, where did Tewa -*bí* come from? Data from Apachean languages suggest that they are the source. Throughout the subfamily we find a third person possessive prefix *bi-*, for example (Chiricahua) *bi-k'à'* [3POS-arrow] (his arrow) and (Navajo) *bi-t'o'* [3POS-water] (his water) (Young and Morgan 1980, 2). Though Apachean *bi-* is a prefix and Tewa -*bí* a suffix, this morphological difference becomes quite irrelevant in constructions where the "possessor" is specified, for example (Navajo) *hastiin bi-ye'* [man 3POS-son] (the man's son), *dził bi-tsíín* [mountain 3POS-base] (the mountain's base), and *bisóódi bi-tsi* [pig 3POS-flesh] (the pig's flesh) (Young and Morgan 1980, 16, 73, 77). Constructions of this type are fully analogous to the Tewa examples of possessed nouns (N-*bí* N) provided above in details of constituent sequence.

In addition to the phonological similarity of the morphemes as well as their common syntactic behavior in possessed nominal constructions, other grammatical evidence exists that clearly establishes the fact that this is not an instance of accidental convergence. In both Tewa and Apachean, these morphemes are employed in postpositional constructions of the type (N-*bi*-PP), for example (Navajo) *tsé bi-yaa* [rock 3:POS-under] (under the rock) and *hastiin bi-ch'ą́ąh* [man 3:POS-front] (in front of the man) (Young and Morgan 1980, 73, 81); (AT) *'é:nu-bí nu'u* [boy-POS under] (underneath the boy); and (RGT) *i sen-bí-'weri* [the man-POS-from] (from the man). Though Tewa restricts -*bí* in these instances to animate objects, such infidelities to the source language are common in instances of grammatical borrowing between such genetically dissimilar languages. Since both the Tewa possessed nominal and postpositional constructions involving -*bí* are Kiowa-Tanoan anomalies, the case for grammatical diffusion from Apachean is especially strong—especially given its ethnohistorical plausibility.

My examination of Spanish sources has provided both direct and indirect evidence of Indian multilingualism in the Pueblo Southwest. Direct evidence occurs in passages from two different documents—*Gallegos' Relation of the Chamuscado-Rodriguez Expedition in 1582* and *Fray Alonso de Benavides' Revised Memorial of 1634*. The former goes so far as to suggest societal multilingualism:

> They [the inhabitants of San Marcos, A Southern Tewa Pueblo] indicated to us that the inhabitants of the buffalo region were not striped; that they lived by hunting and ate nothing but buffalo meat during the winter; that during the rainy season they would go to the areas of the prickly pear and yucca; that they had no houses, but only huts of buffalo hides; that they moved from place to place; that they were enemies of our informants, but nevertheless came to the pueblos to trade such articles as deer skins and buffalo hides for making footwear, and a large amount of meat, in exchange for corn and blankets; and that in this way, by communicating with one another, each na-

tion had come to understand the other's language. (Hammond and Rey 1966, 87)

The latter document, however, suggests that multilingualism may have been more individual than societal by implying that a knowledge of Navajo on the part of Pueblo men may have been restricted to principal captains or some comparable segment of the community (Hodge et al. 1945, 86).

Perhaps more important than these fortuitous, though difficult to interpret, observations are the numerous indirect references to communication networks between Pueblo and Apachean groups. If we attend to the indirect references to interethnic relations between these two groups as they appear in the documents, we find mention of several key institutions that could have promoted considerable bilingualism. These include (1) the existence of stable trade networks between the two groups (Hammond and Rey 1953, 647, 838, 864; Schroeder 1972, 49; Hodge et al., 1945, 66), (2) the tradition of winter settlement by Apachean peoples just outside the boundaries of various pueblos (Schroeder and Matson 1965, 124, 128; Hammond and Rey 1940, 258, 261, 293), (3) the military alliances between Apacheans and Pueblo Indians during outbreaks of inter- and intra-Pueblo hostility (Brugge 1969; Dozier 1966b), and (4) the tradition of seeking refuge among Apacheans by individual Pueblo Indians, their families, and larger social units on occasions of extreme Spanish oppression (Worcester 1951, 105; Reeve 1957, 39–40; Scholes 1938, 63, 94; Hammond and Rey 1966, 200–201, 224).

This evidence of sustained interethnic interaction, which is available in the sixteenth- and early seventeenth-century documents, wanes in later documents—particularly those after the Pueblo revolts. Spanish colonial disruption of precontact inter-Indian relations gradually transformed many of these more amicable relations into the typical raiding patterns and attendant hostile relations between Apacheans and Pueblo Indians in more recent historical times. Thus in Parsons' (1929, 137) Rio Grande Tewa ethnography she reports that the Tewa regarded the Navajo as "traditional enemies." Indeed it is precisely such a characterization that seems to pervade much understanding of Pueblo-Apachean relations—the presentist confusion of the more readily available patterns associated with the recent past with those of a preceding, more remote period. It is, I maintain, just such a confusion which Wick Miller propagates in his characterization of the lack of multilingualism in the Pueblo Southwest (Miller 1978, 612–13). For while he concedes that multilingualism probably existed to a greater extent in aboriginal times than it does today, his conclusions regarding its supposed aboriginal lack seem to be based solely on extrapolations from the very recent past.

The ethnohistorical record, as I have just indicated, does provide evidence of interethnic relations that would have been conducive to substantial individual if not societal bilingualism (Miller 1978, 614). But there is other evidence concerning interethnic relations between Apacheans and Pueblo Indians. One, students of southwestern ethnology recognize the importance of a process that may be identified as the puebloization of the ancestors of the contemporary Navajo and Jicarilla—a process that profoundly embraced both material and ideational culture (Parsons 1939, 1039–63; Dozier 1970, 36; Downs 1972, 10–11).

The second major consideration emanates from an archaeological/ecological understanding of the Pueblo Southwest. In discussions of the ecology of the pueblo area, archaeologists emphasize its marginal agricultural potential, manifold microclimatic and microenvironmental variations, and the general unpredictability of the environment (Plog 1979, 111; Cordell 1979, 133). Variability in resources among social groups as well as conditions of environmental stress are the very conditions that would have encouraged prehistoric trade.

Ford's study of Tewa intertribal exchange amply documents the historic trade of foods, manufactured items, and equally indispensable—in the native view—medicinal and ceremonial materials that was necessitated by unequal access to raw materials (Ford 1972, 22–23). Most notable of all the intertribal exchanges documented by Ford is that between the Jicarilla Apache and the Tewa, particularly San Juan Pueblo. He reports the existence of trade partnerships between many members of each group (Ford 1972, 33). These relationships appear to be quite stable: partners were inherited within families—a practice that at the turn of the last century was at least three generations old (Ford 1972, 33). And Ford observed that "there were people who were conversant at a rudimentary level in the other's language" (Ford 1972, 34).

David Wilcox (1981, 228, 236) has suggested that significant Pueblo-Apachean trade relationships need not be exclusively located in the historical period. He suggests that Pueblo settlement patterns in the protohistoric period (early sixteenth century) may have been in response to the establishment of stable trade networks that permitted, via Pueblo-Plains trade, the exploitation of diverse ecozones while intensifying agricultural production. In other words, trade fostered or enhanced an economic specialization—in agriculture (corn, vegetables, tobacco) by the Pueblos, in hunting and gathering (meat, hides, clothing) by the Plains groups—by providing access to economically complementary goods and services produced by the exchange partner.

This reexamination of pre-Spanish inter-Indian relations, which is prompted by the linguistic evidence of grammatical diffusion from Apachean languages, does reveal a number of institutions and practices that would have promoted the individual multilingualism necessary to produce such borrowing. But is there other linguistic evidence of borrowing that might further support the analysis of grammatical diffusion presented above? Though a definitive lexicographical study has yet to be done, several Arizona Tewa words will likely be found to be loanwords from Apachean languages, including the Tewa words for "deer" (*pę:* from Navajo *bįįh*), "fat" (or "grease") (*ką:* from Navajo *k'ah*), "Coyote" (the story character; AT *bayena* from Chiricahua Apache *ᵐba'ye*) (Hoijer 1946, 59).[4] Given the nature of trade between the two groups and the seasonal nature of their most intense cultural contact, such loanwords make cultural-historical sense. Hunted animals and animal products were traded by Apacheans and other Plains Indians for the agricultural products of the increasingly specialized Pueblos. Winter, the time for Apachean encampment outside various pueblos, is also the time that traditional stories and other entertainments were performed by Pueblo peoples.

The brevity of this list of likely loanwords is no doubt the product of many factors, including the lack of definitive comparative studies, the impermanent nature of contact, and the linguistic conservatism of both groups. Since lexical borrowing is a more salient process than grammatical borrowing, both groups would be better able to restrict and inhibit the former in accord with their local linguistic ideologies (see the discussion of linguistic conservatism in chapter 2). Thus the lack of an abundance of loanwords from Apachean is not an argument against the interpretation of grammatical diffusion from Apachean but rather the expected outcome of prevailing language attitudes which militate against the borrowing of foreign words.

Contact with Spanish

Unlike previous contact between Indian languages, contact with Spanish brought the ancestors of the Arizona Tewa into conflict with a cultural group which sought to dominate them. The assault on Pueblo cultures, which intensified in the seventeenth century after initial exploration and colonization in the previous century, consisted of both economic encapsulation and religious persecution. The agricultural surplus that was previously used to trade with Indians from the plains was now absorbed by the Spanish soldiers and priests. The militant Franciscan missionaries, with the full support of Spanish civil and military authorities, attempted to suppress native religion. From their perspective, they were attempting to abolish practices that seemed to them both pagan and idolatrous. But from the perspective of the Pueblos, sacred rituals necessary for maintaining social and cosmic order were being disturbed by an ignorant and intolerant group of aggressive intruders. Valued masks and other ceremonial paraphernalia were often confiscated and destroyed. Respected ceremonial leaders were burned at the stake as "witches." While the military strength and organization of the Spanish permitted them to impose their hegemonic rule over the Pueblos, this oppressive treatment ultimately led to the Pueblo revolts of 1680 and 1696.

While the Pueblos displayed a unified opposition to the culturally intolerant and exploitative Spanish regime, especially in the first Pueblo revolt, no group demonstrated more resistance than the Southern Tewa ancestors of the Arizona Tewa. Though the acknowledged leader of the revolt was a Tewa man from San Juan Pueblo, it was Southern Tewa warriors who first responded by sieging Sante Fe—the Spanish colonial capitol. When other groups capitulated after reconquest, many Southern Tewa continued to fight a guerrilla war and refused to peacefully resettle their native pueblos. While other Pueblo groups accepted the reconquest of the Spanish after an abortive second revolt in 1696, the Southern Tewa ancestors continued to resist and ultimately defied the Spanish by moving to the Hopi Mesas away from the sphere of their military and cultural influence.

The linguistic repercussions of Southern Tewa resistance appear in a pattern of minimal linguistic borrowing from Spanish. Unlike that of Rio Grande Tewa, Arizona Tewa phonology shows no evidence of Spanish influence. Though neither language displays grammatical influence from

Table 3.1   Spanish Loanwords in Arizona Tewa

Arizona Tewa	Spanish Source	Term
1. bán	pan	(wheat) bread
2. cini	chile	chile
3. ci:yo	cuchillo	knife
4. khape	café	coffee
5. kula:nto	cilantro	coriander
6. kwenu	cabrío	goat
7. limon	limón	lemon
8. mansana	manzana	apple
9. meloni	melón	melon
10. mu:la	mula, mulo	mule
11. mu:lu	burro	donkey
12. mu:sa	miza	cat
13. sani:ya	sandía	watermelon
14. tomati	tomate	tomato
15. 'u:ba	uva	grape
16. wák'a	vaca	cow
17. wa:yu	caballo	horse

NOTE: For further discussion of this table, consult Kroskrity 1978c.

Spanish, they both contain some Spanish loanwords. Table 3.1 lists these loanwords in Arizona Tewa and their Spanish sources.

Perhaps the most noteworthy aspect of this list is its brevity. After more than one hundred years of intensive contact with the Spanish prior to the Pueblo revolts, only seventeen Spanish loanwords can be detected in Arizona Tewa. Qualitative and comparative analysis of these terms reveals the superficial nature of Spanish linguistic influence. They are mostly labels for Spanish imports such as plants and derived foodstuffs (1–2, 4–5, 7–9, 13–15), domesticated animals (6, 10–12, 16–17), and new technologies (3). Unlike Rio Grande Tewa, which has borrowed a considerable amount of religious and governmental terminology from Spanish (Dozier 1956), Arizona Tewa exhibits only loanwords that refer to the material innovations offered by the Spanish. Thus, whereas Dozier provides Rio Grande Tewa examples such as *kumpáre* (from Spanish *com-*

Table 3.2 Contrastive Specification of Spanish Loanwords in Tewa

Spanish	Rio Grande Tewa	Arizona Tewa	Term
vaca	wási	wák'a-kwiyó	bovine-woman = cow
becerro	becero	wák'a-é:nú	bovine-boy = calf
yegua	jewa	wa:yu-kwiyó	horse-woman = mare
caballo	kavaju	wa:yu-sen	horse-man = stallion

SOURCE: Rio Grande Tewa forms are those provided by Dozier (1956) from the Santa Clara dialect. I have removed word-final [h] from each of these forms since it represents a distracting analytical contrivance for the comparisons here. Otherwise I follow Dozier's transcription.

padre, godfather), *konfésa* (from *confesión*, confession) and *pika* (from *fiscal*, official), comparable loanwords are conspicuously absent in Arizona Tewa. In addition to this restriction to a very limited set of semantic domains, Spanish loanwords in Arizona Tewa display a lack of lexical elaboration and specificity in comparison to those of Rio Grande Tewa. In contrast to Rio Grande Tewa, which has admitted loanwords that often preserve the gender and age distinctions of the source language, Arizona Tewa has borrowed only a single term to which native terms are compounded to yield comparable semantic distinctions. Table 3.2 illustrates these differences.

Both the restricted semantic domains and the lack of lexical specification of Spanish loanwords in Arizona Tewa are indexical of their relative scarcity. While Spanish loanwords account for only 5 percent of the Rio Grande Tewa vocabulary (Dozier 1951), they represent less than 1 percent of the Arizona Tewa (Kroskrity 1978c). These quantitative observations suggest that while both languages display a remarkable compartmentalization of Spanish, in accord with local ideologies of linguistic conservatism, Arizona Tewa displays an even more extreme form of compartmentalization which is indexical of their greater resistance to the Spanish.

Though the presence of Spanish loanwords in contemporary Arizona Tewa speech continues to provide a reminder of the influence of the Spanish on their Southern Tewa ancestors, the extremely limited form of this linguistic diffusion also demonstrates their ancestors' successful attempts at resisting the Spanish. Though both the Southern Tewa and their Northern, Rio Grande, Tewa linguistic kinsmen display a common pattern of compartmentalization (Dozier 1956), the more extreme compartmentalization of Spanish by the Arizona Tewa is also a reflection of their unique history. Occupying the eastern frontier of the Pueblo area, the Southern Tewa were middlemen between the Pueblos and the Plains. The encapsulation of the Pueblo economy probably impacted them more than other Pueblo groups by interfering with their trade on the Pueblo-Plains frontier, thus transforming their privileged trade location into one which subjected them to the raids of nomadic groups who sought to obtain by force what they once obtained through more peaceful exchanges. The archaeologist Nelson (1914, 112) contributes to the evidence that the Southern Tewa were especially resistant to the Spanish, by noting the extreme architectural conservatism of Southern Tewa pueblos, which seemed impervious to Spanish influence.

But the more extreme pattern of compartmentalization exhibited by Arizona Tewa cannot be solely attributed to the more resistant stance of their Southern Tewa ancestors prior to the Pueblo revolts of 1680 and 1696. Certainly their refusal to resettle their former villages and their removal from Spanish influence through relocation to the Hopi mesas also distinguish their history from that of the Rio Grande Tewa. Their migration abruptly severed further Spanish influence after reconquest—a time when the Spanish adopted a more tolerant administrative policy to avoid further rebellion, and intergroup relations greatly improved. Of key significance here is the fact that during this longer period of Spanish contact a more peaceful and varied relationship between Spanish and Pueblo groups was effected, thus providing a symbolic environment more conducive to diffusional processes both cultural (Ortiz 1969, 62–71) and linguistic.

One additional factor that should be considered in any account of the disparity of Spanish loanwords between Rio Grande and Arizona Tewa is what language planning specialists such as Jernudd (1973) term *language treatment* on the part of the Arizona Tewa. Language treatment is a native, conscious, and deliberate concern with the speech community's language resources. Note that the scarcity of Spanish loanwords in Arizona Tewa need not be interpreted as evidence of their relative absence at the time of the Southern Tewa exodus from the Rio Grande Valley. Arizona Tewa folk history regarding their migration omits any mention of the Spanish. Spanish loanwords may have been consciously purged from usage because of their symbolic association with Spanish repression. Such terms might have been viewed as symbolic invalidations of the Arizona Tewa folk historical stance that emphasized their migration as the result of a Hopi invitation rather than as flight from Spanish oppression. In any event the heightened awareness of foreign words, which would be a condition of any indigenous movement to purge them, was then, and continues to be, an integral part of the Arizona Tewa culture of language.

A close analysis of the seventeen Spanish loanwords in contemporary Arizona Tewa speech thus yields important insights about their Southern Tewa ancestors and the linguistic consequences of their historical choices. Despite the shared experience of the initial hundred years of Spanish domination before the migration of the Southern Tewa, these ancestors of the Arizona Tewa disrupted the otherwise ongoing acculturative influence of the Spanish that the more tolerant eastern Pueblo adaptation permitted. The relative lack, both quantitative and qualitative, of Spanish loanwords in Arizona Tewa and the absence of any vestige of the Spanish Catholic ceremonial system continue to provide indexes of historical adaptations to Spanish culture contact (Dozier 1958).

Contact with Hopi

Of course what most distinguishes the Arizona Tewa from their former Rio Grande Tewa neighbors is not so much the relative influence of the Spanish as it is the contact and adaptation to another native group—the Hopi. The migration to First Mesa provided not only a new natural environment for the Arizona Tewa but also a novel cultural one. In addition to learning the dry-farming technology necessary for survival in a land without rivers, the early Arizona Tewa had to adjust to Hopi culture and society. Like them, the Hopi too were a Pueblo Indian group, and while there were many similarities between them there were also noticeable differences. These differences could be ignored, even scorned, in the early period of friction between the groups shortly after the arrival of the Arizona Tewa, as described in chapter 1, but as relations between the groups normalized and intergroup interaction, including even intermarriage, became commonplace, the Hopi language, culture, and social organization became increasingly influential.

Though Hopi influence on Arizona Tewa culture and social organization has been significant, the pattern of Hopi linguistic influence on Arizona Tewa appears superficial and highly compartmentalized. This linguistic influence is located in Tewa phonology, lexicon, grammar, and discourse. At each level and as a collective pattern, linguistic influence manifests a circumscribed form, shaped by prevailing language attitudes and the continued maintenance of Tewa as the language of ethnic identity in a linguistic repertoire that, since the latter part of the eighteenth century, has included Hopi as the language of intervillage communication.

Arizona Tewa phonology, as mentioned earlier in this chapter, is remarkably conservative and demonstrates a strong pattern of retention in maintaining patterns attributable to Proto-Kiowa-Tanoan. But within this general pattern of phonological conservatism there is evidence of the subtle influence of the Hopi sound system on the phonetic drift of Arizona Tewa, particularly in its innovation of a palatalized velar stop series {ky}, {ky'}, {kyh}. Hopi does have a palatalized, velar stop [ky]—a phoneme which is conspicuously absent from either Rio Grande Tewa (Speirs 1966) or Proto-Kiowa Tanoan consonant inventories (Hale 1967).

Though Hopi supplied the direction of drift, the distinction between plain, glottalized, and aspirated forms is an elaboration that approximates the four-way contrast of stops that is a central feature of Arizona Tewa phonology and one generally attributed to the ancestral protolanguage as well. In other words, the sound is Hopi but its position and function in Arizona Tewa phonology reflect the operation of a native Tanoan system. The net result of these processes produce phonological correspondences between Arizona Tewa [ky], [kyh], and [ky'] and Rio Grande Tewa [č], [š], and [c'] as indicated in table 3.3.

While linguists would regard these and other correspondences as evidence of slight and systematic divergence, speakers of these languages are struck by the exotic sounds of the other language and usually cannot discern the pattern. Since Arizona Tewa has no [š] and since Rio Grande Tewa lacks all three sounds in the [ky] series, the novel sounds are usually heard as alien aberrations rather than as evidence of a close and systematic relationship between the languages. From the linguist's point of view, however, it is clear that some 250 years of multilingualism with Hopi has had a distinctive but highly delimited effect on Arizona Tewa phonology.

In the lexicon a similar pattern exists. Though almost all adult Arizona Tewa speak Hopi, there are almost no Hopi loanwords in the Tewa lan-

Table 3.3   Phonological Correspondences of Arizona
Tewa [ky] Series

Term	Arizona Tewa	Rio Grande Tewa
to color	kyuwɛ	čuwe
witch	kyuge	čuge'i
chapped	ky'ɛ di	c'aedi
to spill	ky'á:	c'á:
nose	khyu	šu
to flee	khyá	šá

SOURCE: Rio Grande Tewa forms supplied by Kenneth Hale, Anna Speirs,
and Randall Speirs (personal communication).

guage. As mentioned in chapter 2, this lack of loanwords is partially due
to Pueblo linguistic ideology which devalues code-mixing and encourages
linguistic purism—processes that keep the languages, and their associated identities, maximally distinct in that area most subject to conscious
control and manipulation by speakers.

Of the approximately 4,500 lexical entries in my Arizona Tewa file
dictionary, only two words appear to be Hopi loanwords. The first
and most important of these is *ka:khá* from Hopi *qööqa* (older sister).
Though adaptation to the Hopi resulted in very significant changes in the
Arizona Tewa kinship system, this is the only kin term that is a Hopi
loanword (Dozier 1954, 305; 1955). The bilateral, generational system
their ancestors brought from New Mexico was reshaped into a matrilineal clan-based one analogous to the Hopi pattern. But despite the fact
that the Arizona Tewa have borrowed the Hopi kinship system, they have
retained, except for *ka:khá,* their Tewa kinship terms. This terminological retention masks a pattern of wholesale kinship change by preserving
the traditionally used Tewa kin terms while modifying the actual kinship
behaviors in accord with the Hopi model. As such, the retention of kin
terms may have served to insulate the Arizona Tewa from full awareness
of the magnitude and rate of kinship change that their adaptation to their
new Hopi social environment necessitated.

The other term in my sample that appears to be a loanword is *kulasa,*
from Hopi *kolassa* (leather) (Albert and Shaul 1985, 182). In general,

rather than adopting Hopi terms, the Arizona Tewa have opted to extend their native Tewa terms or to compound their own words to create Tewa equivalents of novel Hopi cultural vocabulary. Thus *Maasaw*, the Hopi god of the underworld, is rendered in Tewa as *péní só:yó* (big skeleton), and *Homol'ovi*, the Hopi term for Winslow, Arizona, is *P'o-hulu-ge* (water-canyon-place) in Tewa.

Though Arizona Tewa speakers have minimized linguistic borrowing in the lexicon, they have not similarly resisted Hopi influence at the less salient level of the grammar. Students of language contact (e.g., Gumperz and Wilson 1971; Kroskrity 1982) generally recognize that speakers show a greater awareness of some areas of their language, such as the lexicon, than of others, like the grammar. The Arizona Tewa are no exception. The influence within their linguistic repertoire of one grammar upon the other occurs without significant awareness and thereby escapes their evaluation.

As mentioned earlier, grammatical convergence is the expected product of multilingualism. Almost 300 years of societywide bilingualism in Tewa and Hopi has prompted at least one demonstrable example of such convergence. Though further comparative linguistic research may add other structures to this inventory of grammatical diffusion, only the Arizona Tewa *-tí* passive construction appears to have converged with an analogous Hopi construction. Like Hopi, Arizona Tewa has a passivizing (or detransitivizing) verb suffix that can be employed to make transitive verbs into agentless passive constructions. Examples 10 and 11 below illustrate the similarity of Hopi *-(il)ti* and Arizona Tewa *-tí*.

10. taawi yuk-ilti (Hopi)
    song finish-PAS
    The song was finished. (Kalectaca 1978, 132)

11. p'o na-kulu-tí (AT)
    water 3sgSTA-pour-PAS
    The water was poured.

Example 11 represents a productive means of making transitive verbs into stative ones. While Rio Grande Tewa has the same construction, it uses a different passive morpheme, -n, to form it. Example 12 shows the corresponding Rio Grande Tewa example.

12. p'o na-ku'u-n (RGT)
     water 3sgSTA-pour-PAS
     The water was poured.

Available evidence suggests that Arizona Tewa has retained an indigenous construction but has substituted the Hopi passive suffix for the analogous Tewa form. Such processes of grammatical convergence effect a measure of simplification for bilinguals seeking to store two different languages by reducing the total number of language-specific rules that distinguish them. Though all language behavior reflects both social processes and biological constraints, this type of cognitive pruning suggests the role of more purely grammatical concerns in language contact situations. Societal multilingualism ensures that many if not all other Arizona Tewa speakers will have access to Hopi grammar as a prerequisite to processing Hopi-inspired innovations in Tewa grammar like the function of -tí. In the tripartite Labov (1972b) model of linguistic change, which involves innovation, evaluation, and propagation, the facilitating role of societal, as opposed to individual, multilingualism becomes clear. With societal multilingualism, grammatical innovations inspired by another language in the linguistic repertoire are more likely to occur because of the greater number of speakers who speak both languages. Since grammatical convergence often occurs unconsciously, evaluation is both uniform and neutral and does not inhibit grammatical diffusion by attaching stigma to the convergent innovations. The lack of awareness thus reduces the role of local linguistic ideologies. Finally, propagation is more rapid and complete because of the greater number of speakers who will spread the new form throughout the speech community.

Though grammar and discourse are conventionally, if imperfectly, distinguished (e.g., Scollon and Scollon 1981), they are similar in that they usually operate at the level of the speaker's tacit knowledge. Discourse is another level at which Hopi speech has influenced Tewa language use. Traditional stories in Arizona Tewa have become more like those of their Hopi kinsmen and neighbors than those of their Rio Grande Tewa linguistic relatives in certain discourse conventions. Today, for example, Tewa storytellers repeatedly use the evidential particle *ba,* "(so) they say" at least once in every sentence of narrated discourse. Though this narrative convention will be further discussed in chapter 6 as a means of adopting the voice of the traditional narrator, here it is appropriate to remark the similarity of the Tewa particle to Hopi *yaw*. In a comparative study of Hopi, Arizona Tewa, and Rio Grande Tewa particles, I found that while both Tewa languages use the same *ba* particle in their narratives, Arizona Tewa displayed a pattern of use that it shared with Hopi but not Rio Grande Tewa. Both Hopi and Arizona Tewa narrators used their evidential particles in every narrative sentence and frequently used more than one per sentence (AT 1.32, Hopi 1.49). In both languages, about one-third of the narrated sentences displayed two or more such particles. These multiply occurring evidentials are exemplified in Arizona Tewa and Hopi examples 13 and 14.

13. 'ihɛdám ba, huwa ba, wi' huwa 'i-wínu-di ba, di-khaw-kɛnu. (AT)

     then-FOC EV, again EV, one again 3sgREFL-stand-SUB EV, 3pl-AC-sing-start.

     And THEN so, again so, as one stood up again so, they started to sing.

14. noq yaw 'ora:yvi 'atka ki:tava yaw piw tɨcvo ki'yta. (Hopi)

     and EV Oraibi below:south from:village EV also wren sg:lives

     And wren also lived below Oraibi, south of the village.

     (from Seumptewa et al. 1980)

But in a sample of Rio Grande Tewa stories, the evidential particle was not a required constituent of each narrated sentence. In addition, it occurred at a much lower rate (0.41 per narrative sentence) and only rarely as two or more instances within a given sentence (5 percent). These observations clearly demonstrate that while Arizona Tewa has retained its own evidential particle, speakers now use it in a manner identical to that of an analogous Hopi particle.

This instance of Hopi influence on Arizona Tewa discourse practices is instructive as an example of how differing degrees of awareness of linguistic organization affect both the diffusion process itself and the social meaning of such linguistic products and practices. As an independent discourse particle, *ba* enjoys a popular salience which approaches that of content nouns. For Tewa speakers to have switched from *ba* to Hopi *yaw*, the potential change would have attracted considerable notice and possible stigma as an instance of mixing codes or as some slight to the Tewa culture metonymically associated with the language. But since patterns of use are less tangible to speakers than words, change can occur at this level without attracting comparable attention. For hundreds of years Arizona Tewa children have grown up hearing traditional stories in Hopi and Tewa from their respective relatives. By converging their discursive norms for the two evidential particles, Arizona Tewa speakers have effected a cognitive pruning by reducing the inventory of differences that once distinguished the narrative schemata of the two languages. Though this change dramatically alters the indigenous model of storytelling by transforming *ba* into a genre-marker diagnostic of traditional storytelling, the continued use of the Tewa particle preserves the appearance of maintaining Tewa linguistic and cultural practices. As in the case of kinship mentioned above, the less visible pattern of use is Hopi but the tangible words are unmistakably Tewa.

Concluding Note

These episodes in the linguistic history of the Arizona Tewa and their Southern Tewa ancestors reveal the pervasive influence of Tewa language attitudes as a key mediating factor. When Edward Dozier wrote his well-known article contrasting linguistic borrowing from Spanish in Yaqui and Rio Grande Tewa, he attributed the open borrowing of the former and the extreme compartmentalization of the latter to historical differences in the nature of culture contact (Dozier 1951). He argued that the tolerant policies of the Spanish during Yaqui contact engendered greater acceptance, whereas the repressive regime experienced by the Tewa produced a grudging and highly compartmentalized form of borrowing. The theme of language attitudes is critically undeveloped in Dozier's explanatory scheme. But the history of the Arizona Tewa suggests that factors like language attitudes or linguistic ideologies have a powerful impact on the extent of foreign language influence. The longstanding multilingualism in Hopi creates rather ideal conditions for linguistic borrowing, and yet the pattern of diffusion is so highly restricted that it demands a consideration of local language attitudes. This pattern is explicable only by viewing it as the product of a cultural perspective that values linguistic purism and equates it with ethnic boundary maintenance.

These episodes of language contact examined in this chapter also affirm the essential wisdom of the Arizona Tewa folk saying about the Tewa language being an embodiment of history. These episodes further dem-

onstrate the value of the comparative linguistic approach used to manifest the often covert history behind the words and structures used today.
Evidence of lexical and grammatical borrowing have provided insights
into the historical adaptation of the Arizona Tewa to Apacheans, the
Spanish, and the Hopi. But the process of linguistic change being shaped
by the dynamics of culture contact is not limited to the past. Today,
English has joined Hopi and Tewa in the linguistic repertoire of the
Arizona Tewa. Though their Tano ancestors successfully removed themselves from Spanish influence, the Arizona Tewa descendants have found
the English-speaking world considerably more inescapable.

4

. . .

ON THE SOCIAL DISTRIBUTION OF LINGUISTIC
KNOWLEDGE IN THE ARIZONA TEWA
SPEECH COMMUNITY

The sociolinguistic basis of the Arizona Tewa expression *Na:- bí hi:li na:-bí wowa:ci na-mu:* (My language is my life [history]) is explored in this and the following chapter. How do speakers' linguistic knowledge and speech behavior reflect their biographical differences and similarities? What research strategies can be employed to reveal such sociolinguistic patterns? In this chapter, I will present the results of a series of studies designed to gauge and assess the relevance of some social variables that are considered significant by both sociolinguists and the Arizona Tewa themselves. But why, given the inattention to linguistic variation typical of most Americanist linguistic scholarship, should variation be worthy of scholarly attention for students of Native American languages and for anthropological linguists in general?[1]

Though, historically, students of Native American languages have made valuable contributions to the ethnographic description of such phenomena as "men's and women's speech" (e.g., Haas 1944; Sapir 1949, 160–66), specialized vocabularies (e.g., Newman 1955; Opler and Hoijer 1940), and "baby talk" (e.g., Casagrande 1948; Crawford 1970), little attention has been afforded to intra-speech community variation in casual speech (Voegelin 1960) and its implications for the investigation of language structure in general. A number of factors have contributed to this relative neglect, among them the *salvage principle*. As Brandt notes:

Concern with recording languages before they disappear, although important, has led to neglect in observing ongoing processes of linguistic change. We are aware that some variation in speech occurs in large urban societies, but how often is it noted that variation also occurs in small, relatively unstratified Indian communities? (Brandt 1970b, 46)

A second factor is the practice—with its associated methodological limitations—of employing only one or two native speaker-consultants, collecting data solely by elicitation, and conducting research either away from the relevant speech community or with native speaker-consultants who themselves are either isolated from or no longer possess significant membership in their former speech communities. As Gumperz observes:

The effect of such procedures is the selection of one single variety (Ferguson and Gumperz 1960, 3) out of the complex of varieties which characterize everyday speech behavior. This one variety is then considered to be representative of the entire language or dialect. (Gumperz 1971, 97)

What are the consequences of the inattention to linguistic diversity within the speech community that is fostered by these and other pragmatic factors?[2] As I see it two major consequences logically follow: one, an inability to observe ongoing linguistic change and the sociolinguistic processes that inform it and, two, the problem of analytic accountability in the abstraction of language structure from language use—the "negotiation" of the grammar. The latter problem can be rephrased in the following manner: without a familiarity with the nature and extent of linguistic variation within the relevant speech community, how can the analyst assess the representativeness of the native speaker-consultant's verbal behavior and the degree to which it typifies the grammar of a language or dialect? Certainly a considerable portion of overlap exists in the internalized grammars of all native speakers of a particular language. But just as surely the speech of any linguistic community exhibits competing variant alternations (at multiple subsystem levels), which are the recognized basis of linguistic change (Hoenigswald 1960)—now as in the past—in accord with the *uniformitarian principle* (Labov 1971, 422–23). Thus any analyst's grammar that is based on research informed by the assumption that data provided by any given speaker represents, in microcosm, the speech of the community characterized by its use, will inevitably mask variability in the guise of homogeneity. But this homogeneity is indexical not of actual conditions of the speech community but rather of the analyst's own disregard of that community.

Members' Perception of Variation

Were I not predisposed to view variation—both sociocultural (Wallace 1961; Pelto and Pelto 1975; Gardner 1976; Schutz 1955) and linguistic (Labov 1963; Hymes 1974)—as a significant characteristic of the Arizona Tewa speech community, such a view would have been suggested by the Arizona Tewa themselves. Many Arizona Tewa expressed great concern about how I, the investigating linguist, would choose the "correct" way of saying a particular utterance in instances where the responses of native speakers differed. This concern not only reflected their conception of linguistic description as a *prescriptive* rather than a *descriptive* endeavor but also their awareness of variation as an inherent aspect of the speech community.

In this section I will briefly report the kinds of variation that the Tewa themselves discriminate. In so doing I will provide some basis for comparisons of observations gained from both the perspectives of members of the speech community and that of the analyst. More significantly— since the remainder of this chapter is primarily devoted to a scrutiny of manifestations of but one of several kinds of variation perceived by members of the speech community—I will, in so doing, supply some indication of other variable linguistic phenomena that require additional research if we are to approximate anything like a comprehensive account of the "organization of diversity" within the Arizona Tewa speech community.

The Arizona Tewa attribute variation in their speech to one or more of the following five social variables: the gender, clan membership, age, and idiosyncrasies of the speaker and the nature (sacred or secular) of the speech situation (Hymes 1972, 56).[3] Most variation in the speech community is attributed by its members to the age of the speaker. As in other Pueblo communities like Sandia (Brandt 1970b), Acoma (Maring 1975), and Cochiti (Fox 1959), where similar situations have been reported, the speech of younger members of the speech community exhibits considerable linguistic acculturation or what has been termed, following Weinreich (1953, 1), *linguistic interference*. Most of these younger (up to thirty years old) speakers, in contrast to their elders, employ English as a dominant language and exhibit what is perceived by other speakers as impaired proficiency in Tewa and often little or no proficiency in Hopi except for kinship terms and polite expressions. Two explanations for this apparent *language shift* (Weinreich 1953, 68; Gal 1979), which has enhanced the English proficiency of younger members at the expense of their Tewa proficiency, may be plausibly advanced. One, Arizona Tewa is not a written language, therefore, unlike English it does not receive the "visual reinforcement in the use of a language that a bilingual gets by reading and writing it" (Weinreich 1953, 75).[4] Two, as I will demonstrate, use of English is differently evaluated by Arizona Tewa young people; they endow English with different symbolic associations than do their elders.

Yet despite the fact that older members of the speech community, like their counterparts at Acoma Pueblo (Maring 1975, 480), view the Arizona Tewa speech of young people as defective, they seldom, if ever, offer correction. The perceived deficiencies in the speech of the young are located by older speakers in the phenomenon of lexical attrition and the replacement of indigenous terms by their English counterparts. Though sociocultural change has prompted some adaptive shifts (Herzog 1941) in the lexicons of older speakers, younger Tewa display an abandonment of formerly productive strategies of semantically extending native terms and/or compounding two or more such terms in order to create lexical designations for nontraditional concepts.[5] Older Tewa also cite two additional kinds of evidence in support of their claim that younger Tewa possess a diminished proficiency in their native language. Younger people, they claim, no longer command vocabulary items associated with such native economic activities as planting, herding, hunting, and related activities. Even more serious is their charge that younger people have forgotten all but the morphologically most fundamental verbs. Many younger people openly admit that they no longer know how to "say a whole sentence in one word"—as one young man phrased it—though they view this inability as a consequence of changes associated with modernization and not, as their elders often maintain, as evidence of moral degeneration.

As with other social variables, such as gender (Kroskrity 1983a), the covarying linguistic phenomena are primarily at the lexical level. This finding closely parallels that of Gumperz and Wilson's Kupwar study, in which they observed (1971, 101–2) that lexical items and their inflectional properties appear to provide the phenomenal basis for the folk perception of what constitutes one language as opposed to another—in other words, its criterial attributes. Of course the folk account must be critically regarded. I interpret the prominence of the lexicon in these accounts as evidence of its perceptual salience but not as evidence that all, or even most, linguistic variation is actually located at this subsystem level. Likewise, I interpret the folk account of linguistic variation that is reported here as an initial and tentative first step and not a concluding stride in the direction of a satisfactory analysis of linguistic variation in the Arizona Tewa speech community.

For while the linguistic intuitions of native speakers—those manifested by the speaker in the form of verbalized introspection as well as those inferred by the analyst from the communicative behavior of the native speaker—constitute an important part of the data that the analyst must consult in any grammatical descriptive endeavor, the sociolinguistic intuitions of native speakers must be critically regarded as hypotheses to be tested. They represent the starting point of inquiry rather than the final product of analysis. While both the internalized linguistic and sociolinguistic knowledge of native speakers may be more or less out of his or her awareness (i.e., tacit or taken-for-granted knowledge), a speaker's linguistic intuitions can be reasonably viewed as evidence of the form and operation of his or her internalized grammar. But a speaker's sociolinguistic knowledge must be viewed, in part, as a biased reflection of the speech community, which is indexical of his or her position in its social system. Thus since both the tacit and socially distributed nature of sociolinguistic knowledge militate against its accessibility via self-report, additional research will be necessary to ascertain and verify the existence and extent of variable linguistic phenomena—both those included in the Arizona Tewa self-report and such potentially significant variables as registers (Hasan 1973); culturally defined speech situations (Hymes 1972, 60); genres (Hymes 1972, 65); and other, perhaps neglected, components. Here only age-based variation will be further explored.

The Analyst's Perspective

Though the Arizona Tewa perceive age-based variation as primarily a lexical phenomenon, the speech of younger Arizona Tewa exhibits striking syntactic and phonological differences from the speech of their seniors. In fact, as at Acoma (Maring 1975, 480), it appears that grammatical interference from English is at least as significant at these subsystem levels as it is at those that are more recognized by members of the Arizona Tewa speech community.

The research upon which the original study is based was conducted during summer research over a period of eight years (1973–80). During the first two months of fieldwork performed in the first year, variation was largely ignored as I attempted to familiarize myself with the details of the Arizona Tewa language as manifested in the speech of three native speaker-consultants. Midway through the second summer's research my opportunities to observe more naturalistic speech behavior—as differentiated from the more structured speech of elicitation sessions and interviews—increased considerably. Involvement in some of the practical activities of the residents of Tewa Village—planting, trading with Navajos and Anglos, preparing for dances and ceremonies, conversing with tourists and missionaries, conducting family and tribal matters, going to town for supplies, entertaining visiting relatives, and so on, brought me into regular contact with a greater number of members of the Arizona Tewa speech community and exposed me to some instances of syntactic and semantic variability. Due to my early interest in providing a grammatical description of such phenomena as inverses, conjunctions, and relative clauses, I was especially aware of variation associated with them. During the remainder of that summer and throughout the following summers I recorded instances of variation in the production of the aforementioned phenomena, the speakers who produced them, and details of the speech situation. This strategy was also extended to a number of phonological and morphological phenomena not, initially, because they were research foci but because it was found useful in making sense of various transcriptional problems and the complexity of Arizona Tewa verb prefixes. In this manner I recorded observations of thirty-one individuals. The great bulk of these observations derived from the behavior of fourteen members (nine male, five female, ranging in age from eighteen to ninety years). By the end of the third summer enough data had been gathered to suggest the relevance of age as a dimension of variability that accounted for all the observed variation with only a few exceptions.[6]

During that summer and for the next five summers of fieldwork, special attention was devoted to six individuals (three male, three female),

Table 4.1   Linguistic Correlates of Age

	Group (Age in Years)		
	1 (<30)	2 (30–50)	3 (>50)
Noncasual speech fluency	none	passive	active
Observes NEG assimilation	no	no	yes
Dominant language	English	Tewa	Tewa
Code-switching	no	yes	yes
Lexical replacement	10%	5%	1%

who on the basis of the large sample could be regarded as reasonably representative of their age groups. Age groups were first arbitrarily imposed on the data, utilizing groups that segmented the population at twenty-year intervals (under twenty, twenty to forty, forty to sixty, etc.) as in other studies of Pueblo speech communities (Brandt 1970b; Maring 1975; Fox 1959). These groups were later modified in accord with observed correlations with study-external metrics of linguistic variability and language use. As displayed in table 4.1, three groups were distinguished in this manner. Group 1 consisted of members under thirty years of age. In this group, age correlated with a lack of fluency in noncasual speech styles (e.g., chants, songs, and traditional narratives), use of English as a dominant language and the preferred language of intragroup interaction, and some (10 percent) replacement of basic native vocabulary in the Arizona Tewa code with corresponding English terms.[7]

Group 2 consisted of members between the ages of thirty and fifty. Like the younger group, members of this group displayed no active fluency in noncasual speech forms, though they were proficient decoders of such texts.[8] However, they differed from members of group 1 in two important respects. One, they used all the codes in their linguistic repertoire with approximately equal facility and in accord with local notions of contextual appropriateness. Two, they exhibited greater compartmentalization of codes, as manifested in relatively little lexical replacement of native terms by their English counterparts.

Group 3 consisted of members of fifty or more years of age. They characteristically displayed conversance with noncasual speech varieties—in contrast to the members of both other groups. Like members of group 2 they exhibited a more balanced implementation of all the component codes in their linguistic repertoire and comparable code-switching behavior. In addition, and unlike members of groups 1 and 2, they invariably observe, in careful as well as in relatively unmonitored speech, a morphophonemic rule that assimilates the vowel of the negative prefix /we-/ to the initial vowel of the following pronominal prefix under specifiable conditions.[9] The assimilated form appears to be stigmatized by members of groups 1 and 2, for while they produce the assimilated variant in their spontaneous speech, they purge it from their careful speech—a phenomenon first noted by Yegerlehner (1957, 14).

After distinguishing three groups on the basis of age and nonsyntactic/semantic criteria, I selected two individuals (one male, one female) to represent each group for the purpose of further intensive investigation. Since male and female speech in Arizona Tewa is culturally distinct (Kroskrity 1983a), my inclusion of women in this convenience sample was designed to detect any significant gender differences in speech behavior manifested in those grammatical phenomena under study. (Using a convenience sample is a sociological strategy for gathering data without elaborate random sampling.) Investigation of this intensive study sample assumed two forms. One, all six individuals acted as native speaker-consultants who were interviewed periodically and asked to produce translations of English sentences, some of which were designed to elicit Arizona Tewa phenomena that I had encountered as variable within the Arizona Tewa speech community. Two, in order to supplement "normative data delivered under the influence of conscious reflection" (Labov 1971, 429), as well as to control for the biasing of responses by native speaker-consultants through the use of English as the language of elicitation (Hale 1965), each of these speakers was regularly observed in undirected speech so as to obtain samples of relatively unmonitored speech.[10]

But before I turn to the next section I would like to detail some of the analytical objectives that both motivated and shaped the present study. This study was designed to answer ethnographic, theoretical, and pragmatic questions. The existing scholarship on intra-speech community variation of Native American languages, if not all languages, has concentrated primarily on phonology (e.g., Brandt 1970b; Hinton 1980). Here

I attempted to also focus on instances of syntactic and semantic variation in an effort to complement the small but growing body of scholarship that attends to variation in the speech of Native American communities. Though perhaps less readily accessible than their phonological counterparts (Labov 1972a, 111), these syntactic and semantic indexes are indispensable if we are to more closely approximate a comprehensive account of the sociolinguistic processes that inform language change at all subsystem levels.

The aforementioned ethnographic lack is metonymically representative of a genuine theoretical deficiency in approaches to linguistic variation. Labov has described syntactic change as "an elusive process as compared to sound change" (Labov 1973, 65). A major deficiency of some variationist models—most notably Bailey's *dynamic paradigm* (1974)—continues to be an inattention to syntactic phenomena. It remains far from clear how such models can be extended so as to encompass more than just the phonological component. One of my interests was thus to study the relatively neglected phenomenon of syntactic/semantic change. A final objective was to produce a multidimensional set of measures that would be sensitive to variation in each subsystem level: syntax-semantics, phonology, and morphology.

In addition to such objectives, practical considerations also shaped the present study. Since the research was conducted by a single analyst, who was simultaneously engaged in other linguistic investigations, in a speech community in which a few individuals denounced such research as "the selling of the language," my research procedures must be viewed as an adaptation to the field situation, an adaptation that answered the need for unobtrusive measures while ensuring a satisfactory level of representativeness.

Sociolinguistic Patterns of Four Syntactic/Semantic Indicators

Following Labov (1972b, 178) I define an indicator as a linguistic variable that shows no pattern of stylistic variation and serves as an analytical index—here by statistically significant differences in their display—of membership in group 1, 2, or 3. The following discussion treats these linguistic measures in the order in which they appear in table 4.2.[11]

The three groups demonstrated differential propensities to use phrasal conjunction, or commitative noun phrases, in sentences of the form

Table 4.2   Syntactic/Semantic Indicators of Arizona Tewa Linguistic
Performance, by Age Group (% ER/% SS)

	Group		
Indicator	1	2	3
A. Phrasal conjunctions NP-á-dí NP	90/84	48/44	38/42
B. Inverses under condition S = [+ animate]	74/46	90/84	98/94
C. Relative clauses nonactive prefixes (internal head selected by prefix)	58/48	95/84	94/88
D. Relative clauses active prefixes (embedded S-initial NP coreferential with relativizer)	96/48	62/56	58/51

NOTES: ER = elicited responses; SS = spontaneous speech.

1 = speakers less than thirty-one years of age (actual range eighteen to twenty-nine).

2 = speakers between thirty-one and fifty years of age (actual range thirty-four to forty-six).

3 = speakers older than fifty years of age (actual range fifty-six to ninety).

All ages are based on the speakers' self-reports and reflect their chronological age at the time the study began.

Total elicited responses/total instances of spontaneous speech:

	Group		
	1	2	3
A.	150/75	150/71	185/93
B.	150/50	150/63	200/77
C.	140/63	100/50	160/76
D.	150/88	100/45	156/98

[NP-á-dí NP Verb Complex].[12] For example, "the man and the woman are entering" may be translated into Arizona Tewa as any one of the following semantically equivalent expressions:

1. sen-ná-dí kwiyó da-c'u:de-'ɛ'ɛ
   man-E-OBL woman 3du:STA-enter-come

2. sen-ná-dí kwiyó-wá-dí da-c'u:de-'ɛ'ɛ
   man-E-OBL woman-E-OBL 3du:STA-enter-come

3. sen kwiyó-wa-dí da-c'u:de-'ɛ'ɛ
   man woman-E-OBL 3du:STA-enter-come

Table 4.2A shows that speakers of group 1 display a marked increase in the production of phrasal conjunctions—i.e., use of NP-á-dí NP— over groups 2 and 3, in both elicited responses (ER) and spontaneous speech (SS).

All dialects of Tewa, like Navajo (Hale 1973; Creamer 1974), exhibit semantic constraints on the well-formedness of inverse and active sentences. Inverses are like passive sentences (e.g., English: Fred was hit [by John]) in their foregrounding of information about the patient instead of the agent, which is the usual subject of active voice sentences (e.g., John hit Fred). Inverses differ from passives primarily in the fact that the inverse verb remains a fully transitive construction whereas the passive becomes more like a stative verb or adjective.[13] In the better-known Navajo inverse, entities designated by nouns may be hierarchically ranked so as to provide a basis for a rule of semantic interpretation that declares as ill-formed those sentences in which the subordinate noun precedes the superior noun. The comparable Arizona Tewa phenomenon employs not an elaborate hierarchy but rather a simple binary discrimination between animate and nonanimate noun phrases. Another difference between these languages is that in Tewa, in contrast to Navajo, the logical subject (or agent argument) is marked by the oblique postposition /-di/. Thus linear order of noun phrases in Tewa need not reflect their grammatical relations since this information is morphologically encoded in Tewa inverse sentences. A consequence of these differences is that the rule of semantic interpretation must be restated in the Tewa case so as to refer to the "subject of" an inverse verb rather than to the serial order of noun phrases. These observations are exemplified by sentences 4–7:

4. né'i sen hę'i pę: man-hey
    this man that deer 3sg/3AC-kill
    This man killed that deer.

5. hę'i pę: né'i sen-di 'ó:-hey
    that deer this man-OBL 3sg/3INV-kill
    That deer was killed by this man.

6. hę'i sen né'i p'o mán-su-n
    that man this water 3sg/3AC-drink-TNS
    That man drank this water.

7. *né'i p'o hę'i sen-di 'ó:-su-n
    this water that man-OBL 3sg/3INV-drink-TNS
    This water was drunk by that man.

Sentences 4 and 5 represent an active-inverse alternation in which the inverse sentence is semantically well-formed partially because the surface subject *hę-'i pę:* (that deer) fulfills the condition of animacy. When this condition is violated—as in 7, the inverse alternative of 6—the result is a semantically ill-formed sentence. (The asterisk indicates the sentence is ungrammatical in that language.)

Table 4.2B indicates the percentage of inverse sentences, involving both a third person subject and a third person object, produced by speakers in accord with the semantic condition which states that the subject/patient of a well-formed inverse sentence in Arizona Tewa must be [+ animate]. All elicited responses were in the form of sentences in which both subject and object were fully specified noun phrases, whereas in the spontaneous speech samples instances of pronominalization and constituent ellipsis were also considered, as long as the referent could be inferred with reasonable certainty by the analyst.

Here again group 1 exhibits notable differences in speech behavior from that of groups 2 and 3. Whereas speakers of these other groups consistently observe the semantic constraint in both elicited and spontaneous speech, speakers of group 1 only approximate this in the careful, more self-monitored style permitted by the elicited response—an indication that some stylistic control based on reflection and perhaps recollection of traditional notions of semantic well-formedness of the inverse prompts such a response. But while this knowledge appears to be retriev-

Table 4.3   Diagrammed Arizona Tewa Sentence Illustrating
Relative Clause

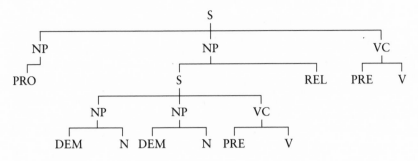

na:	hę'i	sen	né'i	wa:yu	'ų́:-'én	'i	dó-mun
I	that	man	this	horse	3sg:POS -sit	REL	1:sg/3:AC-see

I saw this horse which belongs to (sits in relation to) that man.

able in situations such as translation, the spontaneous speech score indicates that when speech is unself-conscious the semantic constraint approaches random frequencies.

Internal head selection in relative clauses containing nonactive prefixes is the first of two measurements of the speech production of Arizona Tewa relative clauses (table 4.2C). Like relative clauses in most southwestern Native American languages (Gorbet 1977), Arizona Tewa relative clauses are typically headless, or internally headed, in that they lack a fully specified noun phrase in the higher sentence that is modified by the embedded sentence. In a previous analysis of Arizona Tewa relative clauses (Kroskrity 1977, 98–129) I found it useful to distinguish a semantic and a syntactic head. Table 4.3 provides a hierarchically diagrammed sentence that illustrates these concepts.[14]

In table 4.3 'i, the third person independent pronoun, functions as the syntactic head of the modifying sentence embedded in the higher sentence, while nę́'i wa:yu (this horse) represents the internal head—the fully specified noun phrase in the lower sentence that is coreferential with the syntactic head. An important process in the semantic interpretation of Arizona Tewa relative clauses, then, is the establishment of anaphoric relations between the syntactic and internal heads. But just how is this

Table 4.4   Semantic Function and Grammatical Relationship of the
Lower Verb Prefix to the Lower Verb in the Internal Head

Prefix of Lower V	Grammatical Relation to Lower V	Semantic Function
possessive	object	possessed
stative	subject	experiencer
reflexive-reciprocal	subject	agent/goal
inverse	subject	patient
active	indeterminate	indeterminate

accomplished? Why, for example, does the sentence in table 4.3 read "I
saw this horse which is owned by that man" and not "I saw that man
who owns this horse?" The answer is that the nonactive prefixes of the
lower verb control the anaphoric process of semantic head selection. Every Tewa verb must be modified by a member of one of five classes of
prefix (possessive, stative, reflexive-reciprocal, inverse, active), appropriately inflected for person and number (singular, dual, plural). Nonactive
prefixes and not the underlying or surface order of noun phrases determine coreference between syntactic and semantic heads thus permitting
the stable correlations indicated in table 4.4.

In quantifying internal head selection (table 4.2 C) I attempted to gauge
the percentage of times speakers produced relative clauses composed of
embedded sentences with a nonactive prefix in which coreference between semantic and syntactic heads was conditioned by the aforementioned process of semantic head selection—a process in which the identity of the prefix plays a critical role. While the English stimuli-sentences
were designed to elicit the entire range of nonactive prefixes that could
possibly occur in the lower, or embedded, sentence and to secure reasonably even distributions of each (possessive, stative, reflexive-reciprocal,
inverse) in the sample, similar controls were impossible to implement in
the spontaneous speech sample. Thus since relative clauses composed of
embedded inverse sentences occurred more frequently in the spontaneous
speech of all groups than did those composed of embedded sentences
containing the other nonactive prefixes, the two samples are somewhat
differently constituted.

Here again group 1 shows a much lower rate of production of relative clauses in which anaphoric relations between syntactic and semantic heads are determined by the identity of nonactive prefixes. In the spontaneous speech sample for this group the prefix-selected noun phrase head is chosen in less than 50 percent of the instances of relative clause production. The higher percent for elicited responses is probably due to the aforementioned relatively even distribution of nonactive prefix types in that sample. Since some of these prefix types do not co-occur with more than one possible semantic head (e.g., stative prefixes) they do not constitute an instructive test of the anaphoric strategies used in their production. The second measurement of relative clause production—determination of semantic head selection in relative clauses containing active prefixes—was designed to assess the degree to which the speakers employed a *positional* strategy in assigning coreference with the syntactic head to the embedded sentence-initial noun phrase in relative clauses containing active prefixes (table 4.2D). Recall that head selection in such cases is indeterminate and independent of the constituent order of the embedded sentence for most speakers. For example, a sentence such as 8 could be interpreted as either "I saw the woman who made the pottery" or "I saw the pottery which was made by the woman."

8. na: [kwiyó se'ɛ:we mán-pa:] 'i dó-mun
    I [woman pottery 3sg/3AC-make] REL 1sg/3AC-see

This indeterminacy is statistically reflected in the scores of groups 2 and 3, which closely approximate the random values a reliance on disambiguation by the higher verb (or by entirely extralinguistic means) would produce. The results here indicate that a positional strategy appears to have been adopted by members of group 1 since this group exhibits a marked increase in the production of relative clauses that conform to that pattern. The high score obtained in the elicited responses of this group seems to indicate that in careful speech younger Arizona Tewa both use and prefer an anaphoric strategy that is clearly not shared by the older speakers of groups 2 and 3.

DISCUSSION   In contrast to the statistically insignificant differences that prevail between the four measures employed for groups 2 and 3, group 1 manifests consistent and marked differences. Collectively these indicators reveal a pattern of grammatical interference from English in

the internalized Arizona Tewa grammars of group 1. In order to substantiate this claim two points must be adequately addressed. One, the
observed differences must be ones that could have been modeled on
comparable English language structures. Two, some evidence must also
be presented to account for why differential interference exists—since
English is included in the repertoire of all the Arizona Tewa speakers
sampled, why is it that only members of group 1, the younger speakers,
provide demonstrable evidence of linguistic interference. Regarding the
former, an examination of each of the linguistic variables below clearly
demonstrates that the grammar of English does provide a plausible source
of grammatical interference for the observed changes. The pattern of
phrasal conjunction most widely employed by speakers of group 1 is that
which is structurally isomorphic with its English counterpart: [NP-á-dí
NP]NP (table 4.2A). Though aware of the traditional conventions followed by members of groups 2 and 3 in creating well-formed inverse
sentences in both elicited and spontaneous speech, members of group 1
do not systematically follow these semantic conventions in their spontaneous speech (table 4.2B). The fact that less than half of the sentences in
this sample were, from the perspective of older speakers, semantically
well-formed suggests that the Tewa inverse is undergoing reanalysis in
the speech of younger Tewa on the model of the English passive, in which
no comparable semantic constraint exists. Both the abandonment of an
interpretive rule that assigns coreference on the basis of the identity of
the nonactive prefixes of the lower verb and the adoption of a positional
or syntactic strategy for the disambiguation of relative clauses containing
active prefixes also seem to be grammatical innovations on the part of
younger speakers which are inspired by English (table 4.2C and D). In
English relative clauses, coreference between the head noun phrase (in
the higher sentence) and the modifying sentence is syntactically mediated,
not semantically mediated as in the Tewa case. In other words, the head
of an English relative clause immediately precedes the relative pronoun
and the embedded sentence; it is not selected for coreference on the basis
of the semantics of the lower verb as it is in the internally headed Arizona
Tewa examples when such verbs are nonactive.

The speech of younger Arizona Tewa thus represents the innovation of
a new anaphoric strategy based on the syntactic model of English. In
accord with this model the embedded sentence-initial noun phrase of the
Arizona Tewa relative clause is equated with the English head noun

phrase. The remainder of the embedded sentence and the syntactic head are thus equated with the relative pronoun and modifying sentence of their English counterparts. Particularly in table 4.2D we find some cross-linguistic support for Naro's (1981, 97) observation that "syntactic change originates in contexts that admit more than one syntactic analysis with no change in surface form." Despite the production of identical surface structures, members of group 1, on the one hand, and of groups 2 and 3, on the other, assign different interpretations that indicate alternative syntactic analyses.

Collectively, linguistic interference does provide a plausible explanation for the patterned differences in the internalized grammars of Arizona Tewa of younger speakers. The internalized grammatical rules that underlie the production and interpretation of phrasal conjunctions, semantic passive sentences, and relative clauses in English and Arizona Tewa thus appear to have converged (Gumperz and Wilson 1971) or at least to have approximated convergence with respect to these phenomena. The compartmentalization of codes, which accounts for the relative lack of grammatical interference in the speech of groups 2 and 3, no longer acts as a nearly impermeable barrier between coexisting codes in the linguistic repertoire of younger Arizona Tewa speakers. The presence of both lexical interference, of which older members are acutely aware, and less salient grammatical interference, which has been established here, in the speech of younger members testifies to the breakdown of compartmentalization as a symbolic strategy for maintaining the distinctiveness of coexisting codes within the code matrix.

Sociolinguistic Patterns of Four Phonological and Morphological Indicators

In attempting to extend the previous study, I sought phonological and morphological indicators that might further reveal significant sociolinguistic patterns. In studies conducted during summer research from 1977 to 1980, I tested a variety of phonological and morphological phenomena that I had previously encountered as variable within or between individuals.[15] Of these, four yielded significant results when incorporated into measures applied to the linguistic performance of my original research population. These measures and my findings are presented in table 4.5. As in the previous study, I sought data from both elicitations

Table 4.5   Phonological and Morphological Indicators of Arizona
Tewa Linguistic Performance, by Age Group (% ER/% SS)

Indicator	Group		
	1	2	3
A. Preservation of plain consonants—medial	12/28	94/58	96/94
B. Preservation of plain consonants—initial	24/20	98/90	98/92
C. Analogic change of INV prefixes	88/56	0/14	0/4
D. Generalization of *den-* to nontransitive (2)(3):dual	96/84	2/18	0/2

NOTES: ER = elicited responses; SS = spontaneous speech.

1 = speakers less than thirty-one years of age (actual range eighteen to twenty-nine).

2 = speakers between thirty-one and fifty years of age (actual range thirty-four to forty-six).

3 = speakers older than fifty years of age (actual range fifty-six to ninety).

All ages are based on the speakers' self-reports and reflect their chronological age at the time the study began.

Total elicited responses/total instances of spontaneous speech:

	Group		
	1	2	3
A.	150/75	150/71	185/93
B.	150/50	150/63	200/77
C.	140/63	100/50	160/76
D.	150/88	100/45	156/98

and more spontaneous speech. Unlike the previous study, however, the spontaneous speech samples were drawn from all available members of the relevant age group and not merely the two key consultants selected, on the basis of their representativeness, for each age group.

As discussed in chapter 3, Arizona Tewa retains the four-way stop contrast of Proto-Kiowa-Tanoan, distinguishing plain (unvoiced), aspirated, glottalized, and voiced stops. But while this may be regarded as true of the speech of some speakers, these distinctions are not invariably observed by all speakers in every situation. Though speakers of all groups distinguish aspirated and glottalized consonants, there are important group differences in the pronunciation of stem-initial and medial plain consonants. Whereas the oldest speakers preserve this distinction between plain and voiced consonants in their elicited responses and spontaneous speech, group 2 speakers do display a significant difference between these two in their pronunciation of medial plain stops (table 4.5 A). Though they appear to endorse the pronunciation norms of the oldest speakers in the more careful speech of elicitation, their performance in less monitored speech does stray from these norms (i.e., only 58 percent preservation). For a tangible example of the effect of this tendency, verb stems such as -na:pa (to hoe), -cikáy (to ask), and -si:tų́ (to cry) are pronounced, respectively, [na:ba], [cigáy], and [si:dų́] by group 2 speakers in undeliberated speech. The same is true of group 1 speakers, but with two important differences. Not only is the frequency of preservation significantly lower in their spontaneous speech, but their elicited response scores suggest that they have adopted an entirely different pronunciation idea. In other words, speakers of group 1 actually appear to regard the pronunciation of the voiced variant in medial position as the more correct. In table 4.5 B the use of plain-voiced consonants in the stem-initial position is examined. Here we find no significant contrast within or between individuals for speakers of groups 2 and 3. But group 1 speakers contrast markedly by collapsing the distinction between voiced and plain initial stops in the great majority of instances (e.g., only 28 percent retention). Some examples of resulting pronunciation differences are given in table 4.6.

It should be noted that even though this apparent in-progress elimination of the plain stop series seems to be a dramatic and potentially disruptive change, the pronunciation of formerly plain consonants as voiced does not suddenly produce rampant homophony. Since initial voiced stops (in the older, more traditional speech stratum) are extremely rare

Table 4.6   Comparison of Older and Younger Arizona Tewa
Speakers' Pronunciation

Term	Group 1	Groups 2 and 3
rabbit	bu	pu
to plant	-go:	-ko:
digging stick	do	to
to die	-gyu:	-kyu:
rain	gwen	kwen

except in grammatical morphemes such as the pronominal prefixes, the change produces very few homophonous lexical items. What few do occur, such as *dó-* 1sg/3AC and *tó* (digging stick) (pronounced as [dó]) are readily distinguishable on the basis of their disparate morphosyntactic behavior.

Though older speakers sometimes denigrate younger speakers as "speaking Tewa like a whiteman" (*p'o-p'ǫ́-pí'i-bí-wa:ki mán-tewa-hi:li-'o*), from a linguistic perspective the apparent phonological change by the younger speakers does represent a simplifying innovation for their multilingual adaptation. This is especially true when we consider the diglossic situation of the speech community. Though an appeal to pattern congruity and simplification of the signal can supply general, language-internal motivations for such an innovation, no explanation of this process can divorce it from a consideration of contemporary societal multilingualism and, ultimately, the effect of English. It is especially noteworthy to observe that the Tewa phonology of group 1 speakers has converged to a considerable extent with their English phonology. Aside from glottalized stops, the remaining Tewa stop series—aspirated and voiced—function like English voiceless and voiced stops, respectively, to produce the relevant contrast. One could easily argue that these Tewa stop series have become more like their English counterparts. The aspirated stop series of younger speakers may simply be likened to the English voiceless stops which are aspirated in initial position. Similarly the absorption of Tewa plain stops by their voiced counterparts is suggested by the phonology of English in which [±voice] is a much more important

Table 4.7   Arizona Tewa Pronominal Prefixes

A. NON-INVERSE PREFIXES

Subject Person and Number

	1sg	1du	1pl	2sg	2du	2pl	3sg	3du	3pl
POS	dín	gáh	gíh	'úh	dę́h	'óh	'ų́:	dɛn	do:
STA	'o	ga	gi	'ų	da	'i	na	da	di
RFL	déh	an	'íbí	bi	den	'óbí	'i	den	díbí
ACT	dó	'an	'í:	ná:	den	'obí:n	mán	den	dí:

B. INVERSE PREFIXES

	Group		
Patient Person-Number	1	2 or 3	3
1		dí	
2	wí		
2sg			wó:
2du			wó:bén
2pl			wó:bé
3sg			'ó:
3du			'ó:bén
3pl			'ó:bé

NOTE: For purposes of simplification, this table excludes benefactive prefixes. Though some prefixes in B do not distinguish between second and third persons they have been mapped into multiple cells to permit maximal comparability. Finally, all ACT prefixes presuppose a third person object.

contrast. Linguistic convergence thus seems a plausible explanation of available data, especially given the evidence of comparable processes elsewhere in the language and the ethnographic evidence of different generational norms of language use presented in the preceding section.

Table 4.7 displays the asymmetrical morphology of Arizona Tewa inverse prefixes.

Though the prefix stems *wó:-* and *'ó:* 2/3INV and 3/3INV permit both the patient number suffixes *-bén* and *-bé*, dual and plural, no such co-occurrence is permitted with prefix stems *wí-* and *dí-* 2/1INV and 1/-1INV. But here again this is not true of all speakers or even of all regional dialects of Tewa. Table 4.5C shows that group 1 speakers, in contrast to those of groups 2 and 3, appear to have adopted a unitary strategy regarding the morphology of inverse prefixes. In both elicitation and spontaneous speech contexts they will use pronominal prefixes like *wíbén* and *díbé*, 2du/1INV (you two by me) and 1pl/-1INV (we [+ pl] by someone). Such prefixes occur only rarely as *performance errors* in the spontaneous speech of more senior members of the speech community. When given the opportunity to evaluate their prior linguistic performance, as in playback of an audiotape or reviewing a previously elicited text, older speakers (2 and 3) invariably deny the well-formedness of these rarely spoken forms via the process of self-correction.

As illustrated by table 4.7, Arizona Tewa pronominal prefixes typically distinguish the person and number of the subject as well as the clause type, producing unique prefixes for each configuration of these components. An important exception to this pattern is provided by dual number prefixes of second and third persons in reflexive (RFL) and active (AC) clauses. With such configurations all speakers employ the prefix *den-*, as in examples 10 and 11:

10. hę'in sen-en den-hey
    those man-pl (2)(3)duRFL/AC-kill
    Those two men killed each other/him:her.

11. hogu 'ú-n den-tay
    already II-pl (2)(3)duRFL/AC-know
    You two already know each other/him/her.

As the English glosses of these examples indicate, such sentences are ambiguous. They could be reflexive constructions or active sentences with an ellipted object—the choice is linguistically indeterminate and must be negotiated in context. The indeterminacy would be further compounded if the subjects were not specified since the same prefix is used for both second and third person duals.

Table 4.5D illustrates the extent to which this prefix is generalized to similar person and number configurations in nontransitive clause types—

i.e., possessive (POS) and stative (STA)—and reveals that this variable displays a similar pattern to that in table 4.2A. The oldest speakers once again show no significant intraindividual variation in elicited or spontaneous speech. Group 2 speakers show a slight but significant difference in their elicited and spontaneous speech, indicating an endorsement of the norms displayed by the oldest speakers but a slight departure from those norms in relatively unmonitored performance (18 percent). In contrast, group 1 speakers show a very high frequency of generalization to nontransitive constructions in both elicited (90 percent) and spontaneous (98 percent) speech, once again suggesting that they have adopted an alternative linguistic norm.

DISCUSSION   Unlike phonological measures A and B of table 4.5, the morphological measures C and D clearly do not represent instances of linguistic convergence. With respect to the analogic change of inverse prefixes (table 4.5C), there is an interesting similarity between the Arizona Tewa prefixes of younger speakers and those of Rio Grande Tewa. Rio Grande Tewa distinguishes 2/1INV for singular, dual, and plural number: wí-, wǽn-, and wé:, respectively (Speirs 1966, 168–69). In contrast to Arizona Tewa, only 1/-1INV prefixes cannot occur with patient number prefixes in Rio Grande Tewa. These dialect differences suggest that at least one of these dialects has previously changed from the inherited pattern. While a full account of these regional differences must await the reconstruction of the Proto-Tanoan prefix system, these comparative data certainly indicate that change in the prefix system need not necessarily be interpreted as a by-product of language contact.

Elizabeth Brandt (1970a, 123–25) has also observed changes in the prefix system of another Tanoan language—Sandia Tiwa. Unlike the change illustrated in table 4.5D, which involves a simplifying generalization of a prefix to all noninverse clauses with a 2du or 3du subject, the Sandia changes involved the morphological fusion and concomitant lack of analyzability for formerly "transparent" prefixes. Elsewhere Nancy Dorian (1978) has linked a loss of morphological complexity with the phenomenon of language death. But it is unclear whether group 1 speakers can be equated with Dorian's (1981, 155) *semi-speakers,* or whether the simplification effected by analogy (table 4.5C) and extension (table 4.5D) must necessarily be associated with language death, as in Schmidt's (1985, 230) study of "young people's Dyirbal." In regard to the former, it is probably more the rule than the exception that younger speakers, in any speech community display some departures from the linguistic norms of their parents and grandparents. This is, of course, partially an artifact of employing the oldest stratum of speech as the informal standard.

Concerning the apparent loss of morphological complexity and its association with language death, two observations can be made. One, the changes are rather circumscribed and despite their simplification, they preserve category differences (such as dual number) that are not grammatically significant in English—the language of increasing use among young people. As shown in table 4.5C, it is the more complex morphological alternative rather than the less complex (i.e., prefixes uninflected for number) which is adopted by the younger speakers. These observations suggest that these changes have not been influenced by the structure of English although they may reflect simplifications encouraged by their decreasing use of Arizona Tewa in favor of English.

Two, as for language death, it is still unclear whether the language is actually dying. Though most younger speakers prefer to use English in intragroup interaction and reserve Arizona Tewa for vertical communication with the older generation, the crucial question—insofar as the fate of the language is concerned—is which language will be used for the purpose of raising their children. At present the pattern is extremely ambiguous. An unprecedented degree of variation in both residence pattern and household composition currently exists in Tewa Village. In my informal observations, I have found about one half of all children being raised with considerable exposure to the native language. Even where both parents seldom speak Tewa, children in their formative years are still spending considerable time with their grandparents, from whom they often receive informal language instruction (Scribner and Cole 1973).[16] Without clear evidence of abrupt transmission failure, or *tip* (Dorian 1989, 9), it seems premature to describe the sociolinguistic patterns observed in the data as language death.

The Changing Role of English

Taken collectively, the eight indicators of Arizona Tewa linguistic performance illustrated in tables 4.2 and 4.5 clearly indicate the impact of English linguistic structures and increased English usage on the Tewa grammars of younger speakers. Although the morphological simplification appears only to have been facilitated by increased English usage, the measures for syntax-semantics and phonology (table 4.2 and table 4.5 A and B) provide clear evidence of linguistic convergence. Given this convergence and the fact that all three generations of Tewa speakers studied here are fluent English speakers, it seems appropriate to ask: Why does the younger speakers' speech exhibit such linguistic interference? Why do the younger speakers not continue the pattern of compartmentalization observed for their elders? What are the social factors responsible for this apparent change in the perception and use of English? Perhaps foremost among these factors is the formation of a new and influential reference group (Shibutani 1962) that has recruited a significant number of young people—a group that has been fostered by the formal education provided by the government, promoted by the increasing penetration of the mass media into reservation life, and transported from the urban-based boarding schools that many Arizona Tewa attended for the duration of their secondary education. The fact that English is the sole language of instruction as well as the only common language for young Indians of various southwestern tribes, though important, is perhaps not as significant as the removal of younger people from the traditional socializing influences of kinsmen and other community members.

When subsistence agriculture played a major role in the economy of the reservation, activities such as planting, cultivating, and herding constituted an obligatory part of one's informal education—an education that entailed significant intergenerational interaction with kinsmen and community members. Today subsistence patterns have yielded to a cash economy in which the economic security of a household depends on the wage work or salaried employment of at least one of its members. Yet for young people the slim economic base of the reservation affords few opportunities and acts as a *push-factor* (Hodge 1971, 349)—a force that encourages abandonment of the reservation in either a physical (actual urban migration) or psychological sense (e.g., the adoption of a nontraditional, urban orientation).

In keeping with this urban orientation, English is employed as the preferred language of intragroup interaction, and since such interaction comprises the bulk of all their interpersonal interaction—a testimony to the diminished influence of family and other kinsmen—English may be properly regarded as the dominant language of the majority of young people. Gumperz and Cook-Gumperz (1982, 7) have appropriately observed that "social identity and ethnicity are in large part established and maintained through language." Whereas the Arizona Tewa language continues to serve as a badge of ethnicity for older speakers, younger members have adopted English as a symbol of their nontraditional orientation. Their habitual use of English even in response to remarks addressed to them in Arizona Tewa by their parents violates traditional expectations regarding code-switching behavior and both signals the disparity of values attached to the component codes of the linguistic repertoire by members of different generations and symbolically invokes a competing nontraditional perspective from which meanings are differently assigned to actions and objects. By so responding, young people manifest both their rejection of more traditional norms and values—as factors to be considered in the generation of appropriate behavior—and their allegiance to a new reference group from whose perspective they prefer to formulate and evaluate their actions.

For the increasing number of young people who view themselves as members of this group, Tewa identity is variously construed as secondary, peripheral, or irrelevant. In her study of a bilingual Austrian speech community, Susan Gal (1979, 20) noted that "language shift occurs only when new generations of speakers use the new connotations of the linguistic variants available to them in order to convey their changing identities and intentions in everyday linguistic interaction." In the Arizona Tewa speech community, the cultural meanings of English and Tewa as languages have been dramatically redefined, even reversed, by some younger speakers. As the perceived value of Tewa identity diminishes so does the motivation for maintaining a distinct code that conveys that identity. And as a meaningful distinction between the traditional and the nontraditional is obscured by social change, so the significance of maintaining a strict compartmentalization of their associated codes is reduced.

But whether or not this reevaluation of languages will produce a complete *language shift*—total replacement of Tewa by English—depends on whether the radical change in the language attitudes of younger speakers represents a permanent or temporary development. If this is merely a phase in a life cycle that will ultimately lead to their reaffirmation of more traditional values in the future, then the Tewa language is not so severely threatened. But if no such trend is forthcoming in the very near future, language shift, even language death, seems inevitable. Like that of other Indian groups, the Arizona Tewa population is both young and expanding (Stanislawski 1979, 591; Kunitz 1974). Attitudes of the younger speakers affecting home use of Tewa and/or English may have a lasting and powerful impact on their children's generation, greatly accelerating the processes of language change.

As in Sandia Pueblo (Brandt 1970b), social change does account for much of the observed social distribution of linguistic knowledge in the Arizona Tewa speech community. As at Sandia, economic factors have prompted the emergence of English as the language of economic opportunity—on or off the reservation. But unlike the Sandia speech community, the Arizona Tewa speech community does not possess a demographic situation that forces marriage choice outside the reservation thus further encouraging the adoption of English as the language of the home in new households since it is often the only language new spouses have in common.

But for Arizona Tewa young people, it is socioeconomic factors that provide the primary motivation for the increased use of English and the influence of this use on patterns of linguistic grammatical interference. These factors provide the Arizona Tewa young people with little choice— they can remain economically disadvantaged on the reservation (often after acquiring a sense of the material advantages offered outside the reservation through the mass media and their experience in urban-based boarding schools) or they can leave and become "city exiles" (Nagata 1971, 116).[17] At present both the education they receive and the orientation of their reference group provide preparation for the latter alternative and function to make a near economic necessity congruent with their stated aesthetic preference. Of course the economic opportunities often available to young Arizona Tewa in off-reservation settings are usually marginal. It remains to be seen whether or not this risky economic incentive will encourage and sustain a more nontraditional adaptation. The inducement to return to a more secure but conservative adaptation will also play an influential role as younger members grow older and reassess their options.

Implications for Studies of Language Change and Language Structure

In this chapter a synchronic examination of the linguistic production of a cross-section of the speech community clearly reveals, in what Labov

(1972b, 163) has termed *apparent time,* specifiable diachronic tendencies. This Arizona Tewa case study, like its Sandia phonological counterpart (Brandt 1970b), demonstrates the rapidity with which these languages have been changed within the span of a single generation via apparent disparities in the internalized grammars of younger and older speakers. Grammatical interference from English has been plausibly advanced as the shaping force that has altered the grammars of younger speakers. Likewise the sociocultural forces that have begun to decompartmentalize the codes within the linguistic repertoires of younger speakers have also been delineated.

In anticipation of the possibility of a particularistic interpretation of the Tewa findings as merely instances of language change accompanying "rapid acculturation," an observation is worth noting. Language contact and multilingualism are and have been more the rule than the exception. The raw materials for language change are present without as well as within the more or less discrete codes we term languages. If the Tewa study is particularly instructive in any respect it is so in that it delineates—however tentatively—the sociocultural processes (e.g., the symbolic significance of codes to their speakers, the differential evaluation of such symbols, etc.) that underlie ongoing language change. Though internal properties of languages cannot be ignored, as indeed they have not in historical linguistic scholarship, the present study both suggests and reaffirms that language change—conceived in a more holistic sense—is not only a suitable anthropological problem but a necessary one as well. Perhaps valuable insights will come from this and comparable studies that can provide a view of the sociolinguistic forces responsible for areal linguistic phenomena and other apparent artifacts of language contact.[18] While potential limitations abound in utilizing the present to interpret the past, the present in this case clearly affords a view of ongoing processes that is unavailable in our examination of the past (Kroskrity 1982).

Having suggested the significance or potential significance of a study such as this for the investigation of language change and language contact, it seems fitting to conclude with some methodological remarks concerning the anthropological study of language structure. I believe the present study can be instructively viewed as a demonstration of the need for greater attention to selection of linguistic consultants and to field techniques in general. It has long been part of the anthropological linguist's common-sense knowledge to select, when choices were available, older speakers who were recognized members of their communities. The present study clearly indicates the latent wisdom and underlying logic of placing value on the language used by the older speakers, since it is implicitly understood to be the analytical standard against which other social dialects—especially those more subject to linguistic acculturation—can be contrasted. Thus a notion not unlike that of Gumperz's (1968) *language distance*—however unarticulated—is partially responsible for such practices. By studying the speech that is least subject to recently introduced linguistic influences, the sociolinguist can better understand the changes that appear in less distinctive social dialects. It is precisely this pattern of intralanguage variation that is unrecoverable, or barely recoverable, in some polylectal or panlectal models (Bailey 1974), in which the speech community is viewed as a collectivity of competing variants, thus treating the speech of the individual speaker as an unorganized collection of linguistic variants rather than as "acts of identity" (LePage and Tabouret-Keller 1985).

Now, when significant and perhaps unprecedented social changes are continuing to transform many of those Native American speech communities that have persevered, it seems more than advisable to insist on greater analytic accountability—an accountability that acknowledges the role of intraspeech community variation and its impact on grammatical description and interpretation. Even for those linguists for whom variation is not a focal problem it is necessarily a methodological one. The ethnolinguist's responsibility must accordingly be not only the analysis of collected data in a rigorous and principled manner but also the explication of the evidential basis for his or her abstraction of the product "grammar of a language (or dialect)" from the speech of a finite number of speakers. Thus as the present study helps to clarify the traditional practice of anthropological linguistics, it also dramatizes the folly of interpreting Chomsky's ideal speaker-hearer in a completely homogeneous speech community as an implicit sanction of the neglect of variation or a pronouncement of its irrelevance for the practice of grammatical description.

Rather than evade the problem, ethnolinguists interested in grammatical description need to ground their claim for representativeness (of a native speaker, a grammatical construction, or a grammar) and assess its evidential basis. Does this claim issue solely from the analyst's assumption of cognitive sharing, or have measures actually been employed to ethnographically substantiate the manner and degree of linguistic sharing and diversity? If such measures have been employed these too deserve full explication. Should this attention to methodological detail seem alien to the act of grammatical description as it is presently conceived by some linguists, I would suggest that this reflects both the methodological impoverishment of contemporary linguistics and, more generally, its asocial orientation. At a time when greater care has been authoritatively advised in the use and interpretation of documents pertaining to the philological study of Native American languages (Goddard 1976), it seems all the more imperative that correspondingly greater care be devoted to methods and techniques of data collection and interpretation as they pertain to actual native speakers of living American Indian languages and their speech communities.

5

■ ■ ■

EXCEPTIONALLY INSTRUCTIVE INDIVIDUALS
IN THE TEWA SPEECH COMMUNITY

Our natural interest in human behavior seems always to vacillate between
what is imputed to the culture of the group as a whole and what is imputed
to the psychic organization of the individual himself.

(Sapir 1934, 408)

In the previous two chapters, linguistic patterns of "the group," the ancestral and the contemporary Arizona Tewa speech community, have
provided the relevant focus. Following Sapir's suggestion, attention shifts
in this chapter to some Tewa individuals. Jane Hill has examined Sapir's
writings as a forerunner in the linguistic study of the individual and suggested valuable directions for research in this important but relatively
neglected area, noting the need for additional research which recognizes
that "each person speaks, not only with a 'language,' but with a 'voice'"
(Hill 1988, 46).

For the Tewa, this recognition is implied in the saying "My language is
my life"—a cultural recognition of how individual linguistic variation
summarizes an individual's biography. As reported in chapter 4, the
Arizona Tewa speech community is characterized by a pattern of age-
based linguistic variation that is indexical of generational differences in
linguistic knowledge, in the "social meaning" (Blom and Gumperz 1972)
of Tewa and English, and in the degree of convergence (Gumperz and
Wilson 1971) between these languages. While that chapter was designed
to reveal the nature and extent of linguistic variation at a variety of sub-

system levels and to expose some basic sociolinguistic patterns, this one explores the underlying factors which contribute to the apparently anomalous status of those three individuals (of the thirty-one studied) who proved to be exceptions to otherwise pervasive correlations between age and various linguistic variables. Using qualitative methods, I hope to reveal the personalistic basis of these overt correlations by examining those individuals who defy the pattern.

Theoretical Background

In the social sciences, students of language, culture, and society have repeatedly focused their attention away from individual variation in a quest for homogeneity and uniformity at more abstract and presumably more inclusive levels of analysis. In modern American linguistics under both Bloomfield and Chomsky—scholars who occupy antipodal positions in their physicalist/mentalist views—a common disinterest in the individual has prevailed. For the Bloomfieldian structuralists, the assumption of isomorphism between the individual and the speech community transmuted the idiolect into the language of the group (Bloch 1948; Hockett 1958).[1] Under Chomsky, too, individuals and their speech behavior were largely ignored, if not avoided, in part due to the assumption that actual language users were degenerate approximations of the coveted ideal speaker-hearer (Chomsky 1965, 3). Neither linguistic school encouraged the study of individual linguistic behavior, their practices disassociating the individual and his language by extricating language, as an object of study, from social life.

Within anthropology we find a similar evasion of the individual and a comparable avoidance of variation (Pelto and Pelto 1975). Assumptions of cultural homogeneity and cognitive consensus deflected anthropological concern away from intracultural diversity, emphasizing uniformism instead (Pelto and Pelto 1975, 1). Like that of linguistics, much modern anthropological practice has relied on data provided by key informants and has been guided by concern for the presumably shared patterns of a common culture. Historical emphases within the field (e.g., cultural determinism, cognitive anthropology, microeconomic theory) have focused attention away from the individual (Goldschmidt 1972, 67). Ironically, while "much of what any cultural anthropologist collects in the field and on which he bases his professional monographs is biographical in character" (Langness 1965, vi), anthropological analysis is typically construed to be the discovery of patterns that transcend those individuals. A partial exception to this style of anthropological inquiry has been provided by the genre of the *life history* (Langness 1965; Langness and Frank 1981), but the relative dearth of attention devoted to this genre hardly compensates for the pervasive disinterest in the individual of much contemporary anthropological theory.[2]

Contemporary sociology, in Dennis Wrong's (1961) view, has also overemphasized the stability and integration of society, in part, by depicting individuals as *over-socialized*. According to Giddens (1973, 15), the "leading forms of social theory . . . have treated man as *homo sociologicus,* the creature rather than the creator of society, as a passive recipient of social influences rather than an active willing agent." But despite the emergence of many competing, antifunctionalist theories that partially remedy prior neglect of microprocess (e.g., Goffman's [1959] dramaturgical framework, Homans's [1950] neobehaviorism, and phenomenological sociology [Schutz 1932]), Wrong notes "[the] failure of the successors of the now-discredited oversocialized conception of man to remedy the defects of that sociological perspective: the neglect of biography, of the motivational depths and complexities of the human heart, and of the somatic animal roots of our emotional lives" (Wrong 1976, 54).

Though dominant theories in each of these disciplines continue to emphasize relative uniformity and invariant rules or processes, recent and/ or minority movements in each discipline have promoted the study of variation between individuals. As an alternative to linguistic disinterest in variation, sociolinguistics emerged as a means of confronting variable linguistic data and its social patterning (e.g., Labov 1966; 1972b). But while the *quantitative paradigm* (Sankoff 1974) and other approaches to linguistic variation (e.g., Bailey 1974; DeCamp 1971) have offered some methodological refinements to linguistics and illuminated significant correlations between linguistic and social variables, they propagate a disconcern for the individual despite their legitimation of the study of variation. This disconcern is primarily the by-product of a preoccupation with language change—a quest that has narrowed an interest in individuals to their contribution to ongoing linguistic change, typically bartering a more ambitious interest in an individual's biographical details for standardized summaries of their socioeconomic status.[3]

In both anthropology and sociology, a minority of scholars has also promoted the study of previously neglected variation. While the life history genre provides a forerunner for anthropological concern with the individual, the last two decades have provided new support for an alternative to what Sapir (1938) termed the *impersonal* mode of analysis. Wallace's (1961, 27–36) lucid demonstration of the untenability of cognitive sharing as a prerequisite of society and his alternative emphasis on viewing society as an "organization of diversity" helped to redirect anthropological thinking on the relationship of the individual to society. More recently, Pelto and Pelto (1975, 72) have echoed sentiments previously voiced by Sapir (1938, 9–10) that anthropologists need to compensate for a history of preoccupation with cultural groups by examining individuals and their interpersonal interaction as well as intracultural variation. Gardner (1976) and Gardner and Christian (1977) have provided an interesting link between the sociocultural literature on intracultural variation and that of the ethnography of communication by exploring the communicative basis of cognitive sharing and nonsharing through processes of enculturation and interaction. Their work emphasizes the importance of an earlier social anthropological interest in *networks* (e.g., Barnes 1954; Bott 1957; Mitchell 1969) in accounting for the social distribution of cultural knowledge.

In phenomenological, or interpretive, sociology (Wilson 1970) another perspective exists that promotes interests both in individuals and in variation. From Alfred Schutz (1955; 1962, 12–17) comes the notion of *socially distributed knowledge* and the goal of understanding the subjective meaning of an actor's overt social interaction. From such theoretical foundations, *symbolic interactionism* emerged under Blumer (1962) and others as an alternative to preoccupation with reified social categories. For this group, as with Sapir (1938, 9–11), a reversal of priorities was proposed.[4] Instead of starting with the great superordinate categories of *society, culture,* and the like and gradually working down to the individual, the converse was proposed (Blumer 1962). A focus on human interaction, coupled with the use of more inductive means of data collection, could incorporate individuals more effectively into social analysis, discover critical intermediary levels of social organization, and critically test the utility of increasingly more generalized levels of social analysis. A useful concept from symbolic interactionism is that of *reference group* (Shibutani 1962)—the group whose perspective a social actor imaginatively adopts as a vantage point for guiding his or her selection from among culturally available options.[5]

While these developments in linguistics, anthropology, and sociology provide conceptual resources for an interdisciplinary confrontation with variation, it should be emphasized that scholars working in the ethnography of communication tradition have long been advised to view the speech community as an "organization of diversity" (Hymes 1971, 38) and to view variation as an inherent and core interest. This focus on variation has continued to be well represented in contemporary sociolinguistic literature (e.g., Bricker 1974; Ellen 1979; Philips 1976; and Scollon 1979). Considerably more rare, however, are contributions to the study of individual differences in verbal behavior and the sociocultural significance of these differences. As Hymes (1979, 34ff.) has indicated, Sapir's precedent in regard to a personalistic approach to individual speech variation has not been adequately pursued.[6]

Exceptional Individuals and Their Lingual Life Histories

Taken collectively, the sociolinguistic measures discussed in chapter 4 not only provide evidence of linguistic variation at different subsystem levels, they also supply a valuable means of assessing differential fluency in Tewa of individuals in the Arizona Tewa speech community. Like Gardner (1976) and other cultural anthropologists interested in intracultural variation, I regard the mere detection of variation, cultural and/or linguistic, as only an initial step in an account of cognitive sharing and diversity. As Sapir has suggested (1938, 10), "we cannot thoroughly understand the dynamics of culture, of society, of history, without sooner or later taking account of the actual interrelationships of human beings."

While correlations of linguistic performance and overt social categories are useful in revealing gross sociolinguistic patterns, they certainly are not self-explanatory.[7] As mentioned above, only three of the thirty-one individuals exhibit anomalous linguistic behavior when compared to others of the same approximate age. I examine the biographical attributes of these three exceptional individuals in order to construct aspects of their *lingual life histories*—an ethnolinguistic version of what Gardner (1976, 462–64) has called the *cognitive life history*. A cognitive life history employs biographical analysis, especially an individual's interaction with significant others, as a means of accounting for cognitive sharing and diversity in a given social group. According to Gardner (1976, 463), "We might be able to describe the cognitive life history of any person in terms of a series of stages . . . during which the resources for acquiring new concepts and for confirmatory discourse have a certain character." Readers, particularly those familiar with linguistic scholarship, may find the use of "cognitive" here somewhat unusual. In American linguistic scholarship "cognitive" is often opposed to "social" and associated with rather autonomous linguistic knowledge (Ochs 1979b). There are, of course, a number of linguistic traditions, including the Marxists, which challenge the autonomy of linguistic knowledge and its supposed independence from social life, viewing mental activity as inextricably related to interpersonal communication and general social life (e.g., Vološinov 1973, 67–70).

Readers more familiar with anthropology will readily recognize in the notion of cognitive life history a deliberate attempt to combine the tradition of cognitive anthropology (e.g., Tyler 1969), particularly its ideational view of culture and more recent emphasis on cognitive sharing and nonsharing, with the distinctive methods and topical focus of the typical product of anthropological biography—the life history (Langness 1965). As adopted here, the lingual life history is a subspecies of cognitive life history that contains the elements of social learning, personal network, and cognitive sharing and diversity but in which the focus is more exclusively on the biographical acquisition of linguistic knowledge. By linguistic knowledge I mean not only the knowledge of language structure (e.g., grammar and phonology) but also such things as speech levels, language attitudes, and general communicative competence. The lingual life histories that follow are designed to reveal important and sustained interpersonal associations which comprise the individual's informal and formal learning experiences (Scribner and Cole 1973)—either inferentially or explicitly conducted.

Though presented in the condensed, analytical mode of the *analogical* tradition, these cognitive life histories are doubly *dialogical* in nature (Tedlock 1979). Not only are they derived from numerous interviews and conversations between the anthropologist and the atypical individuals and their kinsmen, friends, and associates, but these interactions often focused on past dialogical relationships between the individual and his significant others.[8] Though hardly exhaustive, the biographical details presented below are selected because (1) they can be consistently established as significant by various native consultants in a variety of contexts (reliability), (2) they are useful in attempting to distinguish cultural and idiosyncratic schemata (Agar 1980, 233) via a contrastive analysis of biographical details with other individuals in the same age grade, and (3) they are among those factors that have typically been considered relevant in studies of American Indian language maintenance (Leap 1981, 219). By presenting and analyzing these details in this manner, I hope to locate relevant experiential differences that will provide insight into the relationship of the linguistic knowledge of these exceptional individuals and their personal lives.[9]

MYRON NALA   Though twenty-two-year-old Myron would be placed in group 1 on the basis of age, his performance on the linguistic measures available here suggest that he performs more like a middle-aged speaker (Group 2). His syntactic/semantic scores (table 4.2A: 42/48; B: 94/84; C: 90/88; and D: 56/54) reveal a pattern in the production of phrasal conjunctions, semantic passives, and relative clauses that does not differ significantly from that of older speakers. For the phonological and morphological measures (table 4.5A-B) we find a similar pattern in the majority of cases. The phonological scores (table 4.5A: 92/84 and B: 96/88) suggest that his treatment of plain stops resembles that of older speakers, more closely approximating the oldest speakers (group 3) in the preservation of medial plain consonants. Likewise his elicited response performance on morphological measure C (table 4.5) suggests that he has internalized the norms of older speakers though his spontaneous speech indicates a significantly lower frequency of adherence to these norms (table 4.5C: 0/28). Only on morphological measure D, den- generalization, does he approximate the performance of group 1 speakers (table 4.5D: 88/76).

In addition to his performance on these measures, we should also note that key consultants rate his fluency rather highly, remarking his talent for intergenerational communication. Older speakers report that they enjoy conversing with him. Kinsmen and neighbors find him more approachable than other young men in this regard. Others, they say, seem uninterested or unable to exchange personal stories, to comment appropriately in the role of the listener, or to discuss everyday matters in the Arizona Tewa language. Myron also engages in code-switching of both the situational and metaphorical variety (Blom and Gumperz 1972) in a contextually appropriate manner. In sum, Myron's linguistic knowledge and fluency are unusual for his age. What attributes of his lingual life history might enable us to understand them?

Given the emphasis on early childhood socialization experiences by scholars like Bernstein (1971) and Labov (1979), it seems appropriate to begin a lingual life history with some characterization of the individual's parents. In Myron's case this is especially appropriate. His parents are exceptional in two significant ways. Unlike most parents, they are both Tewa. Given the relatively high frequency of interethnic marriages between Hopi and Tewa (Dozier 1954, 244), this is notable. More rare is the relative age of his parents. Myron's mother and father—parents through the process of intraclan adoption (Dozier 1954, 333)—were forty-five and fifty-five years of age, respectively, at the time of his birth. Not only was Tewa the near-exclusive language of the household but it was also an older variety of Tewa than younger parents would have spoken. Even though the household was not characterized by an extended family as was the case with Myron's parents' generation, the net effect of such older parents is similar to being raised by one's grandparents. Thus despite the fact that Myron's grandparents were either deceased or not readily available, he still received significant exposure to an older stratum of the language than was typical for children his age.

As for the cultural orientation of his parents, we could describe it as eclectic, avoiding the extremes of either ultraconservative traditionalism (rejection of Euro-American ideology and technology) or attempted assimilation. Both mother and father held various service jobs for the tribal council and the Bureau of Indian Affairs. But both also participated in the full range of ceremonial and social activities that characterize village life. Such events were thus witnessed by Myron, knowing that his parents not only approved of such activities but also participated in them. In accord with tradition, Myron was initiated into the kachina cult at about nine years of age. Later, at age fourteen, he was initiated into his kiva group during the *than-tháy*, the winter solstice ceremony. The ceremonial father (*pu:phonun tádá*) he acquired during this initiation was an older, ceremonially active man who took his responsibilities for offering guidance quite seriously. In addition to offering valuable information regarding Tewa folk history, he has also discussed the ceremonial life of the village, providing knowledge not immediately available to either Myron's parents or uncles since they have not held important ceremonial positions. A mutual respect has emerged from this relationship and along with it the likelihood of future recruitment when Myron becomes a mature adult. In Myron's own words:

> I can still hear my *pu:phonun tádá* telling me of our people's *wo:waci* [history]. I can still see him squinting, motioning toward the direction from where we came. His words are clear to me. They come to me when I look over our land from our fields. When others hear only silence or just the wind, I hear him talking. Quietly, slowly, . . . the things that happen to our people. I don't know why these things just stick with me but I can still recall where and when he told me. I guess I'm interested. But right now I can't just listen to the old men [*senó*]. As you know, I'm just beginning a new family, getting used to my new job and everything. There will be time enough later on.

Myron's formal education is rather typical of his age group. After attending the Bureau of Indian Affairs-run Polacca Day School for his elementary education, he went to a boarding school in Salt Lake City. Like many Tewa children, he is remembered as a very promising student— more aggressive, spontaneous, and less anxious than his Hopi counterparts (Thompson 1950, 92–93, 96–97). Though encouraged by his parents and many other relatives, Myron's interest in school waned with each additional year of attendance. According to him, school lessons became pointlessly repetitive and seemed increasingly irrelevant as a preparation for future employment. Upon graduation he joined the Marines, seeking a combination of the military discipline which many Tewa highly value (see chapter 7) and vocational training which might be marketable on the reservation. Though he had hoped to receive training as a mechanic he was ultimately trained to be a food technician—a skill in which he became increasingly interested. It is especially significant to note Myron's motives for such a practical job. According to him, additional formal education would have only contributed to making him unemployable on the reservation. As the youngest of three sons he feels a special responsibility to be near to his parents to assist in planting and other economic activities which have become increasingly more arduous for them as they grow older. In addition to such personal motives, we should also observe that Myron has virtually no role models among his relatives and neighbors for seeking a college education or a white collar job. Guidance counselors at his boarding school never discussed any alternatives to his vocational training objectives.

Myron's teachers remember him well and express considerable disappointment that he did not choose to continue his formal education. One former teacher remembers him as his "best student in over a decade of teaching—excellent language skills." The several available former teachers of Myron all agreed that his reading skills were always well ahead of grade level. Myron himself fondly recalls his experiences with his sixth grade teacher, who both recognized his abilities and made exceptional efforts to develop them. Frustrated by the low quality of textbooks made available by the Bureau of Indian Affairs, Mr. Nickel made a practice of lending his own books to the better students with whom he had established some rapport. He loaned several books to Myron, including some by Indian authors such as Vine Deloria Jr. and N. Scott Momaday. Reading was not such a novelty for him as might be expected. Though his father had only finished elementary school, he was a proficient reader. Well before Myron attended his first year of elementary school, he had already witnessed his father's evening custom of reading newspapers and news magazines while sitting beneath the harsh light of a Coleman lantern suspended from the ceiling of their Tewa village home. But while his father may have imparted a sense of relevance and familiarity to reading, his teacher seems to have been primarily responsible for Myron's discovery of reading as not only informative but also pleasurable.

Returning from military service, Myron was welcomed home by family and friends. He views his experiences on various Marine bases in the United States as valuable in acquainting him with the regional and social diversity of his country. Neither Myron nor his relatives found that his military sojourn had changed him. Though he was, in his own estimation, well treated and well liked by many friends there, he was never tempted to extend his period of service. In conversations with others he often lumped his military and boarding school experiences together. In an informal interview with me, he offered the following assessment of these experiences:

> Yes, there was some good times there but the fun was 'cause of how different things are from here [the reservation]. Different kinds of buildings, music, places to go—you know. But I've done that now and I can still go there now and then. Still when it comes to living somewhere for good I'd rather be here where I know the people and their ways of doing things. This may not be so, so . . . exciting to some people but it is a good life.

Shortly after returning from military service, Myron began living with a Hopi girl from Sichomovi Village. After living with his in-laws for approximately six months, the couple moved to a vacated house immediately adjacent to Myron's parents' home in Tewa Village.[10] Though his wife speaks no Tewa, Myron is surrounded by kinsmen and neighbors who do speak Tewa. His employment as a cook removes him from Tewa Village for wage work in Keams Canyon and Second Mesa, but Myron's personal network aside from work is rather evenly divided between two different groups of people. About half of his interactive time is devoted to younger friends and kinsmen of about his and his wife's age. The other half is spent with older adults, including his parents, who provide a focus for kinship-based interaction through informal but very regular visits that always involve the sharing of a meal. With both types of networks, Myron typically finds himself interacting with someone whom he has known for most of his life.

In contrasting Myron's biographical details with others of his age group, three remarkable differences emerge. One, Myron's parents are rather atypical in both their relative age and the fact that they are both ethnically Tewa. Two, Myron is unusual in his orientation toward the reservation. Rather than use his educational opportunities as a means of preparing himself for a more prosperous off-reservation career, he has instead opted for training in skills that he expects to be marketable on the reservation. What is especially remarkable about Myron's case in this regard is the evidence of future planning involving prioritization of reservation residence. This planning may, of course, reflect a mixture of imposed and intrinsic relevances (Schutz 1964, 124–25). An imposed relevance is the advanced age of his parents. This coupled with cultural norms concerning the caretaking responsibility of the youngest children for their elderly parents does prompt considerably more intergenerational interaction than might otherwise be the case. It is important to note, however, that such ideal norms are often ignored by others of his age who shift this responsibility to the social services personnel of the Hopi Tribe.

But rather than viewing his assistance to his parents in farming or building maintenance as a burden, he instead repeatedly mentions his good fortune in being able to help and be part of a cooperative network of kinsmen. In interviews he consistently emphasizes the importance of his children growing up under the influence of his parents. A valued source of cultural continuity, his parents would also be able to offer an economically valuable service to him. Since both he and his Hopi wife expect to work, such day-care arrangements are important considerations. Thus, instead of an imposed relevance, Myron regards his close relations to his parents as more of an intrinsic interest. In a community that has recently acquired such concepts as "generation gap" and "juvenile delinquency," Myron's orientation is viewed as unusually traditional.

A third pattern concerns his participation in ongoing intergenerational interaction. Most younger speakers interact much more exclusively with members of their own age group. A typical pattern for this group would consist of participation in a non-kin-based network of peers from various villages who have attended the same boarding schools, early marriage, and neolocal residence, that is, setting up an independent household apart from the parents' home village. But in contrast to this pattern, Myron devotes considerable time and energy interacting with older people—his parents and clan relatives in particular. Some people of his own age regard him as friendly but inhibited—lacking any spontaneity. There is also some resentment against him since his example is often cited by parents who chastise their older children. This resentment, however, is entirely absent from Myron's younger clan relations. They know him to be generous in both money and energy and are often inspired by him to participate in various family activities that they might not otherwise attend.

DAN OYOH   Like Myron, thirty-nine-year-old Dan Oyoh is another individual whose linguistic knowledge and performance more closely resemble that of speakers who are significantly older than himself. Dan possesses virtually all the linguistic attributes of group 3 (older than fifty) speakers. His performance on various syntactic and semantic measures reported in chapter 4 (table 4.2 A: 33/44; B: 98/92; C: 90/90; D: 62/48) and the nonsyntactic criteria (table 4.5) originally used in a preliminary attempt to stratify speakers according to language criteria (e.g., DeCamp's [1971] scaling) all typify group 3 speakers.[11] This pattern is sustained by Dan's performance on all four phonological and morphological linguistic variables discussed in the previous chapter. For each of these measures his performance scores are representative of group 3 speakers (table 4.5 A: 98/82; B: 96/94; C: 0/4; D: 0/2).

Dan's parents are somewhat more typical than Myron's in at least two respects. Like most parents in Tewa Village, they were relatively young (late twenties) during their child-raising years. Like an increasing number of parents in Tewa Village, they represented the intermarriage of a Hopi man and a Tewa woman. Though Hopi and some English served as the languages of communication between the couple, the extended family nature of the household insured that Tewa would be the dominant language in domestic activities. In accord with the norm of matrilocal residence, Dan's parents lived with his mother's family. As a consequence of this, Dan enjoyed frequent and significant interaction with his maternal grandparents throughout his entire childhood.

As the second of four children and the first of two sons, Dan spent much of his early childhood interacting with his siblings and the children of neighbors who were mostly from the same localized clan. Even at a young age his older sister (*ka:khá*) assumed the protective role of older female siblings despite the fact that she was only three years older than Dan. His relations with his parents were somewhat indirect and even remote. Strained relations between his parents that would later lead to divorce often deprived him of a close relationship with both his father and his mother. His parents tried to relocate to Flagstaff and later Winslow, leaving their three older children with Dan's maternal grandparents for almost two years. Then when Dan was about nine, his father left their household after a traditional divorce and moved to his own mother's household in Polacca.

Continuity was largely supplied by Dan's grandparents. In addition to giving care and affection, they provided a rich traditional environment for the upbringing of their grandchildren. Traditional stories were related by Dan's grandmother while her husband provided Dan with an early exposure to the folk history of the Arizona Tewa (Dozier 1954, 332). In addition his grandfather, a gifted singer and composer, provided an early introduction to Arizona Tewa song. Many of the melodies to songs that Dan composes today were first learned from his grandfather during his childhood.

Dan's parents, however, were not especially traditional in outlook. His parents had both attended a boarding school in Phoenix and were very impressed with the comparative comfort enjoyed by Euro-Americans in such towns. Both earned some money doing part-time menial jobs and were confident that they could make a living in other towns closer to the

Hopi Reservation. But Dan's father could only find occasional work in the lumber industry in Flagstaff and his wife's wages as a maid were inadequate to support them in town. Rather than bringing their children to the city, they themselves found it economically necessary to return to the reservation. Though frustrated, they were not especially embittered by their experiences. Before their divorce, the couple converted to a Christian denomination, began to use English as the main language of their interpersonal communication, and encouraged their children to attend a BIA or missionary school. Even after their divorce, when Dan's father would occasionally see his son he would always inquire about his schooling and encourage him to apply himself to his studies.

During his later childhood Dan continued his education in two cultural traditions. At eight and fifteen he was initiated into the tribe and into his kiva group, respectively. Each time he was given a ceremonial father. But these men seem to have been selected more by his grandparents than his parents. The formal instruction these men provided concerning ceremonial life was very helpful in making these ritual experiences especially meaningful to Dan. But their advanced age, relative to most ceremonial parents, deprived him of a continuing source of guidance and instruction. Both men died while Dan was still a teenager, denying him a conventional access to highly valued ceremonial participation. Meanwhile, in the BIA school, Dan was performing well. In his first two years he had considerable difficulty adjusting to the highly structured and impersonal nature of classroom instruction. His teachers would write notes home complaining of disciplinary problems. These he would give to his grandparents who could not read. They would admire the unintelligible handwriting before discarding the notes in the wood-burning stove. Only on those rare occasions that the notes made it into the hands of Dan's parents would they be translated into appeals for improved behavior.

Seeing that school was important to both his parents, Dan began to take it more seriously as a source of practical information that might provide valuable survival skills. Since he did not learn very much about farming or ranching from his relatives, he began to view school as a resource which should be efficiently exploited. Having an outstanding memory, he excelled at all the rote learning tasks that his teachers typically provided. This pattern continued through high school and engendered further self-confidence in his capacity for formal education. This coupled with the advice of some of his boarding school teachers prompted him to attend Northern Arizona University in Flagstaff, where he earned an associate's degree after about two years of course work. During this period he received financial assistance from both of his parents and earned other necessary money through odd jobs in Flagstaff. The pressure of parental expectations and competition with Euro-American students, combined with a lack of guidance and anxiety about his future, ultimately led to some problems with alcoholism.

Unable to cope with his rather solitary existence in Flagstaff and his personal problems with alcohol, he left school and returned to the reservation. After a brief courtship, he married a Tewa woman whom he had known throughout much of his childhood. Unlike him, her parents were exceptionally traditional. Despite the objection of his parents the couple was married in a strictly traditional wedding instead of a Christian ceremony. For about one year after their marriage, the couple struggled economically to make ends meet. Suddenly a job emerged at the interface of growing federal and tribal bureaucracies that required some college-level preparation. Dan applied for and received a job as an employment director. The job itself was located in Keams Canyon, a trading-post town that served as the service center for the eastern portion of the Hopi Reservation. The couple moved away from the extended household in Tewa Village and took up residence in a tribally operated trailer court in Keams Canyon.

For several years the couple's relative economic prosperity compensated for their comparative isolation from kinsmen. Aside from regular visits to Tewa Village, the couple and their children also returned for all sacred and social dances. Dan was in fact actively involved in the latter as a singer and composer. He gained a reputation as especially gifted in both of these capacities and was viewed as an indispensable participant in most social dances. He enjoyed the practice sessions, held in the plaza kiva (*mu:nε te'e*), where the men teach each other the songs they have composed as part of their rehearsal for the actual performance.[12]

> I found myself using spare time on the job as a chance to practice the songs (*khaw'*). Between interviews, during breaks. Sometimes even right while talking to an applicant a tune would come to me and my foot would start beating out the time. As we would get closer to the actual time of the dance I found myself, on the job, looking at my watch more and more, hoping for the end of the day so that I could get in my pickup and get over to the kiva for our practice. The other men really enjoyed singing my songs because they have

the old words and melodies revived. Many times they ask me, "Where did you learn these words? Where did you learn the tune?" Much of it must come from my grandfather who is looking down on us now.[13]

While singing became an increasingly rewarding aspect of his life, new problems emerged in his family life. His wife complained of his increasing remoteness and began spending more and more time with her parents— sometimes for two and three days at a time. One of their children died young of a childhood disease. While this brought the couple back together temporarily, the old pattern emerged again after a few months. This time Dan became extremely suspicious of his wife's long absences. On occasion he would investigate her whereabouts by arriving at his in-laws' Tewa Village home unexpectedly. Though his suspicions were never substantiated, his distrustful behavior further damaged their relationship. Then his wife and remaining child were killed in an automobile accident. Dan felt quite alienated from many of his wife's relatives, who according to him blamed him for the misfortune. With the death of his own family, he began relying heavily on the support of his older sister. He would eat with her family, driving from Keams Canyon to their Polacca home. Aside from his sister's household he remained rather aloof and distrustful of others in the village. He feared that others would regard him as a witch (kyuge), who had extended his own life by taking the lives of others.[14]

His diffidence and distrust continued for several months. This extreme aloofness ended with an invitation from a fellow clansman to participate in a social dance that his family was going to sponsor. The next several months were focused on preparation: composition, rehearsal, and discussion with other singers. This activity seemed to offer Dan welcome connotations of acceptance and belonging. His singing on the day of the dance won the praise and admiration of both his fellow performers and the villagers in general. It also led to his recognition by an older, ceremonially active individual—also a singer—who was looking for promising younger men who might be appropriate for ritual training. Dan has found this invitation quite gratifying and has pursued further ceremonial training for the past six years. A considerable portion of his free time is absorbed by interaction with much older, ceremonially knowledgeable men.

His personal network has unique interactional patterns. His job, located in Keams Canyon, is decidedly nontraditional and requires contact with a variety of Hopi and Tewa individuals. Most of these are younger men—his age or younger—with whom he talks in English. Only rarely, when an old man (*senó*), is being interviewed or advised does he use Tewa or Hopi. In his sister's home, he speaks Tewa to her and her children, but because her husband is Hopi, Tewa is not the exclusive language of domestic interaction. Tewa is, however, the only language used in interaction with his network of ceremonial elders—an informal group that meets on many evenings and during the weekend in one of the kivas and in various private homes. Talk varies from informal discussion to formal instruction and is conducted in both major social registers in Arizona Tewa: casual speech, or *t'owa-bí hi:li* (people's speech), and the more obscure ceremonial register, *te'e hi:li* (kiva speech). Through the ceremonial network Dan has acquired conversance with this esoteric speech level.

> This knowledge (*ankhaw*) is important for our people. More important than the work done by our *tribal council*, the police[15] (*pho-t'a-'in*), or the judges. They worry about the things around us but maybe not enough about what is inside. Some of the young ones ask me why I should spend so much time learning these things. "*What will it buy you?*" they ask. "What we need/ want," I tell them. The learning is not very difficult. Usually it's learning that a word used in popular speech has a special meaning when used in ceremonies. Words like "to breathe" (*há:lá*) and "to eat" (*ha'*) are this way.

But for Dan this abbreviated lingual life history reveals not only the biographical source of this esoteric linguistic knowledge but also the source of a traditional orientation. In childhood as in adult life he found in traditional cultural values an anchoring that provided stability in times of emotional turmoil. As a child he relied heavily on his maternal grandparents for a sense of continuity and cohesion at a time when the reservation was experiencing great social change and his parents were experiencing their own marital discord. Similarly, as an adult, this orientation provided an important refuge from personal despair and social disgrace. Here again, as in the case of Myron, two very important aspects of his personal experience can be cited as influences on his exceptional stock of linguistic knowledge.

The first of these involves the influence of a traditionally oriented caretaker. Though Dan's parents did not qualify in this regard, his grandparents certainly did. One could also infer an especially "forceful" (Geertz 1968, 111; Rosaldo 1984, 178–79) influence of his grandparents from a variety of sources, including Dan's own self-report.[16] The diminished influence of his parents in his preadolescent years, his pursuit of singing in village activities as evidence of effective transmission of appropriate skills, his fear of village opinion regarding his role in the death of family members, and his compartmentalization of his modern job suggest a consistency in his orientation and an elaboration of early preparatory experience.

The second factor, also somewhat parallel to Myron's, is Dan's extraordinary involvement in ongoing networks that permit exposure to older forms of the language through frequent contact with older speakers. Though some individuals in his age-grade have similar early childhood experiences involving the participation of grandparents, few seem to have had such intensive experience and none seem to have combined it with active participation in ceremonial networks. Unlike Myron, who is also linguistically exceptional for his age, Dan is often viewed as extraordinary by other members of the Arizona Tewa speech community. This perception emanates from two important facts.

First, Dan's current lack of a family and concomitant inattention to practical concerns are viewed as especially anomalous, even pathological, by some in the community. This coupled with his high visibility as a nearly indispensable performer in the social dances of Tewa Village make him locally remarkable and exceptional not only to the researcher, in the special sense employed here, but to the speech community as well. Since Myron's exceptional linguistic knowledge and fluency are neither accompanied by a lack of family life nor the visibility of a performer, his exceptionality appears to be far less salient than Dan's to members of the community.

NED BAYENAH   The final case to be considered here is that of Ned Bayenah, age forty-one. Unlike those of either Myron or Dan, Ned's linguistic performance on the majority of measures discussed in chapter 4 would locate him in a group typically occupied by younger speakers. His scores on the syntactic measures discussed in chapter 4 are consistently like those of group 1 speakers (table 4.2A: 82/76, B: 76/58, C: 66/58, and D: 84/72). In his performance on the phonological measures, he approximates the scores of group 2—the group that includes his chronological age (table 4.5A: 98/52, B: 90/82). But on both morphological measures, his scores are nearly identical to group 1, or the youngest, speakers (table 4.5 C: 92/68, D: 90/86). Similarly, for those variables presented in table 4.1, including code-switching, native vocabulary replacement, and knowledge of noncasual speech forms, we also find the same pattern as for group 1 speakers. Aside from the voicing of plain stops, his linguistic performance is clearly like that of a group 1 speaker—a speaker typically thirty years of age or less.

As with the others we may begin an abbreviated lingual life history of Ned by examining important influences on his early childhood experience. Like those of Myron, Ned's parents were both Tewa. They were, however, much younger than Myron's. Even though Myron was the fifth of six children, his parents were both in their early thirties at the time of his birth. His father attempted to make a living for his family solely through farming. Since his fields were scattered in a variety of locations, he was seldom available for interaction with his children. In addition to domestic responsibilities Ned's mother also made pottery in order to sell it to trading posts to make a supplementary income. By village standards, their family was rather poor, lacking in both economic means and in terms of ceremonial privilege. Like most children his age, he did enjoy the coresidence of his maternal grandparents. Until Ned was six years old his grandparents lived under the same roof. At that time they retired and moved to the Colorado River Reservation to avoid the more severe winters that are characteristic of the higher elevations in Northern Arizona.[17] They returned to First Mesa only for occasional visits usually coinciding with social dances in Tewa Village.

It is important to note that the language of Ned's home was almost exclusively Tewa. Other languages would be spoken only to non-Tewa participants such as visiting Hopis and Euro-American tourists or in somewhat more rare instances of metaphorical code-switching (Blom and Gumperz 1972; chapter 7 of this volume). According to Ned, he entered grammar school in Keams Canyon with only a minimal knowledge of English. Others in his same-age grade who entered school at the same time as Ned recalled him as especially slow in learning English in school. This appears to be due, in part, to a relative lack of exposure to English. His father was exceptionally insistent that English *not* be spoken in their house. He professed not to speak English at all throughout his life and left all interaction with Euro-Americans to his wife. In view of the often exaggerated claims made about *linguistic conservatism* in the Pueblo Southwest (Kroskrity 1992), we should observe that Ned's father's attitude was somewhat atypical; many Tewa parents already recognized the increasing utility of English even though they themselves were often exposed to it in a rather abusive manner, such as at boarding schools were they were forced to speak only English and punished for any use of the native language.

According to Ned and many others, the move of his grandparents seemed to have a significant impact on him. In his eyes it was only his maternal grandparents—especially his grandfather—who seemed to take a special interest in him. To the others, including his parents, he felt that he was "just another child." Unlike all the other Tewa people from his age grade who were interviewed in the course of my research, Ned alone shunned a nostalgic view and emphasized his personal deprivation. He discusses the deprivations of his childhood in the following manner:

> Naa-bí wo:waci (This is my life) . . . heheh.[18] Well, I'll tell it in *my* own way. The way I see it, people can be rich in two ways. One way . . . they can have a lot of money. The other, the way we Tewas and Hopis are here, is you can be rich in relatives. But my folks didn't seem to have either. Other kids would get a little change for spending money so that they could buy something down here at the store. Not me or my brothers and sisters. Only every so often when my mother might sell a piece of pottery to a tourist, would she give us a few dimes and nickels. But that was rare. Same thing for relations. Except for brothers and sisters who would always tease me, I didn't seem to have much to do with anybody. Nobody seemed to care. That's why I was always getting into trouble.

Village residents tend to verify Ned's account of the relative deprivation of his family, citing the rather asymmetrical exchanges between them and their clan relations that were necessary in order for Ned's family to make ends meet. They also verify his notoriety for mischief and general troublemaking during his childhood days. His reputation earned him a very frightening experience. One winter day, when Ned was approximately seven years old, his home—like the others of Tewa Village—was visited by the ogre kachinas (Kealiinohomoku 1980; Dozier 1954, 327). These creatures, impersonated by fellow villagers, go from house to house asking for children to eat. Their monstrous appearance and growling voices often fill young children with fear. Families will usually bargain with the ogres and offer some food in exchange for the safety of their children. But in the cases of exceptionally mischievous children, the families will hesitate and in unusual cases refuse to bargain with the ogres in order to increase the distress of especially disobedient children.

In the native view, according to Kealiinohomoku (1980, 67), the ritual drama has an effect that is good for children, however anxiety-producing it may be for them. But for Ned, even in retrospect, no lesson was worth the fear and abandonment he experienced when his relatives prolonged his agony by refusing to barter for him. Though ultimately he was retrieved before the ogres could make off with him, his anxiety was deliberately protracted in response to his notoriously unruly behavior.

In his first few years of elementary school, Ned moved from a position of relative deficiency insofar as his knowledge of English was concerned to a position among the better students in his all-Indian, Bureau of Indian Affairs-administered school. In this way he provided his teachers with perhaps their greatest sense of accomplishment. They remarked his exceptional motivation and his general eagerness to learn. Ned thrived on the personal attention and even began to look forward to the times his teachers would call on him to speak. Unlike many other children, he acquired increasing confidence in his ability to perform in such classroom contexts. He received some encouragement from his mother who defended the importance of his schooling to her husband.

Unlike his two older brothers who had dropped out after grammar school in order to take a more vigorous role in assisting their father, Ned was permitted to attend an off-reservation boarding school, where he received vocational training. This led to a Bureau of Indian Affairs-arranged training and relocation program that took him to Albuquerque, where he learned something about heavy machinery and later acquired a construction job.

He found it possible to send home a substantial portion of his paycheck and still have enough money to live on. Though he would return to the Hopi Reservation on occasional visits during long holiday weekends and vacations, he was very satisfied with his personal success and residence away from the reservation. He stayed in Albuquerque for about nine years.

He then returned to the reservation for a variety of reasons. First, he felt that, after rising to a certain level in his company, he was continually being passed over in promotion considerations. Second, he had begun to show signs of a hereditary health problem which, while not life threatening, required ongoing medical supervision—he was a diabetic. He summarizes his return in the mid-sixties in the following way:

> In Albuquerque I was going real well. I had a high paying job working with heavy machinery and was even able to buy a nice house. What finally got to me was paying on everything that either me or my family wanted to do. The pace was just too fast. There I had a lot of things—TV, good pickup, stereo—you know—but hardly one of them I really owned. Here I already own my own home and medical services for all of us are taken care of by PHS [Public Health Service].

Ned's health problem would involve considerable cost off the reservation where he would have had to pay for his own medical attention. Since he had married while in Albuquerque and had begun to raise a family, the cost of treatment seemed to be a severe economic drain to the young family's precious resources.

Another factor not explicitly mentioned was the fact that his wife was a Navajo from the New Mexico part of the Navajo Reservation, adjacent to the eastern portion of the Hopi Reservation. The availability of a better state job involving construction in northeast Arizona seemed to answer several needs. Now Ned and his family live in Keams Canyon. Since Ned's wife is Navajo the multiethnic environment of a trading-post town near the border of the Hopi and Navajo reservations provides a suitable compromise distance between their respective kinsmen. Keams Canyon, as an emerging transitional community (Nagata 1971), also provides a compromise location insofar as the facilities, services, and standard of living are concerned between what is typically available in Northern Arizona towns and what is available elsewhere on the reservation. Given his interethnic marriage, English emerged as the language of interaction for the couple and their children. They have taught their children a variety of kin terms and polite expressions in both Arizona Tewa and Navajo but have not otherwise encouraged their children to learn these languages. Despite the often vocal anti-Navajo sentiment voiced by many Arizona Tewa, Ned's family has accepted their Navajo daughter-in-law and often praise her for her maternal devotion to her children and the responsible manner in which she maintains their Keams Canyon home. Ned's parents will often visit her and their grandchildren on trips to Keams Canyon for various services involving laundry and maintenance of their pickup truck.

Though the couple and their children will often visit their Tewa relatives during social and ceremonial dances, their involvement in village life is rather marginal. Most of their free time is spent in voluntary association with a network of friends and neighbors, many of whom work with Ned. This is a multiethnic group of Euro-Americans and Indians (Tewa, Hopi, and Navajo) who have nuclear families and enjoy their relative economic prosperity. Several families in this group have joined together to purchase a powerboat, which they use for vacation purposes at Lake Mead.

When asked about the significance of his Tewa ethnic identity, Ned usually expresses great pride in how his Arizona Tewa ancestors overcame immense adversity to rise to positions of leadership in greater First Mesa society. But he also adds that ancestry is not as important to him as personal achievement.

> Yes, I'm Tewa and proud of it. But that's not all I am. Even our Tewa ancestors didn't make it simply because they were Tewa. The ones we remember today, like Nampeyo and Yava, really did something with their lives. I'm Tewa ... I guess the way you white people are German, or Irish, or Polish.

Ned's parents and other kinsmen are pleased with his personal success and grateful for the economic assistance which he occasionally provides. They claim to see nothing exceptional about their son, except the fact that he has married a Navajo. Other villagers, however, regard him as extremely marginal to their community. In neither "scope" nor "force" (Geertz 1968, 111–12) does his ethnic identity pervade his daily life in the manner observed for Myron or for Dan. His orientation, like that of many younger members of the Arizona Tewa speech community, is more eclectic than traditional. Like them, he is concerned with fitting his heritage into an increasingly modern world, a concern which requires attention more to economic realities of the present than to past traditions. Similarly, he has less knowledge of the Tewa language. The similarity to group 1 on the majority of linguistic measures employed here is not an indication of increased interaction between Ned and younger speakers but rather a common pattern of relative disuse and diminished interaction with older Tewa speakers.

Though Ned's biographical data are far different from either Myron or Dan, they do sustain previous observations about the importance of early childhood and adolescent experience as well as ongoing adult social networks. In Ned's case we find certain overt factors present that would seem to favor native language maintenance. These include the prominent role of Arizona Tewa as a language of the home and the conservative orientation of his parents. But such factors seem to be undermined by the personally disruptive departure of Ned's grandparents and a sense of alienation from what he perceived as the abusive aspects of his own culture. Rather early in his life, Ned seems to have associated his own sense of deprivation with much of his cultural heritage, finding them both personally unsatisfying. The challenge of English and participation in Euro-American society provided an appropriate medium to display his achievement orientation in a manner relatively unburdened by the baggage of native cultural associations.

Today, his personal network continues to reinforce the linguistic consequences of life choices motivated by his values. Most of his interaction is with his nuclear family and his work associates and is conducted exclusively in English. Visits to his parents, despite their proximity some ten miles to the west, are infrequent and relatively brief. Most often they coincide with plans that involve his parents as baby-sitters for their children.

For Ned, as for Myron and Dan, a mixture of rather overt, readily observable factors and more interpretive considerations of their subjective experience have been provided in an attempt to isolate and assess significant influences. In the next section I will compare and systematize these observations.

Conclusions

Though linguists and anthropologists, representing a variety of perspectives, have acknowledged the personal, biographical, and interactional basis of linguistic knowledge (Ellen 1979, 357; Hudson 1980, 12; Gardner 1976, 446; Becker 1984), few personalistic studies have actually been conducted. The preceding lingual life histories, even in the abbreviated form presented here, provide a rich source of insights regarding the importance and significance of a variety of variables that have been considered significant in processes of language change and language maintenance (Labov 1979; 1980, 264; Leap 1981). In the following pages I will discuss these insights and further explore the general significance of a personalistic approach to sociolinguistic phenomena.

One variable often considered in studies of Native American language maintenance is that of English language fluency. Many analysts assume a type of conflict model that associates increased English language fluency with diminished native language skills. Yet in two of the three cases presented here this pattern does not exist. Both Myron and Dan possess an extraordinary command of their native language for their respective age groups. This is true not only of structural details but also of a use-oriented fluency, in Fillmore's (1979) sense, which includes cultural notions of appropriateness, creativity, and stylistic variation. Only Ned provides any clear support for a conflict model since he is the only speaker in my entire sample of 31 to display language skills typical of speakers of a younger chronological age. Available Arizona Tewa data seems to resemble Stout's (1979) finding for Laguna, a Keresan-speaking pueblo where those students with the strongest English language proficiency (including reading, writing, and speaking) were also those students with the strongest native language skills.

Though a comprehensive treatment of this subject is beyond the scope of this work, some inferences on this subject do warrant brief mention. One concerns the nature of Pueblo enculturation as a preparation for the formal education and literacy of the classroom. Pueblo socialization, especially in the arena of religious instruction, involves explicit verbal transmission, rote memorization, acquisition of a discrete speech level (*te'e hi:li*, kiva talk), and public performance (including rehearsals). This is true not only of those who aspire to membership in esoteric societies, but to a somewhat lesser extent also of all children who are ritually inducted into the tribe. Given this type of socialization and its emphasis on language, one can readily see in these cultural practices a preliterate literacy in Pattison's (1982, 28) sense of a cultural awareness of the relationship between language and the world. Just how compatible this *pueblo literacy* is with the essayist style described by the Scollons (1981) remains to be investigated, but some of the attributes mentioned above certainly must be regarded as significant preadaptations for the Euro-American norms of classroom interaction and literacy.

Other important variables often cited as influential in the maintenance of American Indian languages are the composition and orientation of an individual's family (Leap 1981, 219). Labov, too, places a major emphasis on the role of early social experience in shaping individual variation (Labov 1979, 329). In the case studies presented here, such factors are of undeniable importance. For Myron, the advanced age of his parents and the habitual access to an older stratum of the language that it provided is clearly a significant attribute in any account of his exceptional linguistic knowledge and fluency. For Dan his close apprenticeship-like relationship with his grandfather provided an essential preparation for his extraordinary knowledge of Arizona Tewa.

But Ned's case illustrates that early social experience may be better understood more as a preparation than a determinant of the speech patterns that will characterize one's adult life. He proves especially problematical, given his conservative upbringing in a Tewa-speaking family, for Labov's (1979, 329) claim that profound shifts in social experience and ideology cannot alter the pattern of linguistic variation imposed by one's early social experience. But a careful examination of the relevant data reveals that Labov's claim must be more precisely qualified according to linguistic subsystem in order to encompass the Tewa data. Ned's linguistic performance reveals major differences in his performance on both syntactic/semantic and phonological measures (table 4.2A-D and table 4.5A, B), on the one hand, and on morphological measures on the other. Though his performance on the former reflects the pattern of linguistic convergence and English influence typical of group 1 speakers, his phonological scores are in accord with group 2—the group that he would be assigned to on the basis of his chronological age.

These data suggest that Labov's claim about the relative immutability of one's early linguistic patterns should perhaps be restricted to specific subsystems (like phonology) if it is to mesh with the Tewa data. It is, of course, somewhat unfair to suggest such a modification on the basis of data that Labov's presumably culture-specific claim never meant to encompass. Nevertheless the patterns observed here do illuminate a potential problem in Labov's over-reliance on phonological criteria. It is far from abundantly clear whether linguistic variation in other subsystems, especially syntax and lexicon, would also support his observation even for an urban English-speaking speech community.

Another factor about the family that is often considered to be influential on native language maintenance is its political/ideological orientation, especially as it pertains to modernization and interethnic relations with Euro-Americans. In the available data this factor does not seem very significant. For Ned, the conservatism of his parents has hardly promoted his adherence to that position. Similarly one could not have predicted

Dan's absorption into ceremonial life from the rather progressive orientation of his parents. Perhaps two observations about family ideological orientation are necessary in order to situate this variable into an appropriate ethnographic context. First, kinship and social organization among the Arizona Tewa, as among Pueblo groups in general, provide children with a very large number of potentially significant others—parents, grandparents, mother's brother (*mɛmɛ*), ceremonial parents, and clan relations. Thus any consideration of the family must be ethnographically applied so as to accommodate this rather large number of kin-based, potentially significant others.[19] With this increased number of relevant kinsmen typically comes considerable diversity in ideological orientation (e.g., Yava 1979, 15). Since a variety of culturally sanctioned options are available, it is rather inappropriate to assign a single label like *conservative* or *progressive* as a summary of an individual's family's orientation.

Another factor, much more specific to the Arizona Tewa, that is relevant here is their role as cultural brokers between Hopi and Euro-American society (Dozier 1954, 367). Though some diversity of opinion exists in the speech community, for the most part a willingness to experiment with modern technological innovations and a general attitude of cooperation with Euro-Americans has been characteristic of the Arizona Tewa for most of the present century. Thus, to a great extent, *traditionalism* among the Arizona Tewa is generally reflected in ceremonial adherence and not in antagonism to Euro-Americans and their social institutions.

This general attitude is extended to the related variable of school experience. The Arizona Tewa led the Hopi in their support of Euro-American educational institutions and their recognition of their importance as a means of adapting to an increasingly pervasive Euro-American society (Stanislawski 1979, 601–2). Most Arizona Tewa children attend reservation schools—both Bureau of Indian Affairs and missionary—with considerable support and encouragement from their families. The school experiences of the three exceptional individuals is quite positive. As for most Arizona Tewa, Tewa children seem to adapt well to the classroom. The most significant limitations of their school experience stem not from attitudinal problems nor from conflicting cultural norms regarding learning (as in Philips 1972, 1983) but from a variety of behind-the-scenes problems. These include inadequate pedagogical materials, poorly trained teachers, a lack of role models, and ultimately the lack of economic opportunities on the reservation. The net effect is typically that this type of formal education imparts a useful preparation for future interethnic interaction but, especially given the underdevelopment of the Hopi Reservation, it often fails to provide relevant preparation for the limited economic opportunities available. The underemployment that Myron willingly accepts and Ned's initial off-reservation employment illustrate the two most common economic alternatives that confront young Arizona Tewa people on the Hopi Reservation. The reservation niche (Hodge 1971, 287) occupied by Dan represents a rather rare occurrence of an available job in the service-oriented federal and tribal bureaucracy.

Turning to another variable—the number of American Indian languages spoken—we can observe that all the households of these exceptional individuals are multilingual and that Tewa was the dominant language of each. For both Myron and Ned, Tewa was the nearly exclusive language of the home. But since Dan's father was Hopi, Tewa was not nearly as exclusively spoken. Certainly the case studies presented here demonstrate that even nearly exclusive exposure to the native language during childhood does not guarantee continued command of the language by the adult.

Another factor, not typically considered in studies of American Indian language maintenance but quite familiar in recent sociolinguistic scholarship is that of social network (Milroy and Margrain 1980; Labov 1980, 261). Students of American Indian languages appear to have neglected the social network perhaps because they assume that these speech communities are so traditional that kinship pervades social interaction and minimizes the need to examine an individual's social network (Bott 1957; Mitchell 1969). But social changes that have introduced unprecedented levels of sociocultural variation make network analysis both appropriate and advisable. This is especially true in light of the importance that some scholars have attached to dense multiplex networks as vehicles of linguistic norm-enforcement (Milroy and Margrain 1980).

The present data certainly attest the significance of social networks as a contributing factor in shaping individual variation. For Myron, participation in intergenerational networks combined with the advanced age of his parents are the only extraordinary biographical details for those of his age group that might be associated with his exceptional linguistic knowledge and performance. For Dan, his ongoing participation in ceremonial networks combines with his early introduction to song by his grandfather as extraordinary biographical attributes for those of his age group. Similarly we find in Ned's social network evidence of his marginal membership in the speech community and the relative prominence of job-related interethnic voluntary associations in his personal network. Thus, in all three cases examined here, the age-anomalous networks of these individuals represent a significant, overt contribution to their exceptional linguistic knowledge and performance.

So far, I have considered relatively overt factors in attempting to account for the exceptional status of Myron, Dan, and Ned. Now, however, I will examine the subjective worlds of these individuals,[20] from a symbolic interactionist perspective (Blumer 1969; Bruner 1973). One of the important, perhaps quintessential, premises of this theoretical position is that "people act toward things on the basis of the meanings that things have for them" (Blumer 1969, 2).

At first blush this premise appears indistinguishable from comparable foundational assumptions in symbolic anthropology (Geertz 1973; Schneider 1968) and in cultural anthropology in general. A crucial difference, however, is that anthropologists have tended to emphasize the stable cultural meanings available to members of cultural groups, treating meaning as largely pre-given. In contrast, symbolic interactionism emphasizes the creative efforts of individuals who assign meanings to objects—humans, artifacts, concepts—on the basis of social interaction with others and through an interpretive process. As will be demonstrated below, the interpreted meanings of these individuals are at least as important as culturally pre-given meanings in accounting for the knowledge and behavior of these individuals. Given the situation of extensive sociocultural change and considerable intracultural variation in the Arizona Tewa speech community, this should not be too surprising.

Of special interest here will be the individual's subjective meanings concerning group identity and the largely derivative meanings that he assigns to the different languages he speaks. We can begin this exploration with the concept of the *reference group*—that group to which a person psychologically orients himself and whose perspective he imaginatively adopts in order to generate meaningful behavior. But before attempting to discuss the reference groups of the three individuals, some clarification of this concept in light of recent work on the *self* and on intraindividual linguistic variation is necessary. Ellen (1979, 357) has cogently observed the dangers associated with a *reification* of the individual and the consequent neglect of patterned intraindividual variation that it invites. My goal is not to perpetuate the overly homogenized view of the individual that haunts much of the anthropological literature. (See also chapter 6 for more of a focus on this patterned intraindividual variation). As noted in chapter 2, many Tewa themselves find in their naming practices, which provide them with a repertoire of names (*khǫ́wę́*), a terminological reflection of this multiplicity. Names are acquired at birth, tribal initiation, school, society induction, as artistic pseudonyms, and so on. Most people will have between three and seven names that are used with considerable frequency. My goal is not to falsify the diversity that these ethnographic facts suggest but rather to locate a more paramount social identity. In practice, extending George Herbert Mead's (1934) imagery, I am searching for the reflective *I* that is somehow superordinate to the various *me*s of more compartmentalized social selves. This *I* is distinguishable from any *me* in terms of the greater range of contexts in which it appears, in terms of its more inclusive scope and penetrating force.[21]

Viewing reference groups in this manner, we can examine the lingual life histories just presented in order to locate the *I* of each of these three individuals. Here we can employ the notion of reference group in order to rectify an insufficiency of network analysis. Both Myron and Dan engage in job-related interpersonal interaction that consume about half of their interactive time each working day. If we were to plot their personal networks we would find that job-related service encounters do comprise the majority of their daily interpersonal contacts. But network analysis alone cannot address such issues as relevance and psychological orientation. For both Myron and Dan, these service encounters represent highly compartmentalized interactions and imposed relevances. Their intrinsic relevances (Schutz 1964, 124–25) lie elsewhere and are better reflected in their voluntary, extraprofessional networks and in more general patterns reflected in biographical choices.

For Myron an orientation to the values of older Arizona Tewa pervades these choices. He willingly participates in kin-based networks and assumes the responsibilities for assistance, in both labor and economic support, which such participation implies. His choice of residence clearly reflects this participation. Not only has he chosen reservation residence despite its economic shortcomings, he has also opted to live near his parents. Though the latter choice is culturally guided by ideal norms that place responsibility for aging parents on the youngest available children, it is increasingly rare among younger Arizona Tewa, who tend to channel much more energy into their own nuclear families. Myron's extraprofessional network is intergenerational; he has considerable interaction not only with his parents but especially with older clan relatives. In sum, Myron's integration into family and village life contrasts sharply with the more marginal participation typical of those of his generation. While it is impossible to specify some well-defined, corporate group as his reference group, the available patterns strongly suggest a rather traditional, kin-based orientation best embodied by the oldest generation. In accord with these relevances, he appears to be especially sensitive to their speech patterns, adopting them as his own.

As Labov (1979, 329) has claimed, it would be wrong to suggest that this ideological identification alone would bring about a linguistic convergence of largely out-of-awareness linguistic phenomena. But Ned's case demonstrates that early linguistic socialization is not a determinant of adult speech and that identification, when coupled with significant early exposure to a particular lect, is a critical ingredient in shaping individual variation. Perhaps nowhere are the limitations of correlational sociolinguistics more evident than in discussions of sociolinguistic development. While it may be analytically useful to demark sharp boundaries between the social and the psychological, on the one hand, and language and society on the other, it is especially doubtful that these distinctions capture or illuminate their experiential unity for the individual. Grammars, phonologies, and lexical items are rather effortlessly acquired, but not without a residual symbolic significance that emerges from the very personal nature of the learning experience. Forms are acquired but the meanings attached are not merely lexical or referential (Gumperz 1982, 26). For Myron, as for older speakers, Arizona Tewa was acquired not simply as a language, but the language of ethnicity. Infused with a *sanctity-by-association* (Fishman 1977, 25), it became inseparable from myriad events: attending birth-celebrations, weddings, and funerals; sharing meals with kinsmen; tribal initiation; participation in masked kachina dances; repairing a clan relative's roof; relating history and telling traditional stories; and rehearsing songs in the kiva.

For Dan, as for Myron, job-related networks provide little insight into the nature of his reference group. For Dan, however, his highly focused extraprofessional interaction makes the detection of reference group less problematic, in part because it is closely approximated by a more corporate group—the ceremonial elders. Dan's devotion to this group is nearly complete. Aside from his sister's family, with whom he lives, these individuals virtually comprise his entire personal network. In deep personal crisis after the death of his family, Dan chose a familiar path, relying on the traditional options that provided coherence for him as a child. His knowledge of esoteric speech forms and his knowledge of the more mundane language are clearly shaped by his personal network. But his participation in that network was clearly preadapted by his grandfather's influence. As with Myron, we find in Dan a strong identification with this extraprofessional network, an identification enabled by extraordinary preparatory childhood experiences. For Dan, more so than Myron, linguistic imitation of the ceremonial elders is quite self-conscious. This is especially true of esoteric speech, where imitation is explicitly encouraged so as to maximize ritual continuity. But even in mundane speech, Dan completely endorses the linguistic norms of the elders as the most correct speech. Like Myron he invests Arizona Tewa with a special significance, but unlike him this significance is not so rooted in mundane interaction with kinsmen. For Dan the most significant aspects of the Tewa language are in *te'e hi:li* (kiva speech). For him mastery of this speech level is necessary to ensure ritual continuity and cosmic order for his people.

Of the three individuals discussed here only Ned possesses a reference group that is not approximated by older, traditional Arizona Tewa people. In fact, one could say that Tewa identity has relatively little to do with his personal orientation. His on-reservation residence is more an imposed relevance than an intrinsic one. While he contributes economically to his parents he is rather marginally involved in kin-based or village networks. Having found his own childhood unsatisfying, he has backgrounded those cultural associations in an effort to create a more satisfying self-image—one based on personal achievement. In accord with this orientation, English has usurped most of the functions once performed by Tewa. English is for Ned a language of economic opportunity and a means of participation in a larger American society. Though, like the others, he had significant cultural preparation, his disidentification and consequent educational, residential, and interactional choices prompted him to adopt an alternative cultural orientation.

Coda

Linguists have found it useful to examine the anomalous. As a grammarian I know I am not alone in acknowledging the importance of ungrammatical sentences in delineating the outer limits of a corpus of utterances which must be accounted for via grammatical description (Householder 1973). Gumperz and Tannen (1979, 306) have examined *starred*, or failed, discourse sequences as a means of learning about the interactional prerequisites of successful ones. Fromkin (1973, 1980) has studied speech errors as a clue to the psychological operations involved in grammatical speech. In an effort to disclose the delicate nature of microsociological order, Garfinkel (1967, 37) has studied instances of "making trouble." As an ethnolinguist, I believe this study of exceptional individuals can provide a comparably instructive source of insights. Analytic and etic categories, such as the conventional variables of class and age, may provide convenient explanatory vehicles, but they also offer excuses for the postponement of a more profound understanding of sociolinguistic variation. These abbreviated lingual life histories permit us to penetrate and deconstruct such overt variables as age, revealing the importance of less salient factors like cultural adherence, language socialization, social network, and reference group.

While intensive preoccupation with the over 90 percent of the sample that was not exceptional would also have affirmed the importance of these factors, exceptional individuals—like ungrammatical utterances— seem to provide a privileged access to insights that permits a more profound understanding. Rather than being viewed as a tolerable level of error or as expected imperfections in otherwise neat sociolinguistic patterns, exceptional individuals can be more profitably viewed as instructive challenges to conventional levels of sociolinguistic explanation.

If the present preoccupation with individuals seems unwarranted or excessive, I think this reflects not the inherent worth of the undertaking but rather the state of the art in sociolinguistic treatments of variation. Here, two factors may be briefly mentioned. First, over the last two or three decades most sociolinguistic treatments of variation have focused primarily on the role of speech variation as a reflection of ongoing linguistic change. In such studies the macro-level focus generally blurs out the individual in preference for a more inclusive view of the speech community as the locus of language change. Second, sociolinguistic treatments of variation have reflected if not the divorce then at least the separation from the adjacent social sciences of sociology and anthropology. Formal analysis and the explication of language-internal regularities have become more of a preoccupation than the understanding of socially distributed linguistic knowledge within the speech community. For example, the *variable rule,* once heralded as a means of incorporating social variables in linguistic representation, has been recently employed to account for variation in which sociocultural considerations seem quite peripheral (e.g., Kroch and Small 1978; Rousseau and Sankoff 1978; and Sankoff and Laberge 1978). Rather than illuminating the role of language in social life, variable rules have themselves attracted focal attention in debates over what they can and should represent (Sankoff and Labov 1979; Kay and McDaniel 1979).

I do not want to suggest that there is anything inherently wrong with either of these pursuits. Rather I want to emphasize that such activities do not exhaust the legitimate sociolinguistic investigation of variation. It is unfortunate that such studies have so emphasized quantitative techniques that they have fostered an ignorance of their limitations and a neglect of qualitative methods. In accord with the more intimate relationship between linguistics and anthropology that I have attempted to invoke by reviving the term ethnolinguistics here, I have offered the present chapter as a humanistic alternative to conventional sociolinguistic analysis. The methods and interpretive strengths of anthropology must be incorporated in sociolinguistic analysis if this field is ever to produce genuine understandings about the sociocultural significance of sociolinguistic patterns and not simply persist in telling us things we already know about society (Bickerton 1973, 17). For those whose concern encompasses both languages and their speakers, such undertakings are clearly imperative.

Dell Hymes has encouraged us to think about an individual's speech using the imagery of voices: "One way to think about a society is in terms of the voices it has and might have" (Hymes 1979, 44). My objective in the present study has been to explore the utility of attending to voices that typically go unheard.

6

. . .

HOW TO "SPEAK THE PAST": AN EVIDENTIAL PARTICLE AND THE TEXT-BUILDING OF TRADITIONAL STORIES

In content and form, Tewa *pé:yu'u* (traditional stories) represent an early introduction to cultural knowledge and values. These stories, in the traditional Arizona Tewa view, are regarded as necessary for such seemingly unrelated things as the moral and educational development of young listeners and the maintenance and progression of the agricultural cycle (Kroskrity 1985c).[1] They are fablelike narratives, usually involving Old Man Coyote and other characters, which often contain instructive episodes depicting traditional technologies (e.g., rope-making, food preparation, and hunting strategies). Tewa stories depict a moral universe that rewards "good" characters and punishes the "bad." Dewey Healing expresses this in a definition of stories that he provided while we were engaged in dictionary research:

t'owan díbí-pe:yu-di wihi wo'i dí-mun-de wiyádá
people 3plRFL-story-SUB INDEF good 3plACT-show-HAB also
hele óyyó-pí-yádí dí-khi'o-de.
something good-NEG-also 3pl-reveal-HAB.
When people tell traditional stories, they are showing
something good but also revealing something bad.

As such they promote Tewa cultural values and sanction against the antithetical values displayed by such characters as Old Man Coyote. *Cį́ʼé: Pę́:yuʼu* (Bird Story) provides an excellent example of this duality. Presented in the final section of this chapter, the story can be readily dichotomized into two parallel and opposing lines of narrative action. In the first part, baby birds are being taught to fly by their mother, who leads them in song as they, one by one, attempt their first flights. This scene of intergenerational, intrafamilial teaching and learning is suddenly disrupted by the appearance of Old Man Coyote. But rather than posing an immediate threat to the bird family, Coyote inquires about their learning routine and is told that he, too, can fly, if he simply imitates the baby birds. Gullible as ever, Old Man Coyote willingly participates in this routine, inadvertently jumping to his death while being sung to by the birds. While the legitimate learners acquire a survival skill through traditional transmission, the illegitimate learner meets his death.

But my concern here is more with the meaning of form than with content. More precisely, I am interested in understanding the formal devices that Tewa storytellers use "to speak the past," to construct the authoritative persona of the traditional storyteller.[2] Foremost among these devices is the Tewa evidential particle *ba*. Before exploring its role in traditional narratives, we must understand its place in Arizona Tewa grammar.

/ba/ in Tewa Grammar

The descriptive label *evidential particle* suggests significant facts about its form and meaning. Regarding form, the label *particle* implies a relative independence; it is not a bound form limited to occurrence as an affix of some other constituent, though it often appears in morphological combination with other particles. Regarding the meaning, the label *evidential* conveys its role in qualifying the evidential basis of a speaker's utterance. *Ba* disclaims first-hand knowledge or novelty on the part of the speaker: he or she is merely repeating "prior text." Examples 1 and 2, recorded by John Yegerlehner (1957, 91) from elicitation sessions, illustrate these morphosyntactic and semantic attributes:

1. há: ba díbí-ʼan
    INDEFINITE EV 3plACT-do:PST
    I hear they did something.

2. hę'i-n-dám(-)ba 'ó:bé-t'olo-'an
   III-pl-OBL-F(-)EV 3pl/3INV-tell-PST
   I hear it was they who told them.

In these examples, I have preserved the translations supplied by Yegerlehner. Though these translations into idiomatic English supply the sense of the Tewa sentences, a simple scan of the morpheme-by-morpheme glosses shows that there is no Tewa equivalent to either "I" or "hear" in these sentences. "I hear" could be replaced by "it is said that" or the indefinite "they say." Regardless of translation, the evidential conveys the "hearsay" qualification of the assertion. Example 1 illustrates the independent particle without any phonological influence on contiguous constituents. Example 2 provides an instance of assimilation owing to optional phonological integration in rapid speech. The normally dental-final focus morpheme -án has assimilated to the bilabial position of the initial consonant of the immediately following *ba*. These examples also illustrate the syntax of *ba* placement. In each sentence they appear immediately after a foregrounded noun phrase—indefinite *ha:* in 1 and anaphoric *hę'in-dan* in 2. But where no such foregrounding exists, *ba* may occur in the sentence-initial position or immediately after any time adverbials, as illustrated in 3 and 4, respectively—sentences familiar to me from both naturalistic observation and elicitation:

3. ba 'í'í'-dí na-mε
   EV there-OBL 3sgSTA-go:PST
   They say he left there.

4. thandi ba 'í'í-dí na-mε
   yesterday EV there-OBL 3sgSTA-go:PST
   They say he left there yesterday.

A unified linguistic account of *ba* must also recognize its participation in the morphology of the *direct* quotative *giba*. It is illustrated in 5:

5. 'o-he: gi-ba na-tú
   1sgSTA-sick that-EV 3sgSTA-say
   "I'm sick," he said.

This example can be instructively compared to 6, in which *ba* is removed and a third person prefix replaces the first person, creating an *indirect* quotation:

6. na-he: gi na-tú
   3sgSTA-sick that 3sgSTA-say
   He said that he's sick.

In 6 the speaker is understood to be summarizing rather than quoting another speaker. At first glance the morphological contribution of *ba* to *giba* seems consistent with its use as an independent particle. Where the speaker recites prior text, attributable to either an indefinite or specifiable other, he or she may use *ba*. But there is an additional consistency that partially undermines my translation of 5. Since *ba* also disclaims first-hand evidence, the translation might better be elaborated as, "I'm sick," he is quoted as saying. The implication of a sentence such as 5 is that the direct quote that it contains has been indirectly communicated to the new speaker. According to native speakers, the direct quotation lacks the reliability or facticity of its indirect counterpart. Example 6, the indirect quote, is actually the more likely self-report of a speaker who had participated in a dialogue with the sick person. In actual non-narrative usage in such contexts, indirect quotation is systematically preferred. Similarly in narrative genres other than *pé:yu'u*, such as personal and clan histories, indirect quotation far exceeds direct.

This grammatical introduction to *ba* has aimed at capturing the linguistic knowledge available to speakers that would underlie its grammatical use. Information supplied in the preceding section could be neatly reflected in category symbols and lexical entries that would capture native speakers' knowledge of its morphosyntactic properties and the semantic relatedness of *ba* and *giba*. But this expression of knowledge on the part of an imaginary ideal native speaker of Tewa is especially deficient if we aim for a more ambitious understanding. Paul Friedrich (1979; 1986) has suggested that linguists should not be content in exploring the limited linguistic creativity of Chomskyan ideal speakers but should aim instead at the more inclusive creativity with language that is available to proficient speakers and others who are especially adept in the creative and artistic use of language. Toward this end I will explore what

Tewa narrators know about *ba* and how they display this knowledge in attaining the goal of "speaking the past."

Narrative Fluency and Generic *Ba*

Before adopting the perspective of the narrator as text-builder, it is useful to consider some distributional data concerning *ba* in a sample of three texts—"Coyote and Bullsnake" (Kroskrity and Healing, 1978), "Coyote-Woman and the Deer Children" (Kroskrity and Healing, 1980), and "Bird Story" (Kroskrity 1985c and later this chapter). In approximately 228 sentences there are about 226 instances of *ba*. If we exclude quotations from this sample (where *ba* occurs, but only in the optional *giba*), we find that in 171 narrative verses there are 226 occurrences of *ba*—an average of 1.32 per clause. In more than one-third (34.5 percent) of these verses, *ba* occurs two or more times. This apparent redundancy defies grammatical explanation since the linguistic semantics of *ba* provides no account of why it should multiply occur in a single clause or sentence.

Somewhat less problematic, but still significant, is the relaxation of relatively strict rules regarding the syntactic placement of *ba* in the texts. While many instances do conform to the regularities described above, we find other unanticipated occurrences in the text provided below, including positioning after locatives (e.g., 13, 23), manner adverbials (17, 35), dependent clauses (19, 40, 70), postpositional phrases (18, 60), and so on. I should emphasize that occurrences in these environments are not simply due to the greater length and more diverse constituency of many of these examples. When extracted from the text, comparable sentences will be produced by native speakers with only one *ba* per clause and in accord with the syntactic regularities described above. Two examples, 7 and 8, illustrate this general pattern:

7. ba 'í-wɛ di-powá-dí 'ó:bé-khwó:li-ma:k'a-kan-t'ó
    EV there-at 3plSTA-arrive-SUB 3pl/3INV-fly-teach-do-FUT
    Having arrived there, so it is said, they were going to be taught to fly.

8. kídí ba k'u 'i-yá díbí-khwó:le-n hę:yí'in to' 'í'í
    And:then EV rock there-EMPH 3plRFL-fly-PRES little only

there

And then, so they say, they were flying to the rock bit by bit.

These examples correspond to 23 and 39 in the text below. There are three noteworthy differences between 7 and 23. First, the *ba* which once followed *'í-wɛ* (there-at) has been moved to sentence-initial position. Second, the *ba* which followed the dependent verb *di-powá-dí* (their having arrived) has been deleted. Third, less relevant for discussion here, the subordinator has been removed from the second clause to form an independent clause.[3] Example 8 differs from 39 in only the first of these ways—its lone *ba* has been moved immediately after the temporal conjunct/adverb. *Ba* can optionally occupy sentence-initial position in this example. Thus, in both the number of *ba* permitted and the syntactic position allowed, significant differences exist between non-narrative usage and usage within the *pę́:yu'u* narratives. In order to understand these disparities, we must move beyond a consideration of the grammaticality of sentences to an examination of more encompassing considerations of appropriate discourse. In so doing, we cannot rely on a kind of Chomskyan ideal speaker who produces only grammatical sentences in a single style without considerations of context and prior text. We must instead consider actual narrators, guided by culturally available genres, who are performing before a living audience. Fillmore (1979) has encouraged the exploration of different types of fluency within a culture as a means of assessing not simply what speakers know about their language but also how they use this knowledge. My concern here is with the narrative fluency of storytellers in the Arizona Tewa speech community when they relate traditional stories (*pę́:yu'u*).

As in the acquisition of Arizona Tewa, no formal training is required of Tewa narrators. They "catch on" (*-ma:k'a-'an*) by hearing others tell the stories, absorbing both the form and content of the genre as well as canons of good performance. While many Arizona Tewa people agree on who are adept narrators, they seldom discuss the criteria that motivate such evaluations. Those individuals who did specify criteria offered the following attributes as evaluative criteria in their *oral literary criticism* (Dundes 1966): (1) use of storytelling conventions (*pę́:yu'u tú*, literally "story words"); (2) use of archaic words (*héyé tú*), both in the dialogue of characters and in the narrative itself; (3) use of facial expression (*ce:-po*) in the dramatic imitation of characters; (4) use of prosodic and paralinguistic effects by the narrator, especially in attempts to imitate the voices (*tú*) of characters; (5) use of song (*khaw*); and (6) "carrying it hither" (*-ma:di-ma'a*), which can be paraphrased as situating the narrative for the present audience or, in more colloquial terms, "bringing it home."[4] The storyteller is expected to situate the narrative in a known geographical locale, elaborate or edit episodes as part of recipient design, and add other details, by reshaping texts to new contexts, that contribute to a sense of immediacy for the audience (Becker 1984, 138).

Though detailed discussion of each of these criteria is beyond the scope of the present work, this probing of narrative fluency and the use of *ba* as a means of adopting the voice of the narrator will focus on the first and the last of these criteria—storytelling conventions and interactional aspects of the storytelling process. In accord with this focus I will be primarily concerned with two types of what A. L. Becker (1979, 1984, 1988) has termed *textual relations*. These are *generic* and *medial* relations. Briefly stated, the first of these relates a given text to prior texts (especially those of the same genre), and the second relates texts and text-units to the medium, here oral performance, in which they are produced. As applied here, this dichotomy also distinguishes *discourse schemata* (Fillmore 1979, 97), or generic formulas for text-building, from the medium of text-presentation—oral performance before a familiar audience. As we shall observe, though neither of these relations appear to be part of autonomous linguistics' ideal speaker's knowledge of *ba*, they represent important cultural knowledge on the part of those who know how to tell the stories, and those who have learned to hear them and to respond appropriately.

Regarding generic relations, we can note similar framing conventions similar to those observed by Tedlock (1983, 55) in his study of Zuni *telapnaawe*. But in addition to the formulaic introduction that situates the story and introduces the characters in the initial lines, Arizona Tewa narrators are guided by an additional generic requirement. Informally stated, *ba* must be prodigiously used throughout the narrative. Given its linguistic meaning outside of these texts, it is perhaps not surprising that a *hearsay* evidential be used to maintain the narrator's perspective as one who is relating a traditional story. My own knowledge of Arizona Tewa *pé:yu'u* comes from hearing stories performed by Dewey Healing, Albert Yava, Edith Nash, and others. In their stories, *ba* was extensively deployed in a similar manner, suggesting that its appearance is hardly the product of idiosyncratic practice but rather a genre expectation. The nearly complete lack of linguistic documentation of Arizona Tewa narratives, apart from my own investigations, makes it impossible to compare my collected texts to others in this genre.

One Rio Grande Tewa text collected by Harrington (1947) from Eduardo Cata, "The Girl and the Cow," displays a similar use of *ba*. In neighboring but unrelated languages additional similarities exist. Many Navajo traditional narratives, including those collected by Goddard (1933) from Chic Sandoval, those collected by Haile (1984) from Curly To Aheedliini, and those that represent the collaboration of Barre Toelken (Toelken 1969; Toelken and Scott, 1981) with Yellowman, display a quotative morpheme, *jini* (they say), as the final element in most sentences. Similarly Hopi *yaw*, a quotative, is also used in traditional stories, appearing in every sentence of narratives performed by Herschel Talashoma (Malotki 1978), Evelyn Seumptewa (Seumptewa, Voegelin, and Voegelin 1980), and Michael Lomatuway'ma (Malotki and Lomatuway'ma 1984). Like *ba*, these morphemes appear even when the narrator is not quoting a particular character in the text.[5] This pattern also extends outside the Pueblo southwestern linguistic area in such Native American languages of Southern California as Cupeño (Jane Hill, personal communication). In fact evidential particles in a wide variety of the world's languages do frequently appear in traditional narrative texts (Pamela Downing, personal communication). Given this typological observation, any areal-historical investigation of the narrative uses of evidentials will have to distinguish between relatively common patterns, such as those involving one evidential per clause occurring in a relatively fixed position (e.g., sentence-initial, post-verb, sentence-final), and those that appear to be typologically more rare—multiple occurrences per clause with variable syntactic placement. It is interesting to observe that these more rare attributes are present in both Hopi and Arizona Tewa traditional narratives. Though a detailed areal investigation is beyond the scope of this chapter, these similarities of Hopi and Arizona Tewa narrative traditions strongly suggest mutual influence and clearly warrant further comparative effort.[6]

Though constituents that appear to function very much like *ba* do occur in these neighboring languages, I will confine my discussion of further generic patterning to the Arizona Tewa texts that I have collected over the past six years. Following important precedents by Dell Hymes (1979;

1980) and Dennis Tedlock (1972; 1983), I have detected an ethnopoetic organization of Tewa traditional narratives into verses containing lines. Though Hymes and Tedlock differ significantly on the criteria they use to reveal this organization, with Hymes relying more on features of syntax and Tedlock the pauses of actual performance, this difference need not be interpreted as conflicting. William Bright's (1979; 1980) analysis of Karok texts suggests that the two principles often converge, functioning cooperatively rather than competitively. The same can be said for the Arizona *pé:yu'u* texts, including the one below, especially when an adept narrator performs before a native audience. But the fundamental difference in these approaches is not so much the emphasis on particle or pause as it is the preoccupation with disclosing "scriptal" knowledge of a text, associated with the work of Hymes, versus the appreciation of the narrator's performance of a text, associated with the work of Tedlock.[7]

In Arizona Tewa *pé:yu'u* texts, verses closely conform to the sentence. They typically begin with temporal conjunctives such as *kídí* (and then) *'i-hedi* (after that), or their emphatic counterparts *kídá* (AND THEN), and *'i-hedán* (after THAT). Slightly more than half of all nonquoted verses begin in this manner (50 percent in the story below and 54 percent in the sample of three stories). Locative expressions and discourse introducers, such as *kín* (this) and *kínán* (THIS), combine with the temporal locatives to comprise the great majority of verse-initial elements (85 percent in the story below, 80 percent in the sample). The verses typically end with a sentence-final grammatical pause. Within these nonquoted verses, *ba* serves to distinguish lines of the text, segmenting each verse, apart from the formulaic conclusion and the dialogue, typically into two or three lines. As will be noted in the following section, these occurrences of *ba* are also accompanied by narrative pauses in performance before a native audience.

The ethnopoetic function of *ba* thus appears to explain two important facts regarding its apparent redundancy and lack of syntactic constraint in *pé:yu'u*. Since *ba* is a line marker in these texts it can and must occur more than once in some clauses or verses. Here *ba* is liberated from grammatical constraints in order to serve the discourse expectations of a particular narrative genre. Just as *ba* must often multiply occur in order to do this, so the conditions of its syntactic placement must also be greatly expanded in order to accommodate its line-final placement. This results in the relaxation of syntactic constraints that normally characterize its distribution in everyday non-narrative speech where *ba* is not associated with adopting the voice of the traditional narrator.

Ba in Narrative Performance

In addition to the poetic organization of many traditional Native American narratives, scholarly appreciations of verbal art have observed their similarity to drama (Jacobs 1959; Toelken 1969; Tedlock 1983, 53). In this regard, Dennis Tedlock (1983, 55) specifically notes their concern with the fantastic (as opposed to the prosaic), the parallelism of their organization, and the fact that emotions are evoked rather than described. The oral performance of these narratives often involves gestures, vocal imitations, and other dramatic devices. These observations, coupled with the native criteria for evaluation that I outlined above, strongly suggest the importance of attending to the medium of dramatic performance for further insights into the narrative fluency of Arizona Tewa storytellers. What medial relations of this sort are relevant in accounting for the traditional narrator's knowledge and use of *ba*? Similarly, what does a culturally prepared audience know about *ba* and its consequences for their behavior?

In performance before a native audience, fluent Arizona Tewa narrators will pause briefly at those line demarcations occupied by *ba* in what may be termed *narrative voice*—when the narrator is in the role of the storyteller and not assuming the voice of a particular character. On these occasions, members of an informed and responsive audience may periodically interject the gender-specific form of audience response. These interjections do not occur when the narrator speaks in the voice of a character where verses and lines are discriminated only by grammatical and dramatic pauses, but only in the narrative voice where *ba* serves to segment verses into lines. Thus, *ba* is redefined through the medium of oral performance. As Bakhtin (1986, 95) observed, "Each speech genre . . . has its own typical conception of the addressee, and this defines the genre." For just as the traditional narrator must "speak the past," the audience must attend and respond in an appropriate manner. The use of *ba* is thus further associated with pauses by the narrator and the audience's collaborative interjections. Thus "speaking the past" is not simply a responsibility of the narrator but rather an interactive accomplishment.

In the story below, as in most of the stories that I have collected, only when the narrator utters the formulaic conclusion announcing the end of the story (as in 71 below) does he refrain from *ba* during the narrative.

It is useful to note that when the narrator quotes story characters, he does so in a voice that is prosodically and/or paralinguistically (Crystal 1971) distinct from that of the narrator. Both Mother Bird and Old Man Coyote speak in a slightly higher pitch, and Old Man Coyote speaks with imposed pharyngeal constriction imitative of his advanced age. A consequence of this dramatic effect is the disambiguation of the speakers. Since speakers are simply indexed by third person pronominal prefixes and only rarely identified by the narrator these prosodic and paralinguistic devices, along with shared background knowledge regarding the personalities of the characters, contribute to the immediate intelligibility of the characters' dialogue. Though *ba* itself does not appear in verses containing the dialogue of characters, it still participates in the quotative *giba* that typically follows the dialogue as the storyteller resumes narrative voice.

In performance, *ba* is intimately associated with the voice of the narrator, marking the otherwise unmarked voice of the stories.[8] In the medium of dramatic performance we find in the collaboration of narrator and audience a basis in contexted use for the ethnopoetic structural attributes of generic *ba*. Consider example 9 taken from the beginning of an actual performance that occurred one winter evening in 1981, in which two grandparents are entertaining six grandchildren while their parents are away for several days. The grandfather (GF) and grandmother (GM) have just finished moving chairs around so that grandfather occupies a central position. The segment begins as grandfather rejects a dipper of water offered to him by grandmother and motions to his six grandchildren that he is about to begin. The children, two boys (GS1–2) and four girls (GD1–4), range in age from fourteen to five.

9.   GF: [to GM] Yo, wȯ-'o-na'a-di
         No, I don't want any.
         ne::::
         no::::w
         'ówȩ-he:YÁMMM-ba
         Once upon a time ba
                     [

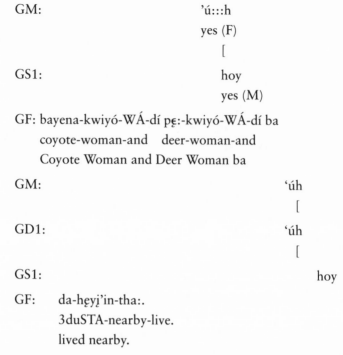

GM: 'ú:::h
      yes (F)
      [

GS1: hoy
      yes (M)

GF: bayena-kwiyó-WÁ-dí pę:-kwiyó-WÁ-dí ba
    coyote-woman-and deer-woman-and
    Coyote Woman and Deer Woman ba

GM: 'úh
                                  [

GD1:   'úh
                                  [

GS1:   hoy

GF: da-hęyị'in-tha:.
     3duSTA-nearby-live.
     lived nearby.

In these ten seconds, the narrator opens with the introductory formula followed by *ba*. This *ba* is overlapped by grandmother's gender-appropriate response, *'úh*, which acknowledges the narrator and ratifies his extended turn at talk. Her response is partially overlapped by the oldest grandson who provides the gender appropriate response for males. After a brief pause, the narrator produces the conjoined noun phrase that introduces the main characters followed by a *ba*. This *ba* also produces overlapping responses from grandfather and two grandchildren. After their response, the narrator concludes the first sentence.

Since *ba* marks pauses that invite audience response, its role in performance complements the structure of the text, further motivating the creative license responsible for its syntactic liberation as the dictates of discourse—here the requirements of genre and oral performance—reshape those of the grammar.

"Speaking the Past, Speaking the Present": Innovation and Convention in Arizona Tewa Narratives

Contemplating speech genres both mundane and artistic, Russian literary critic Mikhail Bakhtin (1986, 63) observed that "not all genres are equally conducive to reflecting the individuality of the speaker (or writer)." Extending this observation to Arizona Tewa *pé:yu'u*, we can add that not all genres appear to be equally conducive to the interactive demands of *contextualizing* (Bauman and Briggs 1990, 72), of fitting a given performance to the unique needs of an audience at a given time. The Tewa narrator of *pé:yu'u* appears to be torn between conflicting values that stipulate highly conventional language, gesture, and song, on the one hand, yet demand that narrators somehow "carry hither" (*-ma:di-ma'a*) their stories to the present audience.

Taking into account a diverse range of culturally shaped forms of casual and noncasual speech, including Javanese shadow theater and American English greetings and closings, Alton Becker (1979, 212–13) rightfully observes that all forms of speech manifest both tradition and innovation, "speak both the past and the present." Though all language activity may consist of both, it is the proportion of each that distinguishes speech genres and their contextualized performances. The genre of *pé:yu'u*, marked by the frequent use of the *ba* particle and the disclaimer of novelty that it encodes, clearly requires Tewa narrators to "speak the past." But what resources does this genre provide to narrators to enable them to "speak the present?" How do Tewa narrators contextualize these highly traditional texts?

Richard Bauman (1986, 78) has identified this general problem as the fundamental question for researchers of oral traditions: "Perhaps the most basic persistent problem confronted by students of oral literature is gauging the effect of the interplay of tradition and innovation, persistence and change, as manifested in the oral text." To investigate this problem, the preferred strategy for Bauman, like other performance-oriented anthropologists (including Briggs 1988 and Duranti 1983) is the comparison of versions of a given story or genre as performed to differing audiences or in disparate social settings. Bauman's analysis of three versions of Texas storyteller Ed Bell's tale about a giant bee tree demonstrates that variation in story length, episode development, degree of metanarrative commentary, and other features are used to contextualize the story for audiences of professional storytellers or of those unfamiliar with Bell and the genre of the *tall tale* that he is performing.

In this section I want to briefly address this issue of tradition and innovation by examining some comparable data. Though almost all of my research on Tewa *pé:yu'u* has been based on elicited texts collected outside the winter months, I had the opportunity during two winter visits in 1978 and 1981 to hear a total of nine stories performed by three different narrators in two domestic settings. Three stories, already familiar to me from prior fieldwork, happened to be performed among the ten to twelve stories that were performed on each of these occasions. I heard "Coyote Woman and the Deer Children" (Kroskrity and Healing 1980) performed by the same narrator on storytelling occasions about three years apart and once again during that latter visit by a different storyteller. I witnessed two different storytellers perform "Ant Story" in the latter visit. Finally I heard two different storytellers perform "Coyote and Bullsnake"—one during each of these visits.

A useful analytical tool for understanding how narrators contextualize their stories is Bakhtin's (1981) notion of *voice,* here used to identify the narrator's speaking persona—the speaking self that is the source of an utterance. Though Tewa *pé:yu'u* may not be as heteroglossic as the Russian novels analyzed by Bakhtin, they nevertheless do have a variety of voices within which the narrator can contextualize his or her performance. The voices in which I found storytellers "carrying [the narrative] here" are those of the traditional narrator, story characters, personal identity of narrator, and also speech event external figures.

By far the most important and most numerous instances of contextualization occurred within the voice of the traditional narrator. Since these contextualizations are viewed as among the least obtrusive, most genre-consistent, and most congruent with a cultural preference for *positional identities* in authentic performance, they provide narrators with resources for innovation that are positively evaluated by informed audience members and the narrators themselves.

Within the voice of the traditional narrator, four distinct means of contextualizing were utilized. The most salient in terms of impact on the text was episode editing and development. In the two versions of "Ant Story" told by two different narrators this was particularly apparent. While both versions contained the same main plot, their narrators devoted special attention to details that they thought would interest their audiences. In summary, the story's main plot consists of a village of ants who manage to convince their nemesis, Old Man Coyote, that their delicate waists are the result of a routine involving the tugging of a rope, wrapped around an individual ant, by two long lines of ants on each side. Since Old Man Coyote envies their shape, he is persuaded to undergo the treatment. He dies when the Ants take advantage of the opportunity and squeeze him to death with a strong rope while pretending to give him a slimming treatment.

In the first version, a grandmother performed before a domestic audience consisting of her husband, their two daughters, and three grandchildren (ages four to nine). The three grandchildren displayed a high involvement with the narrator through eye contact, body orientation, and periodic vocal response. In contrast, the adults in the audience—except for the mother of the children—were manifesting less involvement. They provided appropriate vocal responses but were often looking away, diverting some attention to other activities like cleaning up after dinner and organizing some personal belongings. Playing to her most attentive audience members, the grandmother added some clarifying remarks about Ant social organization that did not appear in either the other performed version or the one I had transcribed from elicitation contexts several years before. While shifting her gaze among the children in a form of audience selection, she noted features of Ant social organization, their clans and village chief, which would enable the children to see parallels between their own community and that of the Ants. This descriptive addition, though presented in the voice of the traditional narrator, is an example of recipient-designed explication offered to scaffold identification with the Ants by the young audience members.

The other version of this story features an elaboration of a subplot in which a search party of Ants ventures off to find a yucca-like plant from which a strong rope can be made. This episode is only briefly mentioned in the previous version, but here the elaboration represents the contextualization of a grandfather who knows of his two grandsons' special interest in native technology from prior experiences in demonstrating farming and trapping techniques to them. A final example of episode editing is illustrated by the two versions of "Coyote Woman and the Deer Children." The only textual difference in these performances by the same narrator is the inclusion/exclusion of a somewhat sexually explicit passage. In this story Deer Children escape from Coyote Woman, who has eaten their mother, and return to their relatives with the help of Old Man Beaver, who carries them across a river in order to be reunited with their kinsmen. Chasing after them, Coyote Woman implores Old Man Beaver to carry her across so that she can care for the orphans. He agrees but almost drowns her in the crossing. In the latter version he not only submerges her on several occasions he also fondles her genitalia. Though the audiences were quite similar on both occasions, my own presence was differentially interpreted, as I later learned from the narrator, and inhibited him in his earlier performance. I questioned the narrator after that performance on the basis of prior research that led to the publication of a version of that story (Kroskrity and Healing 1980). During that research, Dewey Healing hinted that he had left something out of the version we recorded because he did not know how his Euro-American audience would react to the more explicit version. It should be emphasized that many of the Euro-Americans known to the Arizona Tewa and the Hopi are missionaries and that the Arizona Tewa generalize their neo-Victorian attitudes about the body to most Euro-Americans. Though I assured Dewey that he was being unnecessarily conservative in his estimation of his audience he was only willing to insert the following brief sentence rather than elaborate in greater detail.

10.   kida ba 'ı̨:-pó-dí bayena kwiyó ba mán-ma-c'u:n-hon
      and:then EV 3sgPOS-happen-SUB Coyote Woman EV
      3sgACT-hand-enter-about]
      And then while this was happening to Coyote Woman,
      she was fondled by Old Man Coyote.

Though episode editing provides a dramatic means of contextualizing performances, narrators may use other resources that typically result in relatively minor changes in the text yet preserve the highly valued voice of the traditional narrator. One of these devices involves the use of personal names from audience members; the other utilizes place names that are familiar to the audience. An example of the former occurred in a version of "Coyote Woman and the Deer Children" told by a grandmother to an audience of family members, including two grandchildren. Her version of the story was very similar to others I had heard but with two minor differences that contributed to a dramatic change in contextualization. All versions were very similar in adhering to the plot previously outlined but differed in their identification (Burke 1950; Rosaldo 1972) and portrayal of the Deer Children.

Though all versions depict the Deer siblings struggling to follow the admonition of their deceased mother by locating Old Man Beaver and enlisting his assistance, they differ in their gendering of the Deer Children. In stories told by men, the male sibling was presented as the older and the first to give the other moral support on the journey to find their relatives. But in this grandmother's version, the roles were reversed—the sister is presented as the older, the stronger, and the more supportive sibling. It would be wrong to attribute this difference solely to the gender identity of the narrator since other details of her performance strongly suggest that she is recipient-designing the story for her two grandchildren, who are of the same gender and relative age disparities as the "Deer Children." [9] This is further manifested by her use of her grandchildren's names in initially identifying the characters, thus laminating the grandchildren's identities onto specific story characters. Aware that her granddaughter was resentful of her extra responsibilities for her younger brother, this storyteller employed the voice of the traditional narrator to remind her of the special obligation and status associated with being "older sister" (ka:khá). [10]

The use of familiar settings and place names also contributes to the immediacy of the storytelling performance. Comparable phenomena have been described by Dennis Tedlock (1983, 163, 291) for Zuni storytellers. In "Bird Story," for example, many narrators, including Dewey Healing (Kroskrity 1985c), chose to situate the narrative in the familiar topography of the First Mesa area. T'ílí' khyúge (Hawk Cliff) is readily visible from the inhabited part of First Mesa and very experience-near to children who have grown up on the mesas. By utilizing physical locations with which the children have direct experience, traditional narrators engage their young listeners' sense of immediacy and further contribute to carrying their stories to the present audience.

Another resource I saw storytellers use while in the voice of the traditional narrator was *nonverbal communication* or, as Moerman (1990, 9) suggests, *visible communication*. During the performances I saw narrators strategically use such devices as eye contact, tactility, and body orientation while in the voice of the traditional narrator. Though these resources were also available in other voices, my immediate concern is with those that provide narrators with a means of contextualizing traditional narratives while dutifully "speaking the past." Storytellers employed some of these devices in conjunction with other options that have been previously described. In the elaborated version of "Ant Story" that contains the extended episode of journeying for rope-making materials, for example, the narrator made frequent eye-contact with his grandson who had a special interest in native technology. Though it is customary for storytellers to distribute their gaze among the audience, this episode was marked by long periods of mutual gaze between the narrator and his grandson, providing a visible communication parallel to the recipient-designed episode elaboration in the verbal channel. In another instance of strategic visible communication, I observed the storyteller of "Coyote Woman and the Deer Children" engage his oldest grandson in mutual gaze as he introduced the older Deer sibling and then shift his gaze to a younger granddaughter seated next to him. As he touched her shoulders lightly with his outstretched hands, he introduced the younger Deer sibling. Though this use of visible communication rather than the use of names, as in the instance mentioned above, makes the interpretation of these actions somewhat more ambiguous, all audience members attributed a special meaning to it. Rather than viewing it as accidental, they saw it as either or both a deliberate attempt to foster identification with story characters and a means of producing immediacy, of carrying the story hither.

Before briefly considering other voices available to traditional storytellers that would assist them in "speaking the present," it is appropriate to emphasize the importance of this paradoxical cultural preference for "speaking the present" with the voice prototypically associated with "speaking the past." The aesthetic evaluation that prizes this type of innovation above other narrative options is not simply a cultural penchant for subtle rather than for more obtrusive means but rather an expression of a pervasive value on using traditional means to meet the needs of the present. For the Arizona Tewa, and perhaps for other Pueblo narrative traditions, it makes sense to extend Bakhtin's typology of represented speech (e.g., Todorov 1984, 70) and to recognize a *double-voiced* narrator who, according to local narrative ideals, merges the speaking selves of the traditional narrator with his or her personal identity. The devices mentioned above provide resources for recipient-designing, audience-selection and involvement, identification, and other functions that permit storytellers to effectively contextualize traditional narratives for their various audiences and audience members.

Two other types of voices are available to narrators—those of story characters and those of story-external participants. I heard one instance of the former when the narrator laminated various idiosyncrasies of the speech of his grandchildren to various members of the Ant expedition in "Ant Story." So, for example, one Ant spoke with especially exaggerated pronunciation of glottalized consonants, mimicking his granddaughter, while the speech of another Ant was characterized by frequent use of *wemo* (but), a stylistic attribute of her older brother. Somewhat more frequent was the utilization of story-external voices such as the personal voice of the narrator or a voice from the everyday world apart from the traditional narrative. Though Tewa stories typically lack an evaluative coda, some narrators will include one uttered in their personal voice. In example 11 note the concluding sentence of "Old Man Coyote and Old Man Bullsnake," which contains no evidential *ba*—the "emblem" of the traditional narrator.

11.   GF: . . .

      'imo' baaaa

      very EV

      Since, so they say

        [

GS 1, 2:   hoy

           yes

GF: p'o na-kele-di ba

    water 3sgSTA-strong-SUB Ev

    the water was very strong

        [

GS 1, 2:   hoy

             yes

            [

GM, GDs: 'úh

             yes

GF: 'ó:-p'o-hon kídí 'ó:-p'o-hey.

3sgINV-water-carry and:then 3sg-water-kill.

he was carried away and drowned by it.

Néhé 'in-nán né'i-n na:la pé:yu'u na-mu.

This it-EMPH this bullsnake story 3sg-be.

This is all there is to the bullsnake story.

Kínán bayena-senó 'ú:-pó-dí-yán

this:EMPH coyote-old man 3sgPOS-become-SUB-EMPH

Since THIS is what happened to Old Man Coyote

towi' wé-di:-su'o-dε-di.

someone NEG-3plAC-imitate-HAB-SUB.

nobody should imitate others.

GD: [laughs]

                                                        [

GM: mán-mowa

                                                        3sgACT-finish.

                                                        He finished.

This performance contrasts with the published version of a comparable elicited text (Kroskrity and Healing 1978, 168) since in that text Dewey Healing provided the same didactic evaluation but in the voice of narrator, marking the final sentence with two occurrences of evidential *ba*. That the storyteller of 11 has stepped out of his persona as the traditional narrator is manifested not only by the lack of *ba* but also by accompanying visible communication. As he began the final sentence he engaged a young granddaughter in mutual gaze and broke into a broad smile—quite uncharacteristic of the more stylized facial expression and other gestures normally associated with the voice of the traditional narrator. A follow-up interview with the storyteller revealed that he had made this granddaughter a special locutionary target in this mild rebuke since her habit of imitating a variety of TV personalities had offended several members of her family and become a reportable event within that group.

My final example of a story-external voice, considerably more intrusive than the preceding example, is one in which the storyteller simply allows his personal voice to become the speaking self. During one performance of "Old Man Coyote and Old Man Bullsnake," I witnessed the storyteller's growing dissatisfaction with the lack of participation by an older grandchild. While other members of the audience were providing periodic vocalizations in accord with their traditional role expectations, an older grandson seemed a bit indifferent to the storytelling event. In a frame-breaking gesture, the storyteller interrupted his narrative with a code-switch to English, turning to the offending party and asking, "Are you PRESENT, Billy? Say 'PRESENT,'" before resuming the narrative. Invoking the norms of pedagogical discourse associated with the Euro-American educational system, the narrator implicitly questions his grandson's knowledge of the norms of this native form of informal education. But while this abrupt and intrusive voice might have a potent rhetorical effect, this type of innovation is generally negatively regarded by both traditional storytellers and accomplished listeners. For though such voices may help to carry the story here, they cannot do so in a tradition-preserving manner, in a manner that "speaks the past."

In this section I have explored some resources available to traditional narrators that permit them to contextualize their stories. Even the traditional genre of *pę́:yu'u* is sufficiently polyphonic to benefit, analytically, from Bakhtin's translinguistic imagery. Rather than reify the individual narrator, it is appropriate to view his options in selecting and presenting the speaking self. Examining traditional narratives as part of naturally occurring storytelling events complements close textual analysis by providing a privileged site for the study of voice. A limitation of purely literary models is their failure to relate voice, and the selection of the speaking self that it represents, to the interaction of speakers. There is a fruitful parallel in relating scholarly treatments of interindividual variation with those of intraindividual variation. Just as students of ethnicity today find interethnic interaction to be the relevant context for its study, so researchers will continue to find that the interpersonal interaction of storytelling events provide a revealing context for the study of voice.

A Tewa Text: *Cį́'é: Pę́:yu'u* (Bird Story)

12. 'ó:wε:he:-yám-ba [11]
    né-thampe-wen T'íli' Khyúge di-tų́-mε:yu-'i ba

[motions with both hands to the southeast]
cį'é: 'ų:-'e:-kw'ón.

13. Kídí 'i-hange 'i-yɛ ba
hama khe wi:ti na-ná-di 'i-yɛ ba
wada cį'é: do:-'e:-kw'ón-dí.

14. Wɛhę-di ba
hɛ-ge khe na-waki-ná na-khyúge-ná-'i

15. 'i-hɛdi ba
cį'é: di-kele-po-di 'i-h ɛdi ba
'ó:bé-khwó:li-ma:k'a-'o-dɛ.

16. Wɛnge khé khyúge ba
waki da-páy-tí:, we-na-tų̃wɛ-pí-dí ba
pade 'ó:bé-khwó:li-ndɛ.

17. Kídá huwa ba
'i-pu:-ge 'i-n ha: huwa ba
'ó:bé-khwó:li-n-di-yá na-waki-ná-'i.

18. Kídí di-da-kelen 'i-hɛdi ba
'a:khon-ge-pe'e ba
'ó:bé-khwó:li-n-di 'im-bí yíyá-'in-di.

19. Kín ba
díbí-'o-dɛ-di 'ó:bé-tų̃-mɛ:yun-di ba
'im-bí yíyá-dí.

20. [Mother Bird]"Wati wé-'i-kele-pí-dí
neyɛ ma:di Bayena-senó na-mɛn-di.

21. 'i ma:di hɛ̨lɛ̨-wi'-na
hwí:kán'i, k'ologi'i 'i-tų̃wɛ̨-yi-di
'i-do' he:dan 'ú bin-'a:yi-mí
wɛhɛ-di na-'ɛ̨'ɛ̨-di-mo
'i-khyan-me-mí" giba
'ó:bé-tų̃-'an.

22. Hɛdí taye ba
    heyɛ wɛn ba
    cį'é: huwa di-kele-pó-dí[12]
    'im-bí yíyá-dí khyúge-pe'e 'ó:bé-hon.

23. 'i-wɛ ba
    di-powá-dí ba
    'ó:bé-khwó:li-ma:k'a-kan-t'ó-dí.

24. P'ą:nú-dí ba
    di-yi.

25. 'i-hɛdán ba
    wi' ba
    pa:de.

26. [Mother Bird] "Ho hagu pa:de,
    bi-khwole-mí" giba
    'ó:-tų́-'an.

27. Hɛdi ba
    'ų́:-khaw-k'ó né-'i 'im-bí yíyá.

28. Hɛdi 'i-bí-'í'í-dí-mo ba
    di-khaw-'o-dɛ.

29. Hɛdi kínán 'im-bí khaw ba
    na-mu:.

30. 'i-hɛdi ba
    'i-khwóli-t'o-'i ge-pe'e tayɛ na-win khyúge-pe'e.

31. Hę'im-bí yíyá ba
    mán-khaw-kɛnu.

32. [Mother Bird Sings] "Chi:zu, chi:zu,[13]
    "tengi tu:di ni'
    (REPEAT)
    "zi::::yu, zi::::yu,   zi::::yu, zi::::yu"

• 165 •

33. "Ho'o 'o-khwóle," giba
    'ó:-tú-'an.

34. 'i-hɛdán ba
    'ó:-má-p'ege.

35. Taye ba
    'i-khwó:le.

36. 'o:wɛ:-pú:ge-pe'e ba
    na-mɛn ba
    'i-soge.
    [Left hand moves from high left to low right, resting softly in outstretched right palm].

37. 'i-hɛdi ba
    hán wi'i-m-ba
    hán 'ó:bé-'o-dɛ.

38. 'i-ma ba
    di-wí-píde díbí-'ɛlɛ-hón-dí heyin-wen ba
    díbí-khwó:le.

39. Kídí k'u 'i-yá ba
    díbí-khwó:le-n he:yi'in do' 'i'i.

40. 'i-hɛdi di-wí-pí-dí ba
    hám-ba
    díbí-'o-di-ma 'i-wen ga ba
    Bayena-senó-wá 'im-bí-pimpenge-dá do-'ɛ'ɛ-ya.

41. [Old Man Coyote] "Di hán ho bi-'o
    na:-bí thete-'e:?"

42. [Mother Bird] "Né'é né-'in wati di-c'án-kele-pó-dí
    dó-bé-khwó:le-ma:k'a-'o-dán né-kín 'íbí-'o," giba
    'ó:-tú-'an.

43. [Old Man Coyote] "Hagu huwa na-mu:-mí hán ho 'óbí-'o,"
    giba
    na-tú-yi'.

44. 'i-hɛdám-ba
    huwa-ba
    wi' huwa 'i-winu-di ba
    di-khaw-kɛnu.

45. [Mother Bird sings] "Chi:zu, chi:zu
    "tengi tu::di ni'
    (REPEAT)
    "zi::::yu, zi::::yu,   zi::::yu zi::::yu"
    [Makes diagonal motion, imitating flight and landing again]

46. [Old Man Coyote]
    "Di háwákan 'óbí-'o? Némáhá.[14]
    Di:-khehedi-ná hama déh-khwó:le-mí-dí.

47. "Háya há:-wagi-ma déh-'am-mí," giba
    na-tʉ́-yi'.

48. [Mother Bird] "Ho ha:dan hama,
    hama win-khaw-'an
    nɛ́ 'ót'í-dí-mo
    khe wó-tegi-hon-di.

49. Há:dan hen 'ó:wɛ:-waki-we wé-'uh-kwinu-tí:-mí" giba
    'ó:-tʉ́-'an.

50. [Old Man Coyote] "Ho han deh-'am-mi. 'u-m-bí-waki-ma
    déh-na'a-khwi-mɛ:yu 'óbí-khwó:len k'agiwo.
    Gakhwen!" giba.

51. [Mother Bird] "Ho hewe 'o-wínu-di wí-n-khaw-'an.
    'i-hɛdi wati wí-ma-p'ege,
    'i-hɛdi winɛ-pe'e 'u-bí-kho mán-tɛlɛ-di-ma
    'ó:t'í-dí wó-tege-hón-di 'ó:wɛ́:.

52. Há:dán wé-'uh-kwinu-tí:-mí-dí," giba
    'ó:-tʉ́-'an.

53. 'i-hɛdám-ba

'i-ge-pe'e Bayena-senó ba
'i-wínu.

54. 'i-hɛdi ba
'ó:-n-khaw-kɛnu.

55. Kídí ba
cį'é: wemo ba
di-khaw-'o.

56. [Birds Sing] "Chi:zu, chi:zu
    "tengi tu::di ni'
    (REPEAT)
    "zi::::yu, zi::::yu,   zi::::yu zi::::yu"

57. [Mother Bird:] "Ho'o," giba
    'ó:-tų́-'an.

58. 'i-hɛdi ba
    'ó:-ma-p'ege.

59. Taye ba
    'i-kho-tɛ̨lɛ̨ wemo ba
    na-wi'isų:lu.

60. Na-wépí-ketą:be-mɛ-n p'ǫ́-tala-ge-di ba
    na-mɛn.

61. 'ó:wɛ́:-pú:-ge-we ba
    [Narrator imitates rapid descent, clapping left hand against
    outstretched right palm]
    na-won.

62. 'in-gam-ba
    na-k'ó.

63. Guba
    'i-hɛdi-mo 'i-hey.

64. Kínán ba

'i Bayena-senó ba
'ų:-pó.

65. 'i-hedám-ba
di-khwi:-mɛ:yu.

66. [Birds]
"Nɛhe-yán khuwona'a gi-pi gi-yi-mí 'u-bí-'i-wedi.

67. Wé-gi-k'ahagi-yin-dɛ-di ma:di-mo
gi-ci:yindi wɛhedi na:-m-bí thaye
na-khí:-puwa-mí," giba
di-tų́-yi'.

68. [Mother Bird]
"Ho'o ho hoke winge na-khu-mí Bayena-senó.
Yo ho gi-mɛ-mí," giba
'ó:bé-tų́-'an.

69. 'i-hedám-ba
'im-bí di-tha-'i ba
di-mɛ.

70. Kínám-ba
Bayena-senó 'ų:-pó-dán ba
'i-bí wowa:ci 'i-hạ:na.

71. Nɛ́he 'in-nán nɛm-bí pɛ́:yu'u na-mu:.

Bird Story[15]

12'. LONG AGO, so they say
south of here, at a place they call "Hawk Cliff" so
[motions with both hands to south]
a bird had her young.

13'. And there, nearby so[16]
in the same way, on that slope so
too, other birds had their young.

14'.   At one spot so
      there was a slope on that point.

15'.   And then so
      after the little birds became strong enough so
      they were being taught to fly.

16'.   At that spot on the point, so
      where the slope was clear and not too steep so
      the first were being taught to fly.

17'.   And THEN again so
      downward, again and again so
      they were flown on this slope.

18'.   And then, after they got quite strong so
      over to the plain so
      they were flown by their mother.

19'.   This so
      they were doing when spoken to so
      by their mother.

20'.   [Mother Bird] "Since you are not yet grown up,
      Old Man Coyote will be always coming around here.

21'.   He's always looking around for something,
      searching for food or a snack;
      because of THIS, you should be careful
      and, at the moment he arrives,
      you should flee," so this is what
      they were told.

22'.   Then, after a long time so
      sometime later so
      the birds had become stronger so
      they were taken to the cliff by their mother.

23'.   There so

having arrived so
they were going to be taught to fly.

24'.   Five of them so
there were.

25'.   And THEN so
one, so
was first.

26'.   [Mother Bird:] "Now let's have the first
to fly!" so that's what
he was told.

27'.   Then so
their mother had a song.

28'.   Then right to him so
they were singing.

29'.   Then their song so
it goes.

30'.   And then so
the one to fly stood right at the cliff.

31'.   Their mother so
she began singing.

32'.   [Mother Bird Sings] "Chi::zu, chi::zu
"tengi tu:di ni'
(REPEAT)
"zi::::yu, zi::::yu,   zi::::yu, zi::::yu"

33'.   "Now fly!" that's what he was told.

34'.   And THEN so
he was pushed.

35'.   Sure enough, so
he was flying.

36'. Away and downward so
     he went so
     he landed.
     [Left hand moves from high left to low right, resting softly in
     outstretched right palm]

37'. And then so
     that one by one so
     it was done to them.

38'. As for THEM, so
     they came back up walking, sometimes so
     they flew a bit.

39'. And to the rock THERE so
     they flew bit by bit.

40'. And then, having returned so
     in this same way so
     as they continued there so
     OLD MAN COYOTE HAD COME UPON THEM FROM
     THE WEST.

41'. [Old Man Coyote] "What are you doing,
     my grandchildren?"

42'. [Bird Mother]
     "Now that these CHILDREN are just strong enough,
     I'm teaching them to fly like this" so that's what he was told.

43'. [Old Man Coyote] "Maybe you could do it again," so
     that's what
     he was saying.

44'. And THEN so
     again so
     as one stood up again so
     they started to sing.

45'. [The Birds Sing:] "Chi:zu, chi:zu

"tengi tuːdi ni'
(REPEAT)
"ziːːːːyu, ziːːːːyu,   ziːːːːyu, ziːːːːyu"
[Makes diagonal motion, imitating flight and landing]

46'.   [Old Man Coyote]
        "Oh, so that's how you do it! Marvelous!
        I wonder if I could fly that way.

47'.   Maybe I could do it too," so that's what
        he was saying.

48'.   [Mother Bird] "Oh sure, in just the same way
        we will sing for you,
        and the air itself
        will carry you away.

49'.   Surely you'll wind up standing there on the slope,"
        that's what
        he was told.

50'.   [Old Man Coyote] "I'll do it. Just like you,
        I long to fly so beautifully.
        Let's do it," so said.

51'.   [Mother Bird] "After you stand there we sing for you,
        then you are pushed,
        and then you spread your arms apart and
        the air carries you away.

52'.   You can't help but land standing up," that's what
        he was told.

53'.   And THEN so
        there Old Man Coyote so
        he was standing.

54'.   And then so
        he was sung to.

55'.   And so
       the birds, so
       they sing.

56'.   [Birds Sing:]"Chi:zu, chi:zu
                        "tengi tu::di ni'
       (REPEAT)
       "zi::::yu, zi::::yu   zi::::yu, zi::::yu"

57'.   [Mother Bird] "Now!" so that's what
       he was told.

58'.   And then so
       he was pushed.

59'.   Sure enough so
       he spread his arms but so
       he dove.

60'.   He just fell head-first so
       he went.

61'.   Aways down so
       [Narrator imitates rapid descent, clapping left hand against
       outstretched right palm] he landed.

62'.   THERE so
       he lay.

63'.   Unbeknownst to him,
       he had just killed himself.

64'.   THIS so they say
       to Old Man Coyote so
       it happened.

65'.   And THEN so
       they stared down.

66'.   [Birds:]"HERE we lived in fear on account of you,

67'.   never able to live in peace but always

looking out for whenever you would show up
at our home," so that's what
they said.

68'. [Mother Bird] "Now just lie there Old Man Coyote!"
"Let's go now," so that's what
they were told.

69'. And THEN so
to where they lived so
they went.

70'. IN THIS WAY so
it happened to Old Man Coyote so
he wasted his life.

71'. HERE is the end of our story.

7

. . .

AN EVOLVING ETHNICITY AMONG THE ARIZONA
TEWA: TOWARD A REPERTOIRE OF IDENTITY

In previous chapters we have explored various ways in which Tewa language and speech reveal the histories and identities of their speakers. Here I want to explore the changing nature of Arizona Tewa ethnic identity, utilizing the close relationship between speech behavior and identity as an interpretive resource. This changing nature is revealed both by diachronic change in interethnic relations, which has changed ethnic identity for the group, and by intraindividual speech variation in the present which permits individuals to select relevant situational identities.

In ethnographic terms I hope to resolve some descriptive questions provided by the legacy of Edward Dozier (1951; 1954; 1966a)—the most comprehensive of all ethnographers of the Arizona Tewa. The limitation I am most concerned with here manifests itself in a dramatic turnabout in Dozier's characterization of Arizona Tewa ethnic identity. In 1951 Dozier published "Resistance to Assimilation and Acculturation in an Indian Pueblo," depicting the Arizona Tewa as exemplars of ethnic persistence. Just three years later, in his extensive monograph on the Arizona Tewa, Dozier (1954, 259–60) finds the groups to be merging and predicts the eventual assimilation of the Arizona Tewa. I marshal available data to assess these apparently conflicting claims.

While support for this position rests, in part, on the distinction between diachronic and synchronic contemporary trends and on new data that was not available to Dozier, it is also founded on a considerably different theoretical emphasis. To more fully disclose the nature of Arizona Tewa ethnic identity in the present, one must focus on intracultural variation (Pelto and Pelto 1975) and avoid the reification of the individual (Ellen 1979, 357). In other words, assumptions of homogeneity at either the level of the group or the individual must be avoided so as to focus attention on the patterned variability at these levels, which reveals the changing and situated meaning of Arizona Tewa ethnic identity. Even more important, one must adopt a perspective that emphasizes the communicated and negotiated aspects of ethnic and other social identities (Gumperz and Cook-Gumperz 1982, 7).

My objectives, then, are both ethnographic and theoretical. Pertinent to the former goals, I examine several of what Barth (1969, 31) would term *diacritica of ethnicity:* Arizona Tewa folk history, military emphasis, and language. But in so doing we discover certain deficiencies in the associated imagery of *ethnic boundary maintenance,* which, while adequate to describe early inter-ethnic relations, seem excessively brittle to account for the present. I contend that sociolinguistic data concerning code-switching, here the alternate use of available languages for various instrumental and expressive purposes, and the imagery of the linguistic repertoire provide a superior vehicle for understanding the contemporary multiethnic identity of the Arizona Tewa. Finally I situate the present sociolinguistic analogy within the history of the anthropological use of linguistic models.

Hén khí khaw (War Dance Songs)

War Dance Songs provide us with an appropriate introduction to the military emphasis of the Arizona Tewa. My selection of *hén khí khaw* as an informing source on this matter stems not from a preoccupation with the formal properties of the songs themselves but rather from the unique position occupied by their associated performances in the ceremonial system of the Arizona Tewa. For while Parsons (1926) and Dozier (1954, 345) have amply documented the demise of many ritual associations and the depletion of the Arizona Tewa ceremonial calendar, ceremonies involving *hén khí khaw* have exhibited a comparative persistence and social dances that employ them have actually increased. To more fully understand the articulation of these songs with their relevant cultural and

Table 7.1   The Folk Classification of War Dance Songs

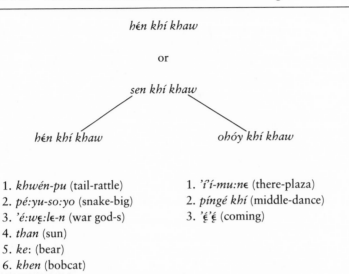

hén khí khaw

or

sen khí khaw

hén khí khaw   *ohóy khí khaw*

1. *khwén-pu* (tail-rattle)	1. *'i'í-mu:nɛ* (there-plaza)
2. *pé:yu-so:yo* (snake-big)	2. *píngé khí* (middle-dance)
3. *'é:wɛ:lɛ-n* (war god-s)	3. *'ɛ'ɛ* (coming)
4. *than* (sun)	
5. *ke:* (bear)	
6. *khen* (bobcat)	

social systems, we need to be aware of a fundamental dichotomy in their native classification. As table 7.1 illustrates, *hén khí khaw*, also known as *sen khí khaw* (brave's or man's dance song), constitutes a superordinate term for a genre of songs that pertain to war—its preparation, conduct, and aftermath; its emotions and actions.[1]

These songs are categorized according to their occasion of use—either esoteric or exoteric. Here *hén khí khaw* contrasts not as a hyponym with other song genres, but in a more restrictive sense—in opposition to *ohóy khí khaw* (exoteric war songs). The *hén khí khaw* (esoteric war songs) are sung in the kiva during the *than tháy*, or winter solstice ceremony. Grouped in six pairs of song types, they represent postmigration increments to a ceremony that predates the immigration of the Tano ancestors of the Arizona Tewa to First Mesa (Fewkes 1899, 274; Parsons 1926, 224–25). These songs constitute not only an obligatory part of the ceremony but also the backdrop for the initiation of boys into one of the two kivas in Tewa Village.

Hopis are not permitted to attend the *than tháy,* even in those years where no initiations are performed (Fewkes 1899, 273). In contrast, the *ohóy khí khaw* are sung in the plaza as part of a social dance in which

Hopis may both attend and participate.[2] Subclassified according to location of the dancers, these social dances are a comparatively modern addition to the repertoire of social dances that can be staged, not according to a fixed ceremonial calendar, but according to voluntary sponsorship by individuals. Thus, despite their symbolic affinity, *hén khí khaw* and *ohóy khí khaw* and their associated performances assume a dichotomous position in Tewa cultural knowledge and use. This divergence necessitates an examination of the disparate sociocultural contexts in which it is appropriate to use them.

But before going on to describe these relevant contexts, an ethnological observation is appropriate. In an article on the war cult in premodern southwestern pueblos, Florence Hawley Ellis (1951) noted that the theme of warfare was more highly developed by the Tanoans than by any other Pueblo group. The Arizona Tewa seem to provide considerable evidence to support this claim. As we shall see, warfare figures prominently in both their history and folk history. Despite the demise of men's and women's war associations, warfare provided a pervasive symbol for the Arizona Tewa that served to distinguish them from their Hopi neighbors. In response to the social disorganization of post-Pueblo Revolt migration, it was warfare and its role in Arizona Tewa folk history, transmitted in part by the sacred and esoteric war songs (Dozier 1954, 345), which permitted the Arizona Tewa to symbolically define themselves rather than be subject to the derisive definitions of the Hopi in the immediate postmigration period. In response to contemporary social change and the Hopi acceptance that it facilitated, the *ohóy khí khaw* represented a modern reaffirmation of the importance of the military emphasis as a symbolic summary of Arizona Tewa identity.

Esoteric War Songs, *Than tháy*, and Folk History

The relevant context of investigation for *hén khí khaw* is both the *than tháy*, of which they are an integral part, and more generally the folk history of the Arizona Tewa. The *than tháy* comprises the most dramatic instance of the transmission of this folk history. On the final night of the ceremony boys of approximately twelve to sixteen years of age are initiated into their kiva group, and along with this initiation comes the revelation of Arizona Tewa folk history in the form of narratives and narrative songs—many of which are the esoteric war songs. It is, of course, no accident that the Tewa should choose to convey their past via such war songs. As Vansina (1965, 108) has observed of oral traditions elsewhere, cultural values influence the selection not only of the events to be recorded but also of the very form of transmission. Since warfare plays such a crucial role in Arizona Tewa folk history, war songs provide a singularly appropriate framing for its display.

To facilitate a succinct description that can be compared and contrasted to the performance of the *ohóy khí khaw*, it is useful to view the *than tháy* as a type of communicative event amenable to analysis along the dimensions suggested by Hymes's S-P-E-A-K-I-N-G acronym (Hymes 1972; Duranti 1985). The acronym stands for the following elements: setting, participants, ends, act sequence, key, instrumentality, norm, and genre.

The setting (S) is both of the kivas located in Tewa Village—*mu:nɛ te'e* (Plaza Kiva) and *p'endi* or *té:wa te'e* (Outside or Tewa Kiva). Each clan in Tewa Village is associated with one of these two semisubterranean religious retreats. Clan membership thus determines which kiva a participant will attend to observe the ceremony.

The participants (P) must include the respective kiva chiefs (*te'e t'ú:yowan*), initiated Tewa men, and uninitiated boys (in those years when a sufficient number of boys have come of age to warrant initiation—every three to five years in actual practice). During those years when the ceremony includes initiation, initiated men will be further divided into those who are simply participants and those who will serve as ceremonial fathers (*puphónun tádá-'in*). According to precedent some women and girls who occupy special clan statuses or who are believed to need the medicinal value of the ceremony for health reasons will also attend (Parsons 1926, 14). Their participation is, however, limited more to that of an audience. Especially relevant here is the fact that no Hopis may attend.

The ends (E), or objectives, of the performance are several. First, the performance ensures the regularity of the cosmic order. According to western Pueblo belief, the winter and summer solstices represent especially precarious occasions when the sun (*than*) requires ritual assistance (Frigout 1979, 574; Ortiz 1972, 161). Toward this end, the manipulation of symbolic effigies by the kiva chief and the singing of war songs by the assembled men and boys are believed to impart energy. Second, the kiva initiations that occur officially admit new members to each kiva. Initiation supplies boys with the fundamental knowledge that is a prerequisite for them to occupy important ceremonial positions in the future.

The act sequence (A) varies slightly between kivas but points of convergence can be observed. The process begins with the sunwatcher who announces the coming of the winter solstice either eight or sixteen days in advance of the actual date (mid-December on our calendar) (Parsons 1925, 12–13).[3] The kiva chiefs and the hereditary village chief (*p'o-'ę́-t'ú:yon*) conduct a planning meeting. Four days later, the kiva chiefs enter their respective kivas to erect appropriate ceremonial altars (Fewkes 1899) and otherwise prepare the kiva. Later that day participants assemble in the kiva and begin a fast. The following morning the men and boys leave the kiva to bathe, have their hair washed in yucca suds, gather appropriate materials, and return to the kiva to make prayer sticks. These sticks with feathers strung to them represent the tangible embodiments of their prayers. In the afternoon, women will enter their kivas to feed the men assembled there. In the early evening men will leave the kivas to distribute their prayer sticks to various relatives—especially close clan relations.

Later that night they enter the kiva to sing the esoteric war songs. The twelve songs from the six genres (indicated in table 7.1) are sung and various folk-historical narratives are related. The assembled men and boys remain in the kiva on the following day, fasting and praying until their kiva chief leads them to appropriate local shrines to deposit his own prayer sticks. Though men and the now-initiated boys may leave the kiva, the kiva chiefs will remain in their kivas for four additional days before disassembling their altars. Having learned to make prayer sticks, to perform the songs, and to recount the history of the Arizona Tewa, uninitiated boys are transformed into ceremonially mature, initiated men.

The key (K), or emotional tone, is very serious as befits a sacred ceremony. Since the ceremony, like most Pueblo ritual, emphasizes correct overt performance and the necessity of proper thinking, it demands complete involvement on the part of participants. Initiates receive explicit instruction on making prayer sticks and are expected to attend to elaborate historical exegesis of the content of the songs. Because of the sacred and esoteric nature of these songs, no examples can be provided here. Though I have been permitted to hear isolated songs, I was forbidden to record them or promulgate any more specific details about them.

The instrumentality (I), or code choice, for this ceremony as for any performed in the kiva is *te'e hi:li* (kiva speech). In this register, as discussed in chapter 2, no foreign words are permitted. Some mundane terms are replaced by ritual-specific terminology. Kinship terms are used for address forms and key participants are called by their ceremonial names. Violation of these norms (N) are overtly censured and may result in physical punishment not unlike that received by Cushing, at Zuni Pueblo, whose use of a Spanish word in the kiva earned him a blow across the forearms with a heavy stick (Cushing 1979, 82).

Having provided this ethnographic introduction to the *than tháy*, let us consider the content framed by Arizona Tewa folk history. When compared to our own tradition of academic historiography, the borders of this frame appear quite restrictive, positioning many events beyond the boundaries of relevance. In the Tewa accounts, for example, no mention is made of the Spanish colonial program, the Pueblo revolts of 1680 and 1696, or their chaotic aftermath (Schroeder 1972) as possible factors in the exodus from the Rio Grande by the Tano ancestors of the Arizona Tewa. But as Sturtevant (1966) implies, the study of folk history should not be limited to a simplistic preoccupation with obvious epistemological differences that inhere in folk history and academic historiography as ways of apprehending the past. For while the latter tradition demands validity in the form of a nonpartisan evaluation of available evidence, the former tradition presupposes validity as a condition of membership and as a manifestation of allegiance to the group. Even though the scholarly tradition affords their ancestors a prominent role in the Pueblo Revolt seemingly compatible with the war-oriented self-image of the Arizona Tewa, this entire event finds no expression in Arizona Tewa folk history.[4]

Instead the Arizona Tewa accounts, transmitted via narratives and songs, unanimously interpret their migration as a response to repeated invitations—four in all—by the Walpi (First Mesa Hopi) Bear and Snake Clan chiefs to protect them from the onslaughts of Ute Indians. In exchange for such service, the Tewa were to receive land and food. Tewa accounts depict their ancestors not as refugees but as invited warrior protectors. In their folk accounts, transmitted in narratives and in *hén khí khaw*, victorious confrontations with the Ute, Apache, and Navajo are documented as celebrations of their military prowess and the potency of their war-magic (Dozier 1954, 345). Not all the songs, however, testify to the bravery of Tewa warriors. Some graphically portray the cruel ingratitude of the Hopi who, in the Tewa view, denied the terms of their pact. Accepting the pacification of their lands by the Tewa newcomers, the Hopi rejected their responsibility to provide the land and food earned in battle.

According to the Hopi, in this immediately postmigration period, the Tewa were uninvited guests. Having fought a protracted guerrilla war against the Spanish from their Northern Rio Grande camps, the Tano ancestors of the Arizona Tewa, who refused to resettle their native villages under Spanish authority, must have presented an intimidating, warlike countenance to the Hopi. Relatively unaffected by the Spanish or the disruption of the Pueblo revolts, the Hopi continued without interruption their preoccupations with agriculture and its associated ceremonial cycle. It is not surprising, given the contrasting cultures and histories of these groups, that the Hopi proscribed interethnic interaction with the Southern Tewa intruders.

But these Arizona Tewa maintained the integrity of their own accounts, interpreting the Hopi response as cruel ingratitude and unjust abuse. Having so depicted the Hopi, the Arizona Tewa interpreted their enforced isolation not as a Hopi refusal to associate with members of a stigmatized minority (Mindeleff 1891), but rather as their own cultural revenge against the Hopi—the linguistic curse (see chapter 1). Denying the Hopi the benefits of their own and in their eyes superior culture, the Arizona Tewa occupied land adjacent to their reluctant neighbors.

Arizona Tewa folk history exhibits a *presentism* (Stocking 1968, 3), an interpretation of the past not for its own sake but rather for some contemporary purpose. Instead of abandoning or symbolically disowning aspects of the military emphasis that was so devalued by their Hopi neighbors, the Arizona Tewa chose to make it a key symbolic manifestation of their ethnic identity. The presentism exhibited by the partisan selectivity of Arizona Tewa folk history thus partially derives from a kind of propagandistic self-defense designed not only to vanquish Hopi definitions of the situation but also to bolster Arizona Tewa self-esteem. They reject an unflattering image of themselves as involuntary actors, preferring to view their immigration and subsequent isolation from the Hopi as consequences of deliberate actions initiated by the Tewa themselves.

In the conflation of the past represented by the esoteric war songs, the vilification of the Hopi persists as testament of former intergroup hostility. The depiction of the Hopi as the tormentors of their Southern Tewa ancestors has at least one especially significant consequence. The knowledge of past persecutions, especially when dramatized in ritual, provides an ongoing symbolic source of alienation from their Hopi hosts and lends significance to a discrete history available only to the Arizona Tewa. Such a source of alienation, when coupled with the proscription of intermarriage by both groups that typified the first two hundred years of their inter-ethnic relations inhibited interaction, creating an environment in which it was easy to maintain the ethnic boundary.

Exoteric War Songs and Social Change

But increasing contact with Euro-Americans in the late nineteenth and early twentieth centuries began to effect massive social change, changes that greatly facilitated the acceptance of the Tewa. As mediators between the Euro-Americans and the Hopi, the Tewa benefited from a willingness to experiment with a cash economy, tribal government, and formal education. In so doing, they provided the Hopi with important models for adapting to the social changes that were the product of ever-diminishing isolation from Euro-American society. These social changes and the related changes in interethnic relations represent the relevant backdrop for the *ohóy khí khaw*.

Previous ethnographic treatment of these exoteric war dance songs is limited to a single footnote (Dozier 1954, 351). Despite its lack of attention, these dances provide important information about the contemporary Arizona Tewa. Unlike sacred ceremonies, no clan owns these ceremonies and no individual is responsible for acquiring (and later transmitting to a successor) the relevant ritual knowledge. Unlike sacred ceremonies, these secular dances and their associated songs are not fixed. New songs are sung every year and the participants differ from performance to performance. Because they are more flexible in regard to change, social dances may provide information about sociocultural change that is less available in the relatively fixed performances of sacred ceremonies. For contrastive purposes it is useful to briefly outline the communicative context of the *ohóy khí khaw* following the S-P-E-A-K-I-N-G model.

The setting (S) for the exoteric war dance songs is the central plaza (*mu:nɛ*) of Tewa Village. The outdoor, public character of the performance contrasts markedly with confined performance of the *hén khí khaw* as part of the *than tháy*. These social dances are not scheduled according to the astronomical observations of the sunwatcher. Like other social dances, *ohóy khí khaw* are staged at any time except during the kachina season. Within this limitation, a sponsor may schedule the dance at any time. Invariably, however, they occur on the weekend—a concession to the forty-hour workweek of most Arizona Tewa wage-earners and a convenience for friends and relatives who must travel to attend.

Unlike the *than tháy,* the key participants (P) typically do not include members of the ceremonial elite. No particular hereditary or achieved status is necessary to sponsor an *ohóy khí khaw,* any villager with sufficient funds to feed all the participants and otherwise reward their participation may sponsor the dance. He or she must obtain permission of a particular kiva chief to use that kiva for rehearsals. Having obtained this permission, word is spread to invite all villagers to participate either as singers or dancers. Young men and women will choose dance partners of the opposite sex. Older men will serve as singers with one or two particularly strong and experienced men selected as drummers. Rehearsals for all these voluntary participants will last up to two weeks. A large audience will typically occupy the perimeter of the plaza. In contrast to the *than tháy,* the essential audience (Becker 1979, 230) is made up of the assembled onlookers and not the supernatural. These dances are open to Hopis, who may participate or attend as audience members. Hopi participation as audience is regular, as dancer occasional, and as singer never. This is, in part, because these songs are in Tewa—a language which no Hopi knows fluently.

The ends (E), or objectives, are utterly unlike the more cosmic considerations of the *than tháy.* Personal success and good fortune are often celebrated by sponsoring a dance. Thus, rather than group-oriented objectives, the motivation for social dances is clearly more personal. Sponsorship does earn an individual and his or her family considerable local prestige and good will and may effectively be used as a deterrent against potential accusations of being overly selfish. The act sequence (A) of the performance consists of an emergence of singers from out of the practice kiva on the first day of the dance. The first song they sing accompanies one or more young couples from the kiva to the plaza. Next they sing a plaza song, which dancers perform to in the central plaza. Finally they dance back to the kiva. This pattern is repeated again and again until all couples have danced the entire three song cycle. Then, depending upon the number of couples, each group may dance again. There is considerable flexibility here. Recently, for example, so many dancers participated in the *ohóy khí* that they had to perform in groups of three in order to permit each an opportunity to dance. Flexibility also exists in the length of the social dance. Audience response may be so positive that the sponsor is coaxed into extending the social dance for an additional day. At the end of each day performers are feasted at the expense of the sponsor.

The key (K), or emotional tenor, of the *ohóy khí* contrasts markedly with the serious, even solemn, nature of the *than thay*. The mood surrounding the *ohóy khí* is festive. While performing, the dancers do concentrate on dancing in time with the music, complementing their partner's movement, and gesturing appropriately. Singers will point to the directions of places named and will imitate actions depicted in the songs. Though they aim at a flawless performance, these performance ideals are not grounded in any demand for ritual perfection. They perform well not to ensure ritual efficacy but to produce a beautiful (*sagi'wo'i* [men's speech], *'asagi* [women's speech]; Kroskrity 1983a, 76) display that will win the audience's admiration (-*ye:mun*). Audience members will alternate from watching intently to commenting on details of costuming, song lyrics, or dance movements. They may leave the plaza periodically to return later to one of the chairs and benches that they have set up for the occasion. During breaks in the dancing, they will converse freely with neighbors and visiting friends and relatives or return to their homes for some shelter from the sun.

The instrumentality (I), or code-choice, for the songs is invariably the Arizona Tewa language. Though the songs sometime employ a poetic license which, along with their musical and dance accompaniment, does make them distinguishable from everyday speech, they are not considered *te'e hi:li* (kiva speech)—the sacred language. However, they do share one attribute with this sacred register: they are exclusively encoded in Tewa. Even though everyday Tewa speech will include various loanwords and code-switches into languages such as Hopi and English, these are usually avoided by the composers in creating the songs.

One norm (N) of interpretation that deserves mention here is the meaning that many Arizona Tewa attach to Hopi attendance at this social dance. They view it not only as a form of admiration and acceptance but also as a kind of validation of the folk-historical view of the Arizona Tewa as the warrior-protectors of the First Mesa Hopi villages.

The relevant genres (G) of the *ohóy khí khaw* are functionally determined in accord with the position of the dancers in the kiva-to-plaza-to-kiva movement of the performers. Songs are divided into (1) *'í'í-mu:nɛ khaw* (there-plaza song) "going to plaza song," (2) *pínge-khí khaw* (middle-dance song), and (3) *'ę́'ę́ khaw* (come song) "coming back song." The middle song is usually distinguishable from the other songs because of its fast tempo. Though these genres constrain musical choice, they do not imply content differences in the lyrics.

It is instructive to examine a representative *ohóy khí khaw* cycle. Since my focus here is on ethnicity I analyze only the relevant lyrical content, ignoring the ethnomusicological or ethnopoetic organization.

1. *Gasínsewe:má Walabi te-'owí:n-ge!*
    Di:gú to:-bí-hi:li-'án-dí ókhú:wa.
    Pó:bí na-sa: tṵ:yǫ́-wan-bí hi:li-'án.

    Pó:yó pó:bí, kwɛ̨-'oyú-pó:bí, seke-pó:bí
    Táyo-pó:bí p'i:liyaw, tṵ:lṵgi
    Kínán ho na-yoge-ná-mí.

    Here it is! Walpi Village.
    I wonder whose authority the clouds are under.
    Flowers bloom to the words of the chiefs.

    Squash flowers, purple flowers, cotton flowers,
    Grass flowers of lavender and spotted hues—
    This is the way our summer should be!

2. *Nán-kɛnu p'ósi:líkway!*
    Di:gú hɛ̨lɛ̨ 'ṵ-k'o:lo-na'a.
    Wonsa:be tṵ:yon-bí t'owa-'an
    Di-khwɛ̨di-kw'ón.

    Yo ho gén-k'e:wen!
    Thay-u:be nṵ́:ge-we.
    Wonsa:be tṵ:yon-bí t'owa-'án
    Di-khwɛ̨di-kw'ón.

Dirt-throwing coyotes!
I wonder what you want to chew.
It's the Navajo Chief's people
Lying smashed and beaten.

So go get them!
There beneath the Hopi Buttes
It's the Navajo Chief's people
Lying smashed and beaten.

3. *Gasínsewe:má Walabi te-'owí:n-ge!*
   'Okhwa-k'edi na:bí k'εmε-'in ho da-wín-di.
   T'é-pí-dán, t'é-pí-dán

   Wi-k'in-dama,
   tayweh na'a-di
   K'u:wah, malan dó-pa:-di
   Wi-k'in-dama,
   ho da-hi:kyan-pówá-mí, tayweh na'a-di.

   Here it is! Walpi Village.
   On the rooftop, my loved ones stand.
   Don't be angry! Don't be angry!

   I show you my love for you,
   surely I do.
   Wearing the black robe, the belt I made,
   I show you my love.
   Now you should be happy,
   surely you should.

These song texts permit a number of significant observations. Both the
going and coming back songs (1 and 3 above) mention Walpi Village—
the oldest Hopi Village on First Mesa. In the first song, the acknowledgment of Hopi religious authorities is the prevailing theme. Their cere-

monial guidance is viewed as causally related to a successful summer growing season and the unmentioned rainfall on which it depends.

The middle song (2) contrasts with the previous one by celebrating not the ceremonial knowledge of Hopi religious leaders but rather the potency of Arizona Tewa war-magic and military might. After a successful battle against the Navajo, the coyotes are invited to dispose of the slain Navajo enemies. The choice of the Navajo is especially appropriate here since they represent, in the eyes of many Arizona Tewa and Hopi, contemporary foes who threaten the security of Hopi lands. Though for the most part litigation has replaced armed conflict as a means of confrontation, most Arizona Tewa interpret their leadership in legal battles with the Navajo as a contemporary manifestation of their ethnohistorical role as protectors of the Hopi.

The final song once again names Walpi, depicting its villagers on their rooftops, seeing warriors off to battle. As men prepare to march off for war, they request that their loved ones understand the necessity of their mission and not harbor any ill-feelings about the hardships such a disruptive departure might impose. Here the act of warfare is viewed as a service to one's loved ones.

Both the song texts and their performance context embody significant sociocultural changes as well as changes in the pattern of interethnic relations. The social organization of the participants, the details of their sponsorship and scheduling, and their popularity amid considerable ceremonial depletion reflect an increasing secularization and absorption into the cash economy of Euro-American society. At the level of song text, we find two very significant observations in regard to the nature of ethnicity and interethnic relations between the Hopi and the Arizona Tewa. One is the persistence of war imagery as a cultural symbol of Tewa ethnic identity. Though warfare continues to be an important theme, there is a marked discontinuity in the nature of interethnic relations depicted. In sharp contrast to the vilification of the Hopi in the *than tháy* ceremony, an identification (Burke 1950, 20, 55) with the Hopi is apparent in these *ohóy khí khaw*. By adopting a Hopi orientation, acknowledging their leaders, and emphasizing a common contemporary enemy, these songs clearly suggest that antipathy for the Hopi has been replaced by empathy with them.

If the songs provided the only evidence of such changed interethnic relations, we could perhaps dismiss them as the products of poetic license or as a type of rhetorical hyperbole. But this is not the case. Today most Arizona Tewa are either married to a Hopi or have a Hopi father and other Hopi relatives. Under such conditions, the either/or ethnicity of the migration period has proven obsolete and even the imagery of boundary maintenance (Barth 1969) becomes too brittle to adequately encompass the changed nature of Arizona Tewa identity.

Ethnic Boundaries Unbound

One of the significant accomplishments of Fredrik Barth (1969) was his explanation of ethnic persistence, not simply as the outcome of geographical and social isolation, but as a process within conditions of intensive and perpetual contact as well. Barth's model (1969, 15–16) predicts a "congruence of codes and values" between the interacting cultural groups that diminishes the total inventory of cultural differences between the two groups. In the case of the Arizona Tewa the adoption of clans, matrilineal descent, and matrilocal residence represent aspects of kinship that were not indigenous to their ancestors in their Southern Tewa homeland. In addition to such congruence, the model also predicts that some of the persisting differences between interacting ethnic groups will be symbolically elevated to diacritica of ethnicity. This symbolic process provides an explanation for why a decrease in overt cultural differences need not be equated with any diminished sense of ethnic identity. In Dozier's (1951) early work, as in my own (Kroskrity 1976), the focus on these diacritica prompted an exaggerated claim about the nature of ethnic persistence. Like Barth's notion of boundary maintenance, we reified ethnic identity, failing to take full account of the variability exhibited by supposedly immutable diacritica—military emphasis, history, and language.

In the preceding sections we have noted the persistence and importance of military imagery as manifested in *hén khí khaw*. Despite this cultural continuity, the exoteric songs clearly presuppose very different kinds of interethnic relations. In one situation Hopis are forbidden to attend, in the other they are welcomed. In one they are depicted as evil antagonists, in the other as respected protagonists, in one as a people contrasted to the Tewa, in the other as a consubstantial people (Burke 1950, 21). These alternations suggest something of the situated nature of Tewa ethnic identity.

Military emphasis is not alone in showing significant variation and change. Karen Blu (1980, 215) has observed the dynamic role of history in ethnically plural societies: "History, as perceived by both insider and outsider, is at the core of ethnic identification, which makes more understandable the urgent demands from ethnic groups to rewrite and expand history." Among both Hopi and Arizona Tewa, history has been significantly rewritten in light of changed interethnic relations. As previously mentioned, both groups traditionally maintained the integrity of their respective folk histories, dismissing the other group's account as fabrication. But as boundaries have diminished between the groups, it has become more difficult to simply dismiss alternative accounts as utterly unfounded. No longer can the proponents of these alternative views be regarded as an evil or immoral *other* and simply dismissed accordingly. The pacification of interethnic hostility has led to a compromise position on the facts of migration. Recently, the Walpi crier chief (Pahona 1977, 1–6) publicly endorsed the Arizona Tewa view that they were invited by leaders of the Walpi Snake and Bear Clan chiefs to protect the Hopi there. Both the Arizona Tewa and the Hopi now recognize a third group, the Tano, as the uninvited refugees of the Hopi accounts. Since no Arizona Tewa identify with this group today, both Hopi and Arizona Tewa accounts have been effectively reconciled.[5] This modification in the form of a diacritic of ethnicity seems unpredicted by Barth's model.

But while warfare and history begin to show the unmanageability of boundary maintenance as a means of describing contemporary Arizona Tewa ethnic identity, it is sociolinguistic data that both provides the best example of its untenable reification and suggests a general model of identification that escapes the unwarranted confinement of the boundary maintenance imagery. This is perhaps ironic since conventional treatments of language and ethnicity (e.g., Fishman 1977) have continued a rather long tradition of viewing language as the omnipresent symbol of ethnic identity.

But such studies have failed to adequately take into account relevant stylistic, or intraindividual, variation. A closer inspection of the facts of Arizona Tewa language use also erodes the supposed imperviousness of the ethnic boundary imagery. Fishman (1977, 25) has appropriately observed that "the link between language and ethnicity is one of sanctity-by-association." But though it is true to say that Arizona Tewa endures as a diacritic of Arizona Tewa ethnicity, it is perhaps equally uninteresting.

Such a statement, by itself, does little more than reincarnate the static correlations of race, language, and culture that immobilized traditional anthropological approaches to the problem of ethnicity. Yes, Arizona Tewa is the language in which folk history is conveyed, the language in which the *than tháy* is performed, and the usual language of intravillage communication. But while Arizona Tewa can be singled out as a kind of metonym of Tewa ethnic identity, it is equally instructive to acknowledge that it is only one of three languages typically found in the linguistic repertoires of members of the Arizona Tewa speech community. Given the multilingualism of the Arizona Tewa, a more appropriate task than mere isolation of the *language of ethnicity* would be the study of patterned alternations in the use of all the languages in their linguistic repertoire so as to reveal when and why members of the speech community find them to be appropriate vehicles for communicative expression.

Code-switching in the Arizona Tewa Speech Community

In chapter 2, I briefly introduced the languages that compose the linguistic repertoire of the Arizona Tewa speech community, detailing some of the basic norms that guide a speaker's selection from among the Arizona Tewa, First Mesa Hopi, and English languages. These norms mostly specify prototypical situational constraints on code-selection and switching. In other words, I focused primarily on the settings (Hymes 1972), or domains (Fishman 1972), and the categories of participants (e.g., other Tewa, Hopi, tourists, government officials) that typically prompt the selection of a specific code. But while the stable association of these languages with such contextual variables clearly influences speakers' attitudes toward these languages, an ethnolinguistic quest for the symbolic meanings attached to these codes by their speakers must consider code-switching data of a rather different kind.

Scholars concerned with code-switching have distinguished between *situational code-switching,* of the type described above, and *metaphorical code-switching* (Blom and Gumperz, 1972; Hill and Hill 1980; Gumperz 1982, 60). While situational code-switching is mostly guided by functional considerations of setting and participants, metaphorical code-switching is guided by more expressive concerns, which provide an important source of insights about the connotative meanings of these codes to their speakers. Since these connotations emerge, in part, from their associations with the ethnic groups with which they are prototypically identified, metaphorical code-switching data can provide significant insights into the nature of Arizona Tewa ethnic identification. This metaphorical code-switching is best studied in conversations among Arizona Tewa themselves, where code-switching is not motivated by considerations of the physical setting or the limitations of an interlocutor's linguistic knowledge. In the examples below trilingual Tewa talk among themselves in informal and semi-formal situations. The code-switches so produced are better understood as expressive rather than as instances of obedience to proscriptive norms regarding physical setting (such as speaking only Tewa in the kiva) or constraints on intelligibility (such as the avoidance of Tewa when speaking to Hopis).

The examples below adhere to Gumperz's (1982, 59) definition of *conversational code-switching:* "the juxtaposition within the same speech exchange of passages of speech belonging to two [or more] different grammatical systems or subsystems." For slightly more than a decade I have observed numerous conversations among Arizona Tewa people in which I could detect abrupt shifts from one language to another. The very different phonologies and grammars of these languages greatly enhanced the salience of the code-switches for me. But I learned from early investigations that though these code-switches were obvious to me, conversational participants were often unaware of this code-switching behavior (Gumperz 1982, 62). This made investigation via self-report quite superfluous. Only when recorded evidence was produced were some speakers willing to recognize this code-switching behavior and able to offer some interpretive guidance in understanding its patterning.

The examples that follow were observed by me in various roles. For conversations in which I was present with the Tewa conversationalists, I was variously defined as audience, auditor, or nonparticipant. For pre-recorded examples I was a nonparticipant limited to retrospective analysis of the data with the assistance of key consultants.[6] In all cases my objective was to ascertain the communicative motives that underlay the code-switches. Such motives may, in theory, be either due to denotative or connotative aspects of the languages being switched. In other words, an individual might switch codes to obtain the most appropriate language in which a given concept or proposition can be encoded. Alternatively, a person might switch codes strictly because of connotative differences implied by code choice. But though there are formal constraints on code-switching of a more purely linguistic type, these constraints are of little relevance here. In all the cases cited below, consultants—often the participants themselves—were able to retrospectively translate their utterances in each of the two languages that were not originally selected. They did so succinctly, accurately, and without hesitation. This evidence from ancillary elicitation suggests that we should examine speakers' connotative, or expressive, purposes in an attempt to understand the data. Since these preferences were not motivated by grammatical or lexical considerations, and since they did not disrupt conversational involvement (Gumperz 1982, 3), they must represent choices that reflect the speakers' background knowledge regarding sociocultural appropriateness (Blom and Gumperz 1972, 417–18).

My objective here is not to offer an exhaustive description of the 279 code-switches,[7] but rather to view metaphorical code-switching as an independent source of insights regarding Arizona Tewa identity, which can be triangulated with previous data so as to refine the interpretation of contemporary Arizona Tewa ethnic identity. Slightly more than two-thirds of the switches (n = 193) are between Tewa and Hopi. Typically, code-switching occurs (1) in the mention of Hopi relatives, (2) in discussions of the Hopi Reservation, Hopi Tribe, or neighboring Hopi Villages, and (3) in evaluative statements where Hopi values are either endorsed or parodied. In the following conversational excerpt, a single speaker switches from Arizona Tewa to Hopi and back to Tewa.

1. Speaker A: *Hę-'i sen dó-tay.* (AT)
    I know that man.
    'i kʷa'a . . . pam pit-'aŋk 'a:pi. (Hopi)
    My grandfather (FAFA) . . . he's related to him.
    Attawo'i sen na-mu:. (AT)
    He's a rascal.

In this example the switch is locally motivated by the topic—the speaker's Hopi grandfather. It is common for Arizona Tewa people to discuss their Hopi relatives, especially those with whom they have a positive affective relationship, in the Hopi language even if this means switching from a different language. Consultants could provide a Tewa alternative but they evaluated it as improper unless they were angry at their paternal grandfather. The return to Tewa signals a change in topic—a return to the unnamed Hopi man mentioned in the first sentence. Though, like the grandfather, this man is also Hopi and he is mentioned only in Tewa since he is not related to the speaker nor endowed by him with any positive affect.

Another pattern which is quite productive is switching to Hopi to discuss Hopi tribal concerns. In example 2 three middle-aged men are conversing about the Hopi-Navajo border dispute. Talk on this subject has occurred with all the men using Hopi. There is some disagreement on the impact of a preliminary courtroom victory and its implications for the disputed territory and Hopi-Navajo relations.

> 2. Speaker B: *Loma-la:vayi!* (Hopi)
>   (It's) good news!
>
>   Speaker A: *Di khé hęyę nǵ'i na-mo:wa-tí:-mí.* (AT)
>   I wonder if this will ever be finished.
>
>   Speaker C: *Pɨma lavayaymɨ'ɨ yiŋwa. Pɨma wihaq*
>   *'ita-tick ay maq'yu'uyani.* (Hopi)
>   They have lawyers. They will get more of our land.

In this sequence, speaker B begins by offering an optimistic evaluation of a legal decision which is favorable to the Hopi Tribe. Speaker A offers a contrast in both mood and language. Laced with considerable pessimism, A's remarks remind B that the recent court settlement hardly represents a successful conclusion of the Hopi-Navajo conflict. Key consultants suggest that the shift to Arizona Tewa here is primarily an evaluative one. Like its speaker's self-image, the Arizona Tewa language is often endowed by them with connotations of a realistic worldview that are not symbolically available with Hopi. Speaker C returns the conversation to Hopi— the language typically selected when aligning themselves with the Hopi in opposition to some third party. It should be emphasized that this alignment is not merely rhetorical. As discussed in chapter 1, the Arizona Tewa share with Hopis the same economic and political interests. They are, in fact, members of the Hopi Tribe, possessing all the rights and obligations which this membership implies.

This other identity is consistently invoked by use of Hopi in discussions of tribal affairs. Only when a role conflict emerges does the conversation switch to Tewa. Examples 3–5 provide three instances of these code-switched signals of a changed we-group. In each of these cases, conversations in Hopi about tribal matters are suddenly switched to Arizona Tewa in order to represent an alternative point of view—one identified with the progressive and practical outlook of the Arizona Tewa. In example 3 below, speaker B expresses optimism over the possibility of a peaceful settlement of the Hopi-Navajo border dispute:

3. [Setting: Same as 2]

   Speaker B: *Tenatyava. Tenatyava. Pay-sen 'ita-m nanami pihi:k'yani.* (Hopi)

   It's come true. It's come true. Maybe now we will live peaceably among each other.

   Speaker C: *'u to'o wi' he:yu-bí-'í'í-dí han ankhyaw 'u-mu:.* (AT) You are one among the few who think so.

His use of Hopi follows a pattern of using the language for topics that pertain to extravillage reservation life, for topics in which no distinction between the Arizona Tewa and the Hopi is necessary because shared interests make the groups consubstantial (Burke 1950, 21). Speaker C's use of Arizona Tewa in 3 is symbolically appropriate for two reasons. At the time of the conversation, most Tewa rather steadfastly demanded an aggressive and definitive settlement of the Hopi-Navajo border dispute with few concessions for the Navajo. The tribal council chairman, a Hopi, was more moderate and still willing to negotiate with the Navajo. This was perceived by many, perhaps most, as a form of weakness that rather than solving the problem sooner would only extend the conflict longer. The switch to Arizona Tewa in 3 thus relies on the association of this contrastive position with the Arizona Tewa and their language. Another connotation of the use of Arizona Tewa in this context is the invocation of the practical and worldly perspective of the Arizona Tewa in contradistinction to the spiritual but naive qualities sometimes attributed to the Hopi

In 4 speaker D reports the continuation of a Hopi Tribal Council meeting, which he has recently left. Shortly after entering E's door, D mentions speech-making in the administrative capital city of the Hopi Reservation—an indirect and somewhat elliptical statement that is understood to mean that the Hopi Tribal Council is or has just been in session.

4. [Setting: D and E talk about recent Tribal Council Meeting. As D entered E's house greetings were exchanged in Arizona Tewa.]

Speaker D: *Kyakotsmovi yɨ'a'tota.* (Hopi)
They are making speeches at New Oriabi.

Speaker E: *Di há:dá na:m-bí nɛkhon-'in wé-dí-n-t'ó:gi-di?* (AT)
How come our representatives were not included?

Speaker D: *'uh-hangim-po.* (AT)
You know.

The switch to Arizona Tewa is primarily motivated by a particular bit of background information. In the summer of 1984, the Hopi *kikmongwi* of Walpi refused to certify duly elected Tribal Council representatives from the First Mesa villages of Walpi, Sichomovi, and Tewa. When these representatives appeared at the next Tribal Council Meeting, they were denied permission to participate by the chairman and other councilmen. The switch to Tewa emphasizes the Tewa "we" in contrast to both the Hopi of First Mesa, personified by the *kikmongwi,* and the Hopi Tribal Council for failure to recognize their representatives.[8] Though representatives from the other villages are involved, the use of Tewa is quite appropriate since the political insult to Tewa Village and its tradition of leadership in Hopi Tribal Government is emphasized. D responds in Tewa, confirming the fact that the anticipated refusal to seat the representatives did occur. The two continue discussion of possible strategies for solving the problem in Tewa.

In example 5, three Tewa men have been discussing recent news of the selection of a site for the proposed Hopi high school. Their discussion has been in Hopi while they have reviewed the complicated and controversial history of why it has taken so long to approve and build a local high school.

5. [Setting: F's home. Speakers are seated around kitchen table. It is mid-morning. A conversation has been going on between F, G, and H about recent news concerning the selection of a site for an on-reservation high school.]

Speaker F: *Tɨtɨqaki-t qa-na:nawakna.* (Hopi)
Schools were not wanted.

Speaker G: *Wé-dí-t'ókán-k'ege-na'a-di 'im-bí akhon-'i-di.* (AT)
They didn't want a school on their land.

Speaker H: *Nɛm-bí 'e:yɛ nɛlɛ-mo díbí-t'ó-'ám-mí kạ:yị' wé-*

di-mu:-di. (AT)

It's better that our children go to school right here rather than far away.

Speaker H recounts the opposition to the school, continuing to use Hopi. His remark is understood by native consultants as nonjudgmental. In contrast, speakers G and H use Tewa to emphasize sentiments that invoke an opposition between the Hopi, who historically have obstructed the building of on-reservation high schools, and the Arizona Tewa. Speaker G distances himself from the Hopi "they" who opposed use of "their" lands as school sites. Speaker H states what has historically been the Arizona Tewa argument for a reservation high school. Since, in retrospect, most members of both groups now recognize the disruptive impact of their children attending boarding schools for the past few decades, H's remark also conveys a note of vindication for the essential correctness of the Arizona Tewa position. In both G's and H's remarks, the code-switch to Tewa clearly invokes their identification with the Arizona Tewa in opposition to the Hopi. While code-switches to Tewa in conversations that are otherwise performed in Hopi often reveal an implicit evaluation from the Arizona Tewa perspective, some code-switches between Hopi and Tewa are explicitly evaluative. Examples 6 and 7 provide brief illustrations of some recurring patterns:

6. [Setting: Speaker C sits among several onlookers at a mixed kachina dance in Tewa Village.]

    Speaker C: *Hi:wo'i díbí-hí-'ó!* (AT)

    They are dancing good!

    Loloma, loloma, lomahin-yinʷa. (Hopi)

    Beautiful, beautiful, they look good!

7. [Setting: Speaker F discusses his health with a visiting kinsman. Discussion on this topic has so far been conducted in Tewa.]

    Speaker F: *Na:m-bí tu'u 'óyyó na-mu:, 'i-wɛ-di gíh-hikyan-po.* (AT)

    My health is good and so I'm happy.

    Nɨ halayti. (Hopi)

    I'm thankful.

In both 6 and 7, the speakers' code-switch to Hopi is primarily reiterative, adding a nuance of evaluation. Arizona Tewa speakers attribute to the Hopi a penchant for ceremonial emphasis and ritual perfection. Native consultants found 6 to be a highly complimentary appreciation of the Tewa Village ritual performance, invoking Hopi standards of excellence through use of the Hopi language. Example 7 illustrates a related pattern in code-switching where switches to Hopi invoke a type of prayerful humility associated with its speakers. Such examples suggest that the Tewa, on at least some occasions, endorse aspects of a reciprocal stereotyping in which the Hopi are viewed as somewhat superior in the spiritual realm whereas the Tewa are seen as masters of the practical world. This interpretation is bolstered by the discussion of the *ohóy khí khaw* above and a recent trend among some younger men to compose new songs in Hopi for certain social dances.[9] But while this folk view concerning the complementary fortes of the two groups approximates the collective anthropological understanding of their symbiotic relationship, it does not satisfactorily account for the code-switching variability exhibited here. As observed above, there are occasions when the Arizona Tewa are consubstantial with the Hopi—when there is no meaningful distinction between them. Yet at other times, the opposition between Tewa and Hopi identities becomes very relevant. Code-switching provides a means of formulating the relevant social identity to be invoked. But though the languages are symbolic of these identities they are, in accord with their complex associations with these groups, quite multivocal.

Some of this multivocality is illustrated by examples 8 and 9:

8. [Setting: Two men are working on repairing a neighbor's roof. Speaker points to something he wants E to hand him.]

  Speaker D: *Na-mɛːgi* (AT)

  Give it to me!

  Speaker E: *Dó-'o.* (AT)

  I'm doing it.

  Tota'ci. (Hopi)

  (You're a) bossy person.

9. [Setting: Speaker A parodies a Hopi traditionalist as part of a lengthy denunciation of him and his followers.]

  Speaker A: *Hanomɨ nɨːnɨkpantɨ. Ni 'okiw. Hopivewa*

> *'ɨːna- toti.* (Hopi)
> The Tewa are uncivilized. I'm humble. They've
> lost the Hopi way. [In English] And so I have
> spoken, my bahana friend, now give me my
> money so I can go home and watch TV.

In both these examples there is a creative imitation of Hopis signalled by a code-switch to the Hopi language. In 8 we find an instance of code-switching between two men outside of a purely conversational context. In response to D's directive, speaker E employs the Hopi expression *tota'ci* (bossy person) (Voegelin and Voegelin 1957, 43) as a form of mild criticism of D. It is important to add that E utters this expression with an exaggerated low pitch, shaking his head visibly in feigned offense. After doing so, E engages D in mutual gaze and both men smile. The switch to Hopi invokes an ideal norm that proscribes the imposition of one's will on another of equal status. The polite avoidance of blunt directives and the irresponsible avoidance of authority are both associated with the Hopi. Native consultants detected an ambiguity about this particular performance. The code-switch could variously be interpreted as an attempt to invoke norms of interpersonal conduct that are stereotypically associated with the "polite" Hopi or as a mocking of Hopis who are, according to the Tewa, easily offended by displays of secular authority. This ambiguity is, of course, an effective face-saving strategy (Brown and Levinson 1978) since it permits an inoffensive protest. Since D avoids blunt directives for the remainder of the job, it appears that this ambiguity was successfully communicated. But beyond the particulars of this example, it is important to observe the ambivalence of the Hopi language as a symbol capable of connoting both virtues and vices associated with the Hopi, often depending upon the intended and communicated identity of the speaker.

In 6 and 7 we observed code-switches to Hopi that attribute the virtues of ceremonial emphasis and ritual perfection to the Hopi. But 9 demonstrates that this positive characterization on which the evaluation is based is not invariable. It provides an obvious example of comic exaggeration as speaker A caricatures a Hopi traditionalist.[10] In an instance of dramatic irony, he impersonates a Hopi traditionalist offering an incoherent moral condemnation of the Tewa for "losing the Hopi way." The incoherence is communicated not only by the semantic anomaly—Tewa losing the Hopi way—but also by prosodic information. Each sentence is issued in short, disconnected bursts bounded by long pauses as if the speaker is carefully choosing his words in a formal speech.

The code-switch to English retrospectively clarifies the performance and unambiguously expresses the Tewa stereotype of Hopi traditionalists who they regard as pretentious, self-serving, and sanctimonious. An absurd incongruity is generated by contrast of professed moral indignation and humility (in Hopi) with the request for a speaker's fee from naive Euro-American audiences and the bald announcement of plans for evening TV viewing (in English). According to many Arizona Tewa, Hopi traditionalists exploit both progressive Hopis and Tewas as well as Euro-Americans, by acquiring undeserved notoriety for obstructionist activities and collecting money for public speeches in which they extol virtues which they do not live up to in private life.

Examples 8 and 9 thus complement examples 6 and 7 by providing a sense of the multivocality of Hopi code-switches. Other ethnographic work, especially that of Blom and Gumperz (1972) in northern Norway has shown how switches to what might be called the marked language of social interaction can be interpreted in a similar manner. Bokmal, standard Norwegian, may convey desired connotations of expertise and officiality but for some communicative purposes it is entirely too impersonal and pretentious (Blom and Gumperz 1972, 419, 427–28). The range of associations that a language can accumulate for a speaker seems to militate against a stable, univocal meaning. Like all symbols, these languages must be interpreted, as above, as part of the communicative context.

So far I have almost exclusively concentrated on Hopi and Tewa as available codes in the linguistic repertoire of the Arizona Tewa. But what about English? Under what circumstances do code-switches to English occur? In contrast to the Hopi cases, switches to English appear to be both less frequent and less difficult to interpret. This is in part due to the more circumscribed role that English plays in Arizona Tewa daily life and to the consequently smaller number of associations that it has acquired for the Arizona Tewa. Three brief examples deserve some attention before turning to the implications of these code-switching data for an account of Arizona Tewa ethnic identity.

Example 10 illustrates two of the connotations of English that prompt speakers to select it in instances of code-switching:

10. [Setting: In H's Tewa Village home. H has been questioned by B about his health and symptomatology. B, a younger clan relative of H, has been called over by H's wife to persuade him to seek prompt medical attention for recent dizzy spells and loss of appetite. Previous discourse has been exclusively in Tewa.]

Speaker H:　*Yo:. Wó-'ó-p'ole-pú-t'ó-dí. 'o-má:yu-po.* (AT)
　　　　　　No. I'm not going to Keams Canyon. I feel tired.

Speaker B.　You better go see a DOCTOR!
　　　　　　Na-ma-mɛn-di, na-mu-mí wo:lo-kán-'i. (AT)
　　　　　　You should go see a doctor.

Here the code-switch to English is largely reiterated by B in Tewa. Because of this, the passage provides something akin to the discourse equivalent of a minimal pair. But rather than the detection of functional contrasts at the phonological level, the goal here is to disclose connotative differences at the semantic level. Consultants judge the English as both more forceful and authoritative than the Tewa version despite the fact that the two sentences are translation equivalents. Here again, as with example 8 above, there is some ambiguity since the use of English connotes pushy and inconsiderate interpersonal behavior such as the Tewa receive at the Public Health Service Hospital and by Euro-American representatives of various federal and state government agencies. But the use of English also connotes a positively valued educational exposure to the modern world and the marvels of science and technology. Though B uses English to invoke the latter connotation, the former seems to necessitate a reiterative code-switch to Tewa in order to resolve ambiguity— English has been chosen not because it is an effective language to order people around in but rather because it invokes an appeal to an educated and informed perspective. In form and substance this code-switch closely resembles the personalized versus objective kind of code-switching in Gumperz's (1982a, 80) typology of code-switching functions. As in his examples, the Arizona Tewa data conform to a pattern in which the indigenous, local language connotes a more personal and subjective touch whereas the superposed standard language invokes an objective detachment.

Example 11 represents another common pattern in which job-related perspectives are invoked by code-switches to English.

11. [Setting: In I's Tewa Village House. Speaker I, an older woman and a potter, sits with her aunt discussing family matters and various economic needs. Prior conversation has all been performed in Tewa.]

Speaker I: *Né-'i na-khá:bén.* (AT)
(This one is broken.) I can sell that little one for ten dollars . . . more, if my paint would stay on right.
'e:-p'í:le-bí'inɛdi 'án-khe-kumɛ-mí. (AT)
(We should buy some clothes for the baby.)

Here, as discussion of the pottery invokes the role of selling to tourists, Speaker I switches to English—the language invariably used for this purpose. As the conversational focus shifts back to family matters, English is discarded for Tewa as the woman mentions the need for additional clothes for her grandchild. Since job-related activities for many Tewa are conducted in English, this language provides an appropriate vehicle for discussion of such concerns. Even though pottery-making is an indigenous craft, today virtually all pottery made on First Mesa is sold to tourists, hence the association with Euro-Americans and English. For service-type occupations of a nontraditional nature it is especially common for discussion of on-the-job encounters to be in English—the language that typically constitutes the medium of these professional communications.

The final example, 12, illustrates a particularly significant role of code-switches to English that involve the establishment of relevant identity as citizen of the United States.

12. [Setting: Speaker E's Tewa Village home. Speaker E is discussing finances with his wife. Discussion of family needs and priorities which precedes this has taken place in Tewa.]

Speaker E: *So:nu kwɛk'u-c'ɛ-'i to'o dín-k'wón.* (AT)
(I only have four dollars.) What is the day? [looking at a calendar on the wall] . . . Tenth. Why is it I haven't received my check?

Here the code-switch to English invokes E's status as a United States citizen as he wonders why he has yet to receive his monthly social security check. Though local identity pervades many more aspects of daily life than does national identity, the Arizona Tewa—like the Hopi—are citizens of the United States and possess the rights and duties which membership in this group implies. Such subjects as taxability, military service, national and state elections, and world news are typically discussed in the English language. In one argument that I overheard but was unable to fully document in August 1984, a Tewa man was complaining to a Hopi relative about the refusal of the *kikmongwi*, or hereditary village chief, to certify duly elected representatives from First Mesa to the Hopi Tribal Council. During this rather long discussion he repeatedly code-switched into English. When I asked about this later in the day he replied, "Doesn't he [the *kikmongwi*] know that this is illegal and against our laws?" In retrospect then it appears that he used English to emphasize the conflict between national democratic ideals and local Hopi political practice.

Taken collectively, these observations of code-switching behavior in the Arizona Tewa speech community further undermine Barth's boundary maintenance imagery and the foundational assumption on which it rests that ethnic identity is profitably understood as a type of *continuous* ascription (self-ascription and/or ascription by others). These code-switching data provide important evidence that Tewa ethnic identity is one among multiple social identities available to the Arizona Tewa. By focusing on intraindividual linguistic variation in the form of metaphorical code-switching, we gain important insights into the microprocess of ethnic identification that begins to unfold its communicated and stylistic (Hymes 1974) nature. By highlighting the active and creative role that speakers take in symboling their relevant social identity, these data encourage us to abandon an inappropriate emphasis on the immutability and coercive nature of particular social identities. As Gumperz and Cook-Gumperz (1982, 2) have observed:

> We customarily take gender, ethnicity, and class as given parameters and boundaries within which we create our own social identities. The study of language as interactional discourse demonstrates that these parameters are not constraints that can be taken for granted but are communicatively produced.

Though Gumperz and Cook-Gumperz (1982, 3) seem to regard this constitutive and interactional role of communicative behavior in signalling relevant identity as unique to "post-industrial society in the urbanized regions of both western and non-western countries," the Tewa data discussed here and in other chapters strongly suggest that this is not the case. Though I defer further discussion of this point to the concluding chapter, it is important to note here that the need for conveying the relevant identity of the speaking self is not unique to speakers in urbanized, bureaucratic states.

A Repertoire of Identity

While code-switching data discussed above provide a valuable case study of the role of language use in establishing and reformulating relevant social identities in a multilingual and multiethnic society, the general view of ethnicity that they encourage is hardly novel to those anthropologists who have contributed to the study of *situational ethnicity* (see reviews of this work in Cohen 1978 and Royce 1982). Moerman (1965; 1974) was among the first to critically challenge the received tradition of much anthropological practice, which often uncritically adopted highly simplified folk categories and, after both decontextualizing and reifying them, pronounced them to be appropriate analytical categories. Writing about the problematic notion of identity as applied to a particular sedentary, lowland Thai group, Moerman (1974, 62) declared, "The question is not 'Who are the Lue?' . . . but rather when and how and why the identification 'Lue' is preferred." This reformulation of basic research questions is entirely appropriate for an evolving theoretical anthropology that has begun in recent decades to compensate for a preoccupation with structural stasis, uniformism, and functionalism through exploratory emphasis on process, intracultural diversity, action or practice (Keesing 1974; Ortner 1984), and sociocultural change. As Cohen (1978, 381) has observed, traditional anthropological treatments of ethnicity were by-products of an equally traditional thrust of the discipline "to understand assumedly homogeneous sociocultural units as entities." Critical of this approach to ethnicity, Joan Vincent (1974, 376) warns of the anthropological penchant for seeking "the embodiment of ethnicity in overly corporate forms." Heeding this admonition as a license for a more phenomenological perspective, we can observe that in a very important sense ethnicity has no existence apart from interethnic relations and interethnic interaction.

Here a focus on intraindividual variation in the form of metaphorical code-switching has revealed significant findings which suggest that just as the proper study of "ethnic" languages is within the context of the linguistic repertoire, so the proper study of ethnicity is the repertoire of social identities available to members of the speech community. In general form this notion of a repertoire of identity has already been approximated by some students of situational ethnicity. Cohen (1978, 395) offers a concise statement of such a view in the following passage:

> The view of ethnicity adopted here is one in which the identities of members and categorizations by others is more or less fluid, more or less multiple, forming nested hierarchies of we/they dichotomizations. . . . So far, however, much less attention has been given to understanding what conditions tend to evoke ethnic identities of particular scale and intensity than to describing what ethnicity is as a phenomenon.

Though this approach captures the multiplicity of identities available to members, it does not acknowledge their agency in selecting from a repertoire of options. The notion of a repertoire of identities would avoid this deficiency and properly attribute agency to interacting individuals who, even when their code-switching is out-of-awareness, display a complex understanding of the linkages between various social identities and their associated linguistic forms. Of course the image of code-switching that I envision in proposing this sociolinguistic analogy is not one in which I uncritically assume that code-switching in various speech communities is a "structurally unified phenomenon whose significance derives from a universal pattern of relationship between form, function, and context" (Heller 1988a, 3). I agree with Monica Heller, who finds that the proper study of code-switching involves understanding how a unique sociohistorical context is tied to language use as a resource for speakers engaged in social interaction. Identity options, like multiple roles, are socioculturally distributed and not uniformly available either across or within cultural groups. Limitations on identity options can emanate from power relations (e.g., Woolard 1988) and the observation that some identities, ethnic identities in particular, possess "double boundaries" (Royce 1982, 29, 185) because they must not only be culturally available within the group but also subject to ratification by (hegemonic) outsiders as in the case of establishing Native American identity in the United States.

At least a partial convergence with the notion of a repertoire of identities is provided by the observations of Albert Yava—an Arizona Tewa individual whom I have occasionally cited in previous chapters. As I have maintained elsewhere (Kroskrity 1983b), it is important to regard Yava not simply as a typical Arizona Tewa from whom we can gain the folk perspective but as an exceptional, privileged source of insights about the Hopi and the Tewa. Certainly no one, whether anthropologist or native, had the experiential basis, as both knowledgeable insider and analytical outsider, that informed his view. As native, Yava received the informal education of his culture, becoming an important clan elder in Tewa Village and a member of a prominent Hopi kiva society. As an outsider, he worked much of his adult life as official translator in Hopi dealings with the federal government and its various agencies. He was also a valued consultant for many anthropologists and linguists on both Hopi and Arizona Tewa languages and cultures. This biographical preparation does not make him especially representative but it does make him especially knowledgeable. In light of the very different framing provided by the present chapter, a reiteration of an earlier quotation from him may not prove entirely redundant.

> We are interrelated with Hopi families in all the villages. Many of us have become members of the various Hopi Kiva Societies. We share dances and festival days with the Hopis. We belong to the same clans. We are usually represented on the Hopi Tribal Council. . . . In many ways we are indistinguishable from them, and often you hear us say in conversations, "We Hopis," not because we have forgotten that we are Tewas but because we identify with the Hopis in facing the outside world. (Yava 1979, 129–30)

While it is gratifying, and perhaps even somewhat validating, to observe convergence with such diverse sources, it is important to consider the theoretical significance of the sociolinguistic model of identification that has been suggested here. Not only does the linguistic repertoire (Gumperz 1962; 1968) provide an appropriate locus for the investigation of languages of ethnicity, it also provides a novel and appropriate source for theoretical imagery regarding ethnicity in general. In contrast to the emphasis on constraints that pervades ethnic boundary maintenance, the repertoire of identity focuses on the interactional and communicated nature of social identity. Rather than an isolated preoccupation with a particular code or identity, the model encourages the study of a given social identity in its interrelationships to other available social identities. Rather than emphasizing the *who,* the model naturally focuses attention on the *when, how,* and *why* of switches within the repertoire of identity. Unlike some studies of situated identity (e.g., Silverman 1988), the model goes beyond the mere recognition of multiple identities by focusing on the interrelationship and interaction between those identities thus better capturing some of the "play between cultures, between realities" that Michael M. J. Fischer (1986, 230) has emphasized in his study of contemporary ethnic autobiography.[11]

Though my main concern in this chapter is substantively ethnographic, it is appropriate to observe two additional virtues of the theoretical model of ethnic identity proposed here. The first of these concerns its resistance to a critique of situational ethnicity that is not without some merit. As Keyes (1976, 202) has properly observed, "If whatever cultural attributes are associated with particular ethnic groups are taken to be entirely situational, then the identification of a group as being an ethnic group is entirely arbitrary and without analytical value." In other words, if ethnic identity is equated with social identity rather than viewed as a special type of social identity, an important analytical distinction may be lost. Even proponents of situational ethnicity, such as Nagata (1974, 333) have suggested that ethnic groups are "special" kinds of reference groups. So far, however, no model has been proposed that can satisfactorily reconcile theoretical demands for a simultaneous recognition of the multiplicity of social identities, and the special characteristics of ethnic identities.

But a model of the repertoire of identities based on the linguistic repertoire may provide a satisfactory resolution of the problem. Among the tasks of the sociolinguist in confronting the organization of diversity posed by a given speech community is the detection of the linguistic distance between the codes of a linguistic repertoire and the discovery of their social meaning as evidenced by instrumental and expressive differences in actual usage of these codes. Like ethnic languages, ethnic identities need not be perpetually invoked to retain their special significance to members. Just as the particular social meaning of each code must be discovered so as to reveal the functional interrelationship of all the codes in a linguistic repertoire, so the corresponding demand to discover the instrumental and expressive choices associated with each social identity permits us to discover the special characteristics of each.

But while the model permits the discovery of ethnic identities, it need not presuppose their existence. Surely the profound givens so often attributed to ethnic identity will be abundantly manifested by members' preference for it in a variety of instrumental and expressive activities. In the Arizona Tewa speech community, for example, the highly compartmentalized invocation of identity as United States citizen and its limited range of instrumental and expressive functions would certainly deny its status as an ethnic identity for most Arizona Tewa.[12] Hopi identity is another matter. Dozier's turnabout on the issue of Arizona Tewa persistence versus assimilation was no doubt due to the recognition that the Arizona Tewa, on many occasions, strongly identify with the Hopi and that this identity was like ethnic identity in character. But Dozier lacked a model like the repertoire of identities or any model of a multiethnic society for that matter.[13] Lacking these, he had no other interpretive option than to construe the acquisition of Hopi identity with the loss of Arizona Tewa ethnic identity.

Another virtue of the model of identity adopted here is the abundance of productive questions that it brings into focus. In addition to the questions of when, how, and why discussed above, it suggests that identity processes comparable to *convergence* and *compartmentalization* observed in linguistic repertoires might be investigated. Just as codes in a linguistic repertoire may converge, so identities may be comparably influenced. We have begun to understand the many factors responsible for why languages may converge or compartmentalize within the linguistic repertoires of multilingual communities (Kroskrity 1982; Kroskrity and Reinhardt 1984) but we lack an analogous understanding of comparable processes of identification. If theories are to be evaluated, in part, by the productivity of the research questions they suggest, then the repertoire of identity would seem to be a potentially valuable theoretical framework indeed.[14]

Linguistic and Sociolinguistic Models In Anthropology

As Hymes (1970) has amply demonstrated, linguistics has played a multiplicity of important roles in American anthropology. In this chapter alone I have relied heavily on the generating, validating, penetrating, and

foundational roles that linguistics has played in the history of anthropology (Hymes 1970, 251–55). But it is the last of these, the role of linguistics as a theoretical inspiration for cultural anthropology, that I would
like to briefly consider in concluding this chapter.

Here preoccupation with sociolinguistic data has, perhaps not so sur-
prisingly, lead me to endorse and develop a sociolinguistic model of identity—the repertoire of identities. But as in any theoretical endeavor, a
historical perspective is advisable. Cultural anthropology has a significant history of borrowing theoretical models from linguistics via the *linguistic analogy*. While it is outside the scope of this brief discussion to
attempt an exhaustive account of this historical tendency, two key examples will permit the explication of a significant pattern.

David Aberle (1968) in his article "The Influence of Linguistics on
Early Culture and Personality Theory" has demonstrated the unity of
method that underlay Boasian approaches to both language, on the one
hand, and culture and personality on the other. He has suggested that
then contemporary understandings about the nature of language (e.g., its
selectivity, unconscious patterning, unique configuration) exercised a
powerful shaping influence on understandings of culture and personality
despite the lack of an explicit awareness on the part of participating
scholars such as Sapir and Benedict.

A few decades later we find a more self-conscious implementation of
the linguistic analogy in the work of cultural anthropologists who were
variously identified as practitioners of ethnoscience, cognitive anthropology, and the new ethnography. Roger Keesing (1972) has effectively
traced the logic and illogic of this attempt to borrow from two seemingly antithetical linguistic theories—Bloomfieldian structuralism and the
mentalism of Chomsky's transformational generative grammar. Keesing's
"Paradigms Lost: The New Ethnography and the New Linguistics" quite
properly traces many of the shortcomings of this theoretical movement to
deficiencies stemming from the incompatibility of ethnoscientific goals,
which emphasized an ideational view of culture, and methods and assumptions derived by analogy from the more physicalist ideology of
Bloomfieldian structuralism.

It is important to observe that in each of these historically important
cases, as in the great majority of linguistic models adopted by anthropologists, the analogy is to language structure not language use. Both
Aberle (1968, 309) and Keesing (1972, 326) trace many of the short-

comings of these linguistic analogies to the preoccupation of the linguistic models with grammatical form and/or competence rather than with communicative performance. Yet anthropologists have always admired the rigor of linguistic analysis, often ignoring the atomism, formalism, and misguided materialism (Friedrich 1975, 215–18) that so sanitized many leading linguistic theories. Rigor was too often attributed to superior models when it might better have been attributed to more restrictively bound ones. Absolving themselves of accounting for communication between speakers, most linguistic theories have instead dedicated themselves to the explication of a disembodied code—a task that both permits and encourages formally elegant analysis but is hardly compatible with the typically more holistic appreciation that has been traditionally valued in anthropology.

The repertoire of identity model proposed here differs from most applications of the linguistic analogy in that it invokes language use and not language structure.[15] Rather than relying on the model of grammar and the uniformity that it invokes, I have drawn theoretical inspiration from the model of the linguistic repertoire—a model that is metonymically related to the view of a given speech community as an "organization of diversity" (Hymes 1962; 1974). For more than three decades now, sociolinguistics and the ethnography of communication have complemented linguistic preoccupation with uniformity and invariance by exhorting researchers to study the contributing role of inter- and intraindividual variation in communicative processes. The comparatively recent reawakening of anthropological interest in intracultural diversity (e.g., Pelto and Pelto 1975) thus has potentially instructive precedents in the ethnography of speaking tradition.

As for the Tewa, they have not only provided the data that occasions this study of their changing ethnic identity but also an instructive folk theory of language—one that emphasizes language, history, and both personal and group identities, one that not only enlightens us in our attempts to understand Tewa communicative behavior but also implicitly challenges and critiques the comparatively narrow vision of language manifested in much conventional western linguistic theory and practice.

8

■ ■ ■

CONCLUDING REMARKS

What can we learn from this tiny group of Native Americans? While the Arizona Tewa people have taught me a great deal about such diverse topics as family values, farming, and tradition, two concerns stand out here as especially worthy of further discussion. The first of these concerns language attitudes and linguistic ideologies. On this point, these studies clarify past misconceptions of Pueblo *linguistic conservatism* and examine the Arizona Tewa *culture of language* as a powerful and irreducible force in language contact and general culture change. Related to the first, the second concern is the relationship of language and identity. On this point, I believe the Arizona Tewa provide an instructive allegory for theoretical conceptions of the mutual relations of the linguistic formulation of the speaking self and, perhaps on a more practical level, a parable for those confronting minority language policy issues.

Language Attitudes/Linguistic Ideologies: *Linguistic Conservatism* Revisited

One way in which the Arizona Tewa case studies can prove particularly instructive is in illuminating language attitudes, especially in refining the often misunderstood notion of linguistic conservatism. Both Wick Miller (1978) and Joel Sherzer (1976) rely heavily on such a notion in claims they made about the Pueblo Southwest in their respective works on Native American multilingualism and linguistic diffusion. Miller regards three factors as most important in determining patterns of multilingualism in aboriginal North America: (1) degree of diversity, (2) native evaluation of second language learning, and (3) usefulness of learning a particular second language. Though he regards the Southwest as sufficiently diverse to support multilingualism, he finds it comparatively inhospitable because of the second and third dimensions. Since I have already addressed the issue of utility in chapter 3, it is best to focus on native evaluation here. On this point it has become conventional to invoke extreme ethnocentrism and general linguistic conservatism as the cause of disinterest in and denigration of other languages.

Regarding ethnocentrism, I quite agree with Miller (1978) that it represents an important factor but one that, as these studies show, influences the form which diffusion takes rather than inhibiting it altogether. The concept of linguistic conservatism warrants further focal consideration since it represents a characteristic often ascribed to the Pueblo Southwest yet seldom critically examined by interpreters of the macrosociolinguistic situation there, such as Miller and Sherzer (Sherzer 1976, 233; Miller 1978, 613).[1] In fact the notion has served to discourage the study of language contact by masquerading as an accurate and comprehensive assessment of native language attitudes. Since neither of these scholars investigated the problem ethnographically nor attempted to understand native language attitudes as an aspect of local cultural knowledge and practice, these studies provide new perspectives from which to rethink the issues.

Since a long tradition of usage has burdened the term with the baggage of new associations, premises, and assumptions, it will be necessary to analytically deconstruct linguistic conservatism into its component parts in order to actually assess their adequacy and utility. I regard this as necessary because as presently reified, the notion refers ambiguously to language attitudes, mechanisms of enacting these attitudes, and the linguistic consequences of these mechanisms.

As a starting point we can examine a representative recitation of received knowledge on the subject offered by Joel Sherzer (1976). In his discussion of the Southwest he remarks on the apparent anomaly posed by a culture area with the third highest population density of any Native

American culture area, a high degree of genetic linguistic diversity, yet little apparent diffusion. He says:

> The explanation of this situation may be found in a sociolinguistic factor about which we rarely have data—attitudes toward language. The southwest is one area for which many observers have reported attitudes toward one's own language and that of others, perhaps because these attitudes are often quite explicit. Southwest Indians are very conservative with respect to language . . . taking pride in their own languages and sometimes refusing to learn that of others. Especially noteworthy is the compartmentalization of their own language. When they do learn other languages, they seem consciously to avoid allowing alien linguistic traits to penetrate their own linguistic system. (Sherzer 1976, 244)

This passage presents two problems. One is the mistaken confidence that Sherzer seems to have in the existing scholarship and its ethnographic adequacy. The Arizona Tewa data presented here is the first comprehensive argument for viewing local language ideology and practice as shaped by the model of kiva speech rather than by extreme xenophobia and ethnocentrism. The other problem is the assumption that all aspects of language might be equally subject to native regulation and thus uniformly influenced by compartmentalization. This position is untenable in light of the evidence presented in chapters 3 and 4 and my previously published conclusions on the contact history of the Arizona Tewa (Kroskrity 1982), which show a pattern of resistance to diffusion in the lexicon yet provide discernible diffusion at the more out-of-awareness levels of the phonology, syntax, and discourse.

Concerning the variable of language attitudes, two claims are made in previous areal scholarship. One, native languages were attributed a privileged status by their speakers in accord with the ethnocentrism often attributed to the Pueblos. Two, non-native languages were denigrated, thus making second-language learning an undesirable alternative to monolingualism. The first of these claims simply amounts to the statement that Pueblo groups viewed their languages as exceptional affective resources beyond their instrumental uses. In other words they endowed their languages with a profound affective significance. I find this claim uncontroversial. But while such beliefs are to some degree more the ethnologic rule than the exception, the degree to which the native language symbolizes ethnic identity in the Southwest may be enhanced by its function in *ethnic boundary maintenance* (Barth 1969). In other words, the general cultural similarities of the Pueblos would highlight any linguistic differences, making the languages likely candidates as *diacritica of ethnicity*. While I have found specific faults with Barth's imagery as applied to the multicultural Arizona Tewa, the notion still has explanatory value in accounting for why a few cultural differences can be endowed with new meanings as badges of ethnicity in situations of sustained interethnic contact and interaction. Good evidence for such a claim is provided by my own sociolinguistic investigations of Arizona Tewa code-switching and intraspeech community variation (chapter 4). Yet while the strong bond between language and ethnicity is incontestable in the Southwest, native language practices should not be simply equated with *linguistic purism*. As maintained in chapters 2 and 4, the cultural ideals of kiva talk, including linguistic purism, are only approximated in the practice of casual speech. In their evaluation of everyday speech, the Arizona Tewa clearly recognize such a social distribution of knowledge and behavior. This observation is not limited to the Tewa. Thus Trager discovered the following:

> In everyday speech the Taos use many more loans, especially of English origin, but these I was never able to record because there was—once it was known that I knew something of the language—little free conversation in my presence, and what there was I could not write down but only try to remember. My informants reacted to many loan words with a kind of purism that made it difficult to get them to repeat the words. The items treated here were either recorded in texts . . . or were caught on the wing as it were. (Trager 1944, 144)

His observation appears to confirm my statement regarding the disparity between cultural ideals—"that which people say they should do"— and actual practice. Those who have reported language purism for the Pueblo Southwest have often uncritically assumed that this ideal is automatically and uniformly approximated in everyday speech when in fact its enactment is both socially distributed and dependent on the amount of attention the speaker pays to his or her speech.

Having confronted native language attitudes, it seems appropriate to focus attention on Pueblo attitudes toward other languages. Some apparent support for second language denigration can perhaps be gleaned from Dozier's (1951) study of Spanish loans in Rio Grande Tewa and my own study of comparable loans in Arizona Tewa (Kroskrity 1978b). It should be noted that both these instances involve the special case of Spanish—a language symbolically linked to former political repression and religious intolerance (Simmons 1979, 180ff.). Dozier observed that Tewa speakers appear not to attach comparable significance to borrowing from English. Cushing, in *My Adventures in Zuni*, provides a more graphic example (1979, 50). As he first approaches Zuni Pueblo, he is met by a group of men, one of whom addresses him:

> "How-li-loo?"
> "Pretty well," I replied. "How are you?"
> "At's good," said he, and this useful phrase he employed until I reluctantly concluded that it was the extent of his English. It was amusing to see his efforts, by constantly repeating this phrase, ducking his head and grinning, to convince the other Indians that he was carrying on a lively conversation with me.

It would seem that this behavior on the part of the Zuni man makes sense only if a knowledge of English is valued, not stigmatized. Both Dennis Tedlock (personal communication) and I have had similar and recent experiences in the different pueblos in which we have conducted research, which strongly suggest that foreign languages are valued. At Zuni, Tedlock occasionally met older villagers who would ask his permission to let their children sit on his lap in the hope that they would absorb some of his English language skills. I experienced similar situations in my earliest fieldwork in Tewa Village and observed comparable treatments of other foreigners (e.g., visitors from Germany, Scandinavia). Today, as presented in chapter 4, older speakers criticize younger not for their knowledge of English but rather for the interference of English in their everyday speech and, more importantly, in their use of English in contexts where the native language is traditionally viewed as appropriate.

But what of attitudes toward other Native American languages? So far I have only discussed attitudes toward Spanish and English. It seems difficult to contend that other Native American languages were necessarily despised or devalued in light of the following practices: one, frequent borrowing of songs—words and music (Charlotte Heth, personal communication; Paul Humphreys, personal communication) and, two, as Leslie White noted (1944), the presence of loanwords from other Pueblo languages in many Pueblo ceremonial vocabularies. (More on this below.) Ethnographically I find that the Arizona Tewa continue to place a value on knowing languages such as Hopi and Navajo—the former as the language of greater First Mesa society and Hopi religion, the latter as a still useful trade language that helps one obtain substances as diverse as sheep dung and ochre. While these languages are valued more for their instrumental significance, perceived mixing of Hopi with the native Arizona Tewa language is widely frowned upon and said to be character-istic of women's speech. Since women are relatively culturally removed from the ceremonial realm—the locus of the most prestigious variety of Tewa—this association with what may be termed *linguistic interference* (Weinreich 1953), is both symbolically and behaviorally appropriate.

A principled interpretation of these observations would, I conclude, discourage adherence to the view that native language attitudes in the Pueblo Southwest devalued learning other Indian and non-Indian lan-guages. While it is true that these languages suffer in comparison to the native language, they are not stigmatized as potential objects of second language learning. A more accurate assessment would locate such deni-gration not in the cultural devaluation of other languages but rather in violations of the ideal norms that informally proscribe conscious lan-guage mixing. It appears that aesthetic considerations should be subor-dinated to pragmatic ones in any adequate account of the lack of multi-lingualism in the Pueblo Southwest. In those situations where stable multilingualism does represent a genuinely adaptive response—the ac-quisition of Spanish and English throughout the pueblos, the acquisition of Hopi by the Southern Tewa ancestors of the Arizona Tewa—it was adopted. In the Arizona Tewa case, as Ed Dozier found, the Tewa view the fact that they speak Hopi but few Hopi speak Tewa as a cultural victory on their part.

Having cast some doubt on the adequacy of current notions of Pueblo language attitudes, it is appropriate to conclude this discussion of lin-guistic conservatism by examining both mechanisms of enactment of these attitudes and the linguistic consequences of this enactment. Regard-ing the mechanisms of enactment, it is generally assumed that both soci-etal and individual multilingualism were quite rare in the Pueblo South-west. As long as this is not viewed as the product of native cultural aesthetics, I quite agree with this insofar as societal multilingualism in the proximate past is concerned. For more remote periods, such as that investigated in chapter 3, I seriously doubt that we can dismiss societal multilingualism or discount the significance of individual multilingualism in producing areal patterns. Since ceremonial varieties are viewed as prestigious, words first introduced in ceremonial contexts or by ceremonial practitioners would stand a better chance of propagation throughout the speech community because of the positive cultural evaluation they would gain by that association. At present, however, this statement is better understood as hypothesis than as ethnographic fact since the lack of relevant sociolinguistic studies or ethnographic documentation prevent an accurate estimation of the linguistic consequences associated with this or other instances of individual multilingualism. Lacking such ethnographic analogies in the present, there is little to guide an interpretation of the past. This lack calls attention to the need for what the indologist Franklin Southworth (1971, 256) has termed "a more precise sociolinguistic typology of outcomes of language contact"—one that is capable of accounting for diffusion whether it is the result of either societal or individual multilingualism and one which treats language attitudes as an inherent part of the diffusion process.

Finally I turn to the consequences of the expression of these attitudes in the form of diffusional patterns. Here the platform of linguistic conservatism includes the following assumption: an adequate examination of a sufficient body of materials has been accomplished, finding no significant linguistic diffusion at either lexical or grammatical levels of analysis. It is important to recall that a general lack of dictionaries in the Pueblo Southwest has militated against any areal-comparative analysis of lexical resources. Zuni (Newman 1958) and Hopi (Voegelin and Voegelin 1957; Albert and Shaul 1985; Seaman 1985) are the only Pueblo languages for which published lexicons exist.[2] For Keresan, Tewa, Tiwa, and Jemez no comparable materials exist. Even so, a brief inspection of Wick Miller's Acoma grammar, which I conducted recently, disclosed two obvious instances of lexical borrowing (Acoma examples from Miller 1965, 9, 13):

TERM	TEWA	ACOMA
pipe	sa:-k'u:	sa:k'u
butterfly	bulakaka (AT)	buur'aika

Since the Tewa word for "pipe" is readily analyzable into the morphemes for "tobacco" and "stone," it is the obvious source of the Keresan term. In the case of "butterfly," the Tewa form represents something of a morphological anomaly, at least in the Arizona Tewa dialect, which clearly indicates its foreign origins. These loanwords may well be indicative of inter-Pueblo linguistic borrowings which appear to reflect nonutilitarian uses. For while the Pueblos were relatively independent as political units, they were and are ceremonially cooperative and, on occasions, even dependent on neighboring ceremonial practitioners (as in the case of a reinstatement of a lapsed society, and so forth [Lange et al. 1975, 415, 447]).

Like the grammatical evidence presented in chapter 3, these lexical examples suggest the efficacy and potential significance of further areal linguistic pursuits in the Pueblo Southwest. Rather than assuming the futility of detailed investigation, we need to examine processes of linguistic diffusion in the present so as to acquire an understanding of such sociolinguistic phenomena in the past and their ethnological and ethnohistorical significance. As these studies indicate, however, we should acknowledge the profound importance of a correct understanding of Pueblo linguistic ideology in shaping patterns of language contact and diffusion of linguistic forms and discourse practices. Here the identification of kiva speech norms as a cultural model for Arizona Tewa linguistic ideology refines an understanding of areal linguistic processes in the Pueblo Southwest by permitting a much needed deconstruction of its linguistic conservatism and by locating its origins in native cultural ideals rather than in intercultural rivalry and conflict.

Another contribution of the Arizona Tewa data is as a demonstration of the influence of popular awareness on processes of language contact. Though compartmentalization of languages has served the speech community well as a strategy for maintaining distinctive languages, it has clearly only been successful at those levels, most notably the lexicon, that are most subject to speakers' self-conscious manipulations. This recognition is an important corrective both to Sherzer's apparent assumption of *uniformist* compartmentalization and, more generally, to what Heath (1989, 194) has described as "the axiom of structural determinism"—a principle he attributes to earlier contact theorists like Haugen (1956) and Weinreich (1953) for their expectation that diffusion was a mechanical, consistent, and especially systematic process quite largely predictable from the structures of the two or more grammars in question. While

Heath's study of Moroccan Arabic questions just how systematic and consistent diffusional processes are on a more purely linguistic level, this work has concentrated on disparities between phonological, grammatical, and lexical processes as evidence of speakers' manipulation of the more accessible linguistic levels and as further evidence that contact processes are culturally regulated by local linguistic ideologies.

Regarding such ideologies it might be appropriate to ask, if the Arizona Tewa provide a model of Pueblo linguistic ideology, why are they unique in representing the only Pueblo group displaced during the Pueblo Revolts which has retained its native language? We know, for example, of several groups, including the Tigua of Ysleta del Sur (in El Paso, Texas), who opted for linguistic assimilation with their larger host groups after their emigration from their Rio Grande villages (Houser 1979). I think it is most useful to understand the Arizona Tewa as displaying a typical Pueblo linguistic ideology which was subject to historical circumstances that have actually enhanced and even fortified the pattern. The distance marched by their ancestors from the Rio Grande Valley to the easternmost Hopi Mesa was considerable, yet this distance was not as great as the cultural distance between the Hopi and the Southern Tewa. Their Hopi hosts knew how to live in what for the Tewa was an unusually harsh environment, one without rivers to irrigate their fields. Yet these Hopi stigmatized the Tewa mercenaries despite their usefulness as guards of the Hopi village of Walpi. By using their language as a means of both rejecting the Hopi definition of the situation and conserving their collective identity, the Arizona Tewa were able to simultaneously define themselves in much more flattering terms and to begin an inevitable process, however masked, of adjustment and accommodation to their Hopi hosts. This dual service of the Tewa language as a symbol of group identity and as a means of concealing historical change in kinship and social organization to accord with the Hopi model supported the need of the immigrant Southern Tewa to ultimately win the acceptance and cooperation of Hopis without sacrificing their group identity and the cultural control of constructing their own history. For the Arizona Tewa, the expression of a Pueblo linguistic ideology has been historically enhanced and enforced by the special role of Arizona Tewa as an enduring ethnic boundary marker—one of few differences (and by far the most omnipresent and tangible one) that still distinguish the Arizona Tewa from the Hopi.

Language, History, and Identity: the Arizona Tewa as a Multicultural Model

Though Barthian ethnic boundaries and diacritica of ethnicity provide useful notions for understanding how a few cultural differences between interacting groups can be symbolically transformed into ethnic emblems, they need to be supplemented by a conceptual framework like the repertoire of identities to better capture the multicultural adaptation of the Arizona Tewa. For in Barth's (1969) scheme, ethnic identity is a continuous, and presumably exclusive, self-ascription. The advantage of a *repertoire of identities* approach is that it permits us to attribute to members a multiplicity of *alternating* identities, and directs analytical attention to (1) when and how identities are interactively invoked by sociocultural actors and (2) the relations between various identities (e.g., the compartmentalization or convergence of ethnic, social, and culturally available voices) as well as the means by which they are communicated between members.

Though Gumperz and Cook-Gumperz (1982) suggest that the importance of communicated identity has been especially enhanced by the conditions of a bureaucratic, urban, industrialized society in which "unprecedented ethnic diversity" exists, these ethnolinguistic studies of the Arizona Tewa clearly demonstrate and exemplify the intimate association of language and identity in a so-called small scale society that is decidedly nonurban. Though the Tewa display some similarity in this regard to members of urban society, they also display important differences. A key source of similarity to the urban context is what could be understood as a consubstantiality or multiplicity of identities. Members of urban ethnic groups have membership in a larger sociocultural group as well as in more specific ethnic groups and often will employ linguistic and communicative styles that signal the situationally relevant interactional identity. Even before the spread of Euro-American cultural influence to their area, the Arizona Tewa were beginning their multicultural adaptation to the Hopi and using the associated languages to invoke membership in each of these groups.

But what most distinguishes the Arizona Tewa use of communicated identity is not this alternation of ethnic and other national identities but rather the somewhat different nature of interpersonal relationships in urban as opposed to small-scale societies. In the former an individual, apart from a small number of family members, interacts with many anonymous others and knows many relevant others primarily in simplex role relationships. But in Tewa Village and the greater First Mesa area, interactions with anonymous others are rare. Since one is related to almost two-thirds of one's neighbors, and since relationships are typically multiplex (involving a variety of kinship, ceremonial, administrative, business, and other practical roles), linguistic and communicative means often supply important evidence of selection from within an individual's repertoire of identity.

Certainly, there are times when the communicated identity is redundant or harmonious with nonverbal aspects of the speech event, as when a ceremonial leader employs kiva speech to his followers within a kiva sanctified by an altar for a sacred ceremony. But there are also instances, as portrayed in the code-switching examples of chapter 7 and the story-telling events of chapter 6, when evidence of formulated identity is primarily, if not exclusively, revealed through selection of language choice and communicative style. When an individual, for example, switches, in discussing reservation matters, from Hopi to Tewa, issuing a verbal condemnation of past Hopi policy regarding on-reservation high schools, language choice iconically indicates the speaker's situational selection of Arizona Tewa ethnicity as a relevant identity. In such cases the *marked* choice of Tewa from an individual's linguistic and identity repertoire is tantamount to framing one's statement by saying, "Speaking as a Tewa. . . ."[3]

It is perhaps this cultural preference for maintaining and reproducing distinctive linguistic forms corresponding to the various invokable social identities of the Arizona Tewa that makes a theoretical framework like the repertoire of identity so ethnographically warranted. Approaches to languages of ethnicity merely fetishize the obvious symbolic relationship between a language and an ethnic identity that exists in many communities (e.g., Fishman 1989). But rather than claiming that ethnic identities are exclusive, continuously ascribed, or automatically expressed by particular languages, a repertoire approach focuses attention on speakers' alternation, or selection, of codes and identities, both intracultural and intercultural. In understanding the Tewa data such an approach seems useful and even necessary, but there is also some theoretical motivation for emphasizing speakers' selection. Recent theory in the social sciences (e.g., Ortner 1984; Giddens 1984) has supported an agentive view of cultural actors that acknowledges their creative work in producing and reproducing structures which have been the obsession of conventional sociocultural analysis.

But just as these theories also acknowledge the role of historical constraints and the social distribution of resources as factors that shape an individual's actions, so recent theories of code-switching (and identity-selection) also recognize this dialectic duality of structure. In understanding code-switching we must appreciate the history of language contact relations and how this has permeated the social meanings of the associated languages. We must also observe that the nature and function of code-switching varies both across and within cultures. Collective research on the subject (Heller 1988a, 7) suggests that access to multiple roles and role relationships within a variety of social domains that are distinguished, in part, by distinct languages is a necessary but insufficient condition for code-switching. Woolard's (1988; 1989) studies of Catalonia, for example, suggest that even when these conditions exist, the social boundaries between domains may militate against any linguistic behavior that does not reproduce a comparably strict compartmentalization.

Within the same cultural group, code-switching may be socially distributed. As Heller (1988b, 270) observes, "the study of code-switching is also the study of the maintenance, change or breakdown of social barriers, and of the consequences of these processes for individuals' access to important social and economic resources." Just as codes within a speaker's linguistic repertoire converge or compartmentalize, so too their associated identities can be similarly treated. Myron and Ned, discussed in chapter 5, exemplify the diversity that can exist within a speech community. Whereas Ned does not code-switch and his spoken Tewa provides strong evidence of convergence with English, Myron exhibits an older strategy, within the community, of code-switching highly compartmentalized codes. As Heller (1988b, 266) observes, code-switching is typical of only those members of a community who find themselves "at the boundary of social groups." For Myron, as for many older Arizona Tewa people, it is important to locate this boundary not so much "between" groups as "within" individuals and to view it as less a preexisting imposition and more a continuously achieved creation. Code-switching serves to maintain a variety of maximally compartmentalized codes that provide continued access to discrete sets of cultural resources, both indigenous and nonindigenous, and invoke appropriate claims to membership in multiple cultural groups. In contrast, convergence—at both the level of linguistic code and social identity—represents the transformation of structures through the routine use of new linguistic and social practices. Where, for example, Myron has opted for a strategy of maintaining diversity, Ned's eclectic pose invites a more synthetic outcome involving a reshaping of codes and identities.

For some this reshaping assumes the form of replacement. Just as *language shift* represents the abandonment of indigenous languages so a parallel process, *identity shift,* can be recognized in the rejection of local cultural identities in favor of those supplied by Euro-American culture. Fifteen years ago, at the time of my last systematic survey, about twelve of twenty-one Tewa (extended) families contacted were raising their children with significant exposure to Tewa (either as a first language or as one of at least two languages regularly employed in Tewa households). At present it is still somewhat unclear whether this is evidence of sociolinguistic tip (Dorian 1989, 9)—a terminal language shift that would result in the death of Arizona Tewa or perhaps its survival as a liturgical language limited only to ritual performance.

Though discussions of language death may be premature, it is perhaps not too soon for the Arizona Tewa community to consider a program of *language renewal* (Leap 1988, 285). Language renewal would be a community-based effort to provide opportunities to people to restore fluency in the native language. During my early fieldwork I heard many Arizona Tewa speak out against any type of bilingual or multicultural education that would bring Tewa into the classroom. Though this was probably as much a statement about local schools as it was a conviction that all native language learning should be of the informal, or "from the home," type, it does suggest a source of resistance toward a renewal effort aimed at those who are not receiving sufficient instruction in their early years to become fluent speakers. For while the Tewa attach great cultural significance to their language, language learning, like all learning, is seen as properly kin-regulated and indexical of clan and kiva group membership.

Though Tewa language attitudes may exercise a partially contradictory effect on community efforts toward language renewal, at present it is very clear that Tewa people will have to control their own linguistic destiny. Federal policy recognizes—in principle—the importance of Native American languages but offers no substantive contribution to the enhancement of their survival. On October 30, 1990, President George

Bush signed into law the Native American Languages Act, which contains the following excerpted statements:

> The Congress finds that—(1) the status of the cultures and languages of Native Americans is unique and the United States has the responsibility to act together with Native Americans to ensure the survival of these unique cultures and languages; . . . (3) the traditional languages of Native Americans are an integral part of their cultures and identities and form the basic medium for their transmission, and thus survival, of Native American cultures, literatures, histories, religions, political institutions, and values; . . . (5) there is a lack of clear, comprehensive, and consistent Federal policy on treatment of Native American languages which has often resulted in acts of suppression and extermination of Native American Languages and cultures; . . . (8) acts of suppression and extermination directed against Native American languages and cultures are in conflict with the United States policy of self-determination for Native Americans. . . . It is the policy of the United States to preserve, protect, and promote the rights and freedom of Native Americans to use, practice, and develop Native American Languages.

No doubt, this act—as a law of the land—will assist Native American communities at a time when "English-only" legislation and intolerance for cultural diversity both propagate and escalate through the fifty states. But the Tewa, like other Native American groups, have long known the intimate relationship of language, history, and identity acknowledged by this law. This is hardly a revelation. Whatever spiritual solace and legal precedent this recognition provides, it provides no substantive economic support for language programs of any type. Clearly, if the language their ancestors brought from the Rio Grande Valley is to endure, it will be mainly through the continuing heroic efforts of the Arizona Tewa themselves.

Coda: The Voice of the Linguistic Anthropologist

If this work has succeeded in revealing something new, useful, and important about Arizona Tewa language and identity then perhaps it is appropriate to conclude with a few words about the professional identity of the author as a linguistic anthropologist. Wary readers may have already recognized that this volume contains not only the allegory of ethnography, but also another allegory. The skills necessary to reveal the various language-linked identities of the Arizona Tewa are today not conventionally those of the cultural anthropologist or the theoretical linguist. I would argue that this combination of historical linguistics, ethnography of communication, linguistic analysis, textual analysis, discourse analysis, and ethnography is only the tool-kit of the linguistic anthropologist. While these studies speak primarily about a people and their language they also provide a telling demonstration, as in the unraveling of Dozier's paradox, of the value of attending to language and communication, not merely as reflections of culture and social process, but as critical resources and activities in the continuous fashioning and refashioning of culture and society.

Yet as I conclude this volume, linguistic anthropologists would seem to be an endangered species confined to almost token representation in most departments despite the centrality of language and communication in all human endeavors. In bringing forth this volume I have deliberately kept back several chapters that seemed accessible to only a handful of specialists, in the hope of reaching a wider audience. But are my remarks an invitation or a challenge? Like a Hopi man issuing a grievance chant, I have climbed my ladder and from this rooftop chanted my complaint. To all, to no one in particular. As they say at the end of some eastern Pueblo stories, "And now, I throw it to you."

APPENDIX I

LEXICAL COMPARISON OF ARIZONA AND RIO GRANDE TEWA

	TERM	RIO GRANDE TEWA	ARIZONA TEWA
1.	all	t'æhki	t'ɛhkí
2.	and	heri, herá	kídí, kidá
3.	animal	hae:pan	pan
4.	ashes	nû:	núh
5.	at	-ge	-ge
6.	back	t'ú:	t'ú:
7.	bad	yæ	óyyó we-na-mu-dí[1]
8.	bark (of tree)	te:xowa	te:kho:wa
9.	because	herânho	he:dán
10.	belly	sik'u	siku
11.	big	só'yó	só:yó
12.	bird	círé	cį'é
13.	bite	-xu:gi:	-khun
14.	black	ɸéndi'	phén'i

15.	blood	'ûn	'uh
16.	blow	-siɸe:	-si:liphen
17.	bone	ɸéh-xú̧	phé-khú:
18.	breast	wâ:	wá:la
19.	breathe	-hâ̧:	-há̧:la
20.	brother²	tí'úu	tí'éy
21.	burn	-koye'	-koyɛ
22.	children	'é:ñæ̂:	'é:yɛ́
23.	claw	ma:ñæ̂:	ma:yɛ̧
24.	clothing	'a:	khe:
25.	cloud	'oxúwá	'okhúwá
26.	cook	-hæ̧:há:-'an	hawo:wa-pa:
27.	cool	-o:t'î:	-o:t'í
28.	count	-ma:pa:	-mapa:
29.	cut	-c'â'	-c'á:la
30.	dance	-šáre	-hi'
31.	day	ʈa:	thaw
32.	die	-ču:	-kyu:
33.	dig	-šæ̂:	-khyɛ̧lɛ̧
34.	dirty	-xá̧:-mu:	-khá̧:la-mu
35.	dog	cé	ce'é
36.	drink	-su̧wæ̂	-sun
37.	dry	-t'a:	-t'a:
38.	dull	k'e-pî'	k'e-pí-'i
39.	dust	taɸú:gî'	t'aphulu
40.	ear	'oye	'o:yɛ
41.	earth	nan	nan
42.	eat	-hú̧:ñan	-hwíyan
43.	egg	wá:	hwá
44.	eight	xâ:ve	kha:be
45.	eye	cí:	cí:
46.	fall	-kanu	-kanu
47.	far	kañi	ka̧yi'

48.	fat/grease	ka̱:	ka̱'
49.	father	tárá	tádá
50.	fear	-xuwô:da'	-khuwó:na'a
51.	feather	ɸe:	phele
52.	few	hi̱:ñæ̂:	hi̱:ye
53.	fight	-na'	-yá:la
54.	fire	ɸa:	pha
55.	fish	pa:	paw
56.	five	p'á̱:nu	p'á:nu
57.	float	–	p'o-yi'
58.	flow	p'o:-mæn	p'o-mɛn
59.	flower	póvi	pó:bí
60.	fog	sô:xuwa	só:p'okhuwa
61.	foot	'ân	'án
62.	four	yô:nu	só:nu
63.	freeze	-'o:yî:	-'o:yu
64.	fruit	be:	p'e:-'i
65.	full	p'íre	p'í:de
66.	give	-mǽgi	-mɛ́gi
67.	good	híwǫ́'	híwǫ́'i
68.	grass	tá:	tá
69.	green	cǎ̱wǽ̱'i	cǎ̱wɛ̱'i
70.	guts	si:	si:
71.	hair	ɸó	phó
72.	hand	man	man
73.	he[3]	'i'	'i
74.	head	p'ôn	p'ón
75.	hear	-t'o:	-t'o:
76.	heart	pín	pín
77.	heavy	-xá:	-khala
78.	here	næ:	né'ɛ
79.	hit	-xʷǽ̱ri	-kwɛ̱di
80.	hold	-ca̱:	-ca̱:la

81.	horn	sen	sen
82.	how	há:rí	hádídá
83.	hundred	tægintæ	tɛgintɛ
84.	hunt	-wó	-wo:'
85.	husband (spouse)	son[4]	on
86.	I	na:	na:
87.	ice	o:yí:	o:yi'
88.	if	-ráho'	gu
89.	in	íve, búge	íbe, múlúge
90.	kill	-he:	-hey
91.	knee	xų́mañæ	khųmele
92.	know	-ta:	-tay
93.	lake	p'okᵘ̂in	p'okwáy
94.	laugh	-p'âyi'	-p'áyi'
95.	leaf	ka:	ka:la
96.	left side	ñǽ'mængérí	yénédi
97.	leg	xų́:	khų́:
98.	lie	-k'ó	-k'ó
99.	live	-ɬa:	-tha:
100.	liver	hada	ha:la
101.	long	he'yi	heyi'in
102.	louse (flea)	šuwa	khyuwa
103.	man	sen	sen
104.	many	báyékí	máyén
105.	meat	tû:[5]	tú:
106.	moon	p'ó:	p'ó
107.	mother	yíyá	yíyá
108.	mountain	p'in	p'in
109.	mouth	só:	só:
110.	name	xą́wǽ	khą́wę́
111.	narrow	se:gi'	philigi'
112.	near	co'wa, nú'	cohwa, núlú

113.	neck	k'é:	k'é
114.	new	c'a̜:bi'	can'i
115.	night	xu̜:	khu̜:
116.	nose	šu	khyu
117.	not	yo:, wí-	yo, wé-
118.	old	-ke:yi:	-ke:yi
119.	one	wî'	wi'
120.	other	wíyá	wíyá
121.	person	t'owa	t'owa
122.	play	-'árâ:	-'á:ta
123.	pull	-ta̜æ:	-te̜le̜
124.	push	-se:	-map'egi
125.	rain	kwan	kwen
126.	red	p'î'	p'í'i
127.	right/correct	há'wa:	ha:wakan
128.	right side	kó'ríngérí	khódidí
129.	river	p'o'k'e:	p'o-maen
130.	road	p'ô:	p'ó:lo
131.	root	pú:	pú:
132.	rope	pa̜'[6]	pa̜'a̜
133.	rotten	-si:	-si:yɛ
134.	rub	-hu:	-hu:lu
135.	salt	'a̜:ñæ:	'a̜:yɛ:
136.	sand	'oxân	'okhán
137.	say	-tu̜	-tu̜
138.	scratch	-ma'c'æ:	-ma'c'ɛ
139.	sea	p'o:so'o	p'o-'akhon
140.	see	-mû'	-mún
141.	seed	tân, ko'yi	tán, koyi'
142.	seven	cé	cé
143.	sew	-pæn	-pɛlɛ
144.	sharp	-k'e:	-k'e
145.	shoot	-tón	-thón

146.	short	híñậ:'i'	-híyɛ:'i
147.	sing	-xa'wan	-khaw'an
148.	sister[7]	pá'rê:	pádéy
149.	sit	-ǽn	-ɛ́n
150.	skin	xowa	khowa
151.	sky	makówá	'ó:pa
152.	sleep	-yǫ́'k'ó:	-yóhk'ó
153.	small	hį́ñae'i	hįyɛ'i
154.	smell	-sun	-sun
155.	smoke	į:ñæ	į:yɛ
156.	spear	yúnɸé	yúmphé
157.	smooth	anae'i'	aya:we
158.	snake	pæ:nu	pɛyu:n
159.	snow	ɸon	phon
160.	some	wí, wên	wí, wên
161.	spit	-'ohɸe:	-'ophen
162.	split	-páve	-pábe
163.	squeeze	-ma'p'i	-ma'p'ili
164.	stab/pierce	-yún	-yun
165.	stand	-win	-wín
166.	star	agóyó	agáyó
167.	stick	ɸé	phé
168.	stone	k'u:	k'u
169.	straight	ta'ge	tayige'i
170.	suck[8]	-p'ohcǽ:	-p'ocɛ̧
171.	sun	ťan	than
172.	swell	-ti:	-ti:
173.	swim	-kohse:	-p'o-k'uwon
174.	tail	xʷǽn	khwén
175.	ten	(wé:mû:)tæ	(wému)tɛ̧
176.	that	hæ'i'	hɛ̧'i
177.	there	'i-we	'i'i-we
178.	they	'in	'in

179.	thick	k'a:'i'	k'ala-'i
180.	thin	t'a:'i'	t'a:-'i[9]
181.	think	'án-ša:	'án-khyaw
182.	this	næ'i'	nɛ́'i
183.	thou	'ʉ:-n	'ʉ:-n
184.	three	po:ye	poye
185.	throw	-čǽnu	-kyɛnu
186.	tie	-xʷi-'an	-kwí-'an
187.	tongue	hæn	hɛn
188.	tooth	wæ̣:	wɛ̣:
189.	tree	te:	te:
190.	turn	-bí:	-mí:li
191.	twenty	wétæ	wiyutɛ
192.	two	wíye	wíye
193.	vomit	-'enu	-'enu
194.	walk[10]	-ạhtuye	-'ạ'tuy
195.	warm	-súwá	-súwá
196.	wash	-'owiri	-'owí:di
197.	water	p'o:	p'o
198.	we	na'in	na:'in
199.	wet	-p'o:mu:	-p'ocimʉ
200.	what?	hán	hán
201.	when?	hæ̣:ri	he:yɛ
202.	where?	wǽhæ̣:	we:he
203.	white	c'æ'i'	c'ɛ́'i
204.	who?	toan	towan
205.	wide	ɸa:gi'	pha:lagi'i
206.	wife	kwiyó	kwiyó
207.	wind	wạ:	wạ:
208.	wing	k'un	k'un
209.	wipe	-píri	-pídí
210.	with	-árí	-ádí
211.	woman	kʷi:	kwiyó

LANGUAGE, HISTORY, AND IDENTITY

212.	woods	wǽ'k'a	wɛnk'a
213.	work	-t'ô:-'an	t'ó:lo-'an
214.	worm	puvǽ	pu̜:bɛ
215.	ye	'u̜'	'u̜:
216.	year	pa̜:yo	yo:ge[11]
217.	yellow	c'é:yi'	c'éy'i

NOTE: Cited Rio Grande Tewa (RGT) forms were provided by Randall and Anna Speirs. Unless otherwise noted, all RGT forms are in the San Juan Pueblo dialect. Arizona Tewa (AT) forms appear in the same orthography used elsewhere in the volume.

[1] The AT form is "it is not good."

[2] For "brother" I have substituted the term in the Tewa languages which means "younger sibling."

[3] This is "third person." The Tewa languages do not use gender distinguished forms like English "he," "she," and "it."

[4] The word for "spouse" which is more widely used in AT is a less common form in RGT.

[5] This is a Nambe Pueblo term. San Juan uses *pivi*.

[6] In RGT this term is restricted to thread or string.

[7] For "sister" I have substituted the form for "older sibling."

[8] In RGT this also means "to nurse" and "to kiss."

[9] Derived from "to dry."

[10] In RGT this word means "to step forward."

[11] In AT the primary meaning of this term is "summer."

■ ■ ■

A	agent
AC(T)	active prefix class
DEM	demonstrative
DIM	diminutive
du	dual person number (e.g., we two, you two, etc.)
E(MPH)	emphatic particle
EV	evidential particle
F(OC)	focus morpheme
FUT	future aspect
HAB	habitual aspect
HORT	hortative
INDEF	indefinite
INV	inverse prefix class
N	noun
NEG	negative
NP	noun phrase
OBL	oblique, or nonsubject, marker
PST	past tense
pl	plural (more than two) person number

POS	possessive morpheme
PRE	pronominal prefix
PRO	pronoun
REFL	reflexive/reciprocal prefix class
REL	relativizer or nominalizer
sg	singular person number
S	sentence
SUB	subordinate clause marker
TNS	tense-aspect marker
V	verb
VC	verb complex
1, 2, 3	person number as encoded by prefixes
1/3, etc.	first person acts on third person, etc.
I, II, III	person number of independent pronouns

■ ■ ■

NOTES

CHAPTER 1

1. The native text and its morpheme-by-morpheme translation appear below. Punctuation follows the translation. See the "Guide to Pronunciation of Tewa Terms" and the "Abbreviations Used in Tewa Glosses" for further details on orthographic and other representational conventions.

Kạyị-'iwe Kạyị-'iwe 'o:k'a 'akyan p'o-kwin na-k'ó,
far-there:at far there:at shell shake water-spring 3sgSTA-be
'iwɛ-dám-ba té:wa t'owa khú:lú-wokan wo:waci-in-kán
there-from:EMPH-EV Tewa people corn-bearing life-PL-with
ho 'íbí-khá:di-ma'a.
already 3plREFL-move-hither.
Kín ha:wan na:mbí senó: ho díbí-tụ́-ma'a.
This INDEF:EMPH I:POS elders already 3plREFL:say-hither
Kín ha:wan na:mbí sá:yá-'in ho díbí-tụ́-ma'a.
This INDEF:EMPH I:POS grandmother-PL already 3plREFL:say-hither.
He:dán kwɛn 'imbí hi:li-'an 'í:-t'ó-yan-di,
Then:EMPH if III:PL:POS word-EMPH 1plAC-listen-TNS-SUB
nɛwe sengi-tụ́ sígí-tụ́ wa:kan ho 'íbí-hụ́-mí!
here greet-word kind-word this HORT 1plREFL-live-OBLIG!

Wę̨hę̨ hę̨yáma nembí té:wa hi:li-yán ho 'i:-hų́-mí,
distance how I:PL:POS Tewa language-EMPH HORT 1plAC
wę̨hę̨ hę̨yáma na:-'in senó ho 'íbí:-ka-mí.
distance how I:PL elders HORT 1plREFL-live-OBLIG.
Kín ha:wan na:-bí 'ankhyaw déh-mún-dí na:-bí thété:-'e
This what I-POS thought 1sgSTA-see-SUB I-POS grandchild-DIM
na:-bí pápá:-'e ho de:-samɛ-'an.
I-POS great:grandchild-DIM already 1sgSTA-embrace-PERF.
Gasinewe:yan t'owa t'émɛ́ ho dí:-kwo-mí!
May-it-be people all HORT 3plSTA-live-OBLIG!

2. Scholars familiar with the literature on ethnicity may note a superficial similarity between the title of this section and that of a well-known article by my colleague Michael Moerman (1965)—"Who are the Lue: Ethnic Identification in a Complex Civilization." While the form of the title is indeed similar, the objectives of each associated work are quite different. In Moerman's article, the adequacy of conventional anthropological labels for specific ethnic groups is challenged in favor of a recognition of the multiplicity of situationally invoked social identities. Rather than viewing ethnic units as part of strictly anthropological practice, I am attempting to suggest the relative invisibility of the Arizona Tewa to nonanthropologists. In chapter 7, I examine Arizona Tewa data as evidence of the need for revising contemporary theories of ethnic identification.

3. *Hano* is the Hopi term for both the Arizona Tewa and their home village. It is most probably a loan from Tewa *Thanu*—the term which, according to Dozier (1951, 57), represents the self-designation of the older Tewa at the time of his initial fieldwork.

4. Especially pertinent to the resolution of this ethnohistorical problem is an accurate assessment of the "linguistic distance" between Arizona Tewa and the various New Mexican dialects. My ongoing comparative work, reported briefly in chapter 3, suggests that Arizona and Rio Grande Tewa, the cover term for the different dialects of Tewa spoken in various New Mexican Tewa pueblos, are now minimally divergent languages. In 1700, the Southern Tewa spoken in *Thanu* pueblos was probably even more like Rio Grande Tewa than Arizona Tewa is today. At that point Southern Tewa was simply a dialect of Rio Grande Tewa. Historical sources (Espinosa 1940, 76–80) also support this position.

5. The native term for San Cristobal appears in Dozier's transcription (which I would normalize to *c'ę́wa:de*, "White Band"). There are, however, competing alternatives to this place name that are current in Tewa Village. These include *c'ę́kwade* (White Line) and *c'ę́wa:ge* (White Sash). This latter form is preferred by Albert Yava and written as *Tsewageh* in his book.

6. For exhaustive description of the Pueblo Indians see such classic sources as Dozier (1951; 1954; 1966a; 1970), Ortiz (1969; 1972; 1979), and Eggan (1950).

7. The kiva serves as location for both sacred and mundane activities. When major ceremonies are performed there, priests will erect appropriate altars and reenact the emergence of humans. At other times the kiva serves as a men's club where men go to perform such solitary activities as weaving and sleeping or such joint activities as conversation and rehearsal for ceremonies.

8. For readers unfamiliar with the Hopi-Navajo border dispute, Kammer (1980) provides useful background. It should be noted, however, that this is a rather partisan account that seems considerably more sympathetic to the Navajo than to the Hopi.

9. The notion of culture brokers as culture-members who mediate between two cultures is discussed in such works as Wolf 1956, Geertz 1959, and Press 1969. The Arizona Tewa provide an especially interesting ethnographic application of the concept because of their participation/mediation in three cultures: Tewa, Hopi, and Euro-American.

10. Clifford specifies six ways in which ethnographic writing is determined: contextually, rhetorically, institutionally, generically, politically, and historically.

11. A dearth of theoretical options existed both in then contemporary theories of cultural change and of ethnicity. In the former, especially as applied to American Indian data, acculturation theory assumed a unilineal path from an intact, precontact culture through a period of cultural disorganization leading to complete assimilation. As for ethnicity, the emphasis on homogeneous sociocultural units as entities directed attention away from ethnographic confrontation with multiethnic societies (Cohen 1978, 381) and the theoretical challenges they embodied. Such theories provided Dozier with little of value in his attempt to understand a multiethnic society that defied characterization as either completely resistant or fully assimilated.

12. Discussions with Walter Goldschmidt and Alfonso Ortiz about Dozier's performance as a graduate student at UCLA and his relationship to his home community of Santa Clara, respectively, suggest that Dozier's own bicultural adaptation was characterized, at times, by self-conscious and somewhat limited participation. Dozier's critical regard for both his inherited cultures—the native culture of his Santa Clara mother and the Euro-American of his Franco-American father—clearly predisposed him to attend to similar critical voices in his own research.

13. Another source of evidence regarding Dozier's use of Arizona Tewa as a field language and the access to the native perspective that it may have provided emanates from the analysis of Arizona Tewa phonology revealed in his discussion of "orthography" in his monograph (Dozier 1954, 261–62). This analysis suggests that Dozier did not appreciate fundamental differences between the phon-

ologies of the two languages since he records many phonological units that exist in Santa Clara but not in Arizona Tewa and omits several distinctive Arizona Tewa phonemes that are not present in his analysis of Santa Clara Tewa (Hoijer and Dozier 1949). The flapped "r," for example, while quite prominent in Santa Clara does not exist in Arizona Tewa at either the phonetic or the more abstract phonemic level of analysis. Missing from his phonological inventory are the aspirated stops (ph, th, kh, kyh, kwh) as well as other phonemes like [hy] and [hw], which most linguists would attribute to Arizona Tewa. The overall pattern suggests that Dozier had an incomplete understanding of Arizona Tewa phonology and tended to confuse its distinctive properties with those found in his familiar native language. While the exact impact of this deficiency on his ability to use or process Arizona Tewa as a field language remains unclear, it further suggests the problematic nature of his use of Arizona Tewa in his research. This is significant since many anthropologists, like the Spindlers cited above, quickly dismiss this as a problem area because of Dozier's fluency in Santa Clara Tewa.

CHAPTER 2

1. Hymes (1983, 348) has warned that an attention to the "folk linguistics" of cultural groups, including ourselves, is methodologically advisable since its inattention promotes ignorance of terms and notions that have a potential relevance for linguistic research. We can further observe that such notions are important whether or not they are culturally shared or quite idiosyncratic. The Scollons's (Scollon 1979; Scollon and Scollon 1979) analysis of the descriptive efforts of Li and his Chipewyan consultant Mandeville demonstrates how their respective understandings of the goals of linguistic description contributed to the creation of a very artificial product. While Cook (1991) has challenged the interpretation of the general patterns of Chipewyan variability, preferring to view available data as evidence for intralinguistic divergence rather than linguistic convergence, his findings do not necessarily undermine the Scollons' interpretation of the Li-Mandeville collaboration.

2. -tų́ occurs as both a stative and transitive verb. In the latter form, -tų́—like hi:li—occurs with pronominal prefixes from any of three classes (inverse, active, and reflexive-reciprocal) and an auxiliary verb that encodes tense-aspect information (e.g., tų́-'an, "did," and tų́-'o, "doing").

3. See Kroskrity 1992, 305–7, for a discussion of a fourth dimension—the linguistic indexing of person. I have not chosen to develop this aspect further here because it is, to a considerable extent, redundant with the running theme of the volume concerning the use of language as a resource for creating and displaying identity.

4. Silverstein (1979, 193) identifies a "linguistic ideology" as "sets of beliefs about language articulated by the users as a rationalization or justification of perceived structure and use." It should also be noted that previous scholarship on Pueblo southwestern language attitudes fails to elucidate the cultural basis for its notorious "linguistic conservatism" and attributes this phenomenon to extreme ethnocentrism and a denigration of other, non-native languages.

5. This opposition between "power" and "solidarity" in language function can be traced back to Brown and Gilman (1960). While the dichotomy is too simplistic to capture the subtle manipulation of linguistic symbols that can characterize interpersonal interaction, it has proven to be of value at a more macro-level of analysis, where it is merely intended to reflect statistical norms. In addition to the reincarnation of the dichotomy here, readers can find its application to other multilingual situations in the works of Gal (1979) and Hill and Hill (1980, 1986) for the Austrian (Hungarian and German) and Mexicano (Nahuatl and Spanish) speech communities respectively.

6. This folk view, which emphasizes form over meaning and reduces meaning to reference, has obvious counterparts in academic linguistic theory and practice, as Silverstein suggests. This cultural critique cuts in two directions, simultaneously questioning the limited goals of contemporary theoretical paradigms and arguing for alternative models of linguistic inquiry based on other cultures of language.

7. A grammar, in linguistics, is conventionally understood as a descriptive device that systematically relates form and meaning. The focus on grammatical form has led to a relative neglect of such obviously integral parts of language as the lexicon and the sociocultural significance of grammatical forms and lexical items.

8. By "homogenized" here I mean language in which variation due to genres, stylistic levels, and interindividual differences has been ignored or minimized by research strategies.

CHAPTER 3

1. Some aspects of the internal classification of the Kiowa-Tanoan family of languages have been strongly influenced by the lack of complete documentation on all the relevant languages and the general history of scholarship on this family. Trager's view of Tiwa, for example, as the core of the Kiowa-Tanoan family, is perhaps best understood as the expected product of his having researched Taos Tiwa and knowing a great deal less about languages like Tewa and Towa. In recent years as new information has been generated and our knowledge reflects a more balanced documentation, the consensus among specialists has switched to a view of the family consisting of four coordinate branches.

2. For further discussion of the Arizona Tewa prefix system see relevant tables and discussion in chapter 4.

3. Arizona Tewa *bí* and Rio Grande Tewa *ví* are cognate grammatical morphemes. [b] and [v] are in free variation in Arizona Tewa. Since both Tewas have the morpheme, its entrance into the language must be traced to a point no later than immediately preceding the Spanish colonial occupation of the Rio Grande pueblos.

4. It is useful to remember that the Young and Morgan orthography in which Navajo is conventionally rendered is not equivalent to the phonemic orthography in which I am representing Arizona Tewa. In that orthography, for example, *b* is an unaspirated bilabial stop. Thus the phonetic proximity of the Navajo and Tewa forms is greater than their orthographic representations convey.

CHAPTER 4

1. Researchers who recall the pre-"translinguistic" 1970s (Hill and Hill 1986, 387–401), will remember the relative paucity of models for those of us who shared coordinate interests in sociolinguistic variation, ethnography, and grammatical description, yet found few genres in which these interests could be simultaneously engaged. In the presentation of this chapter I have opted for retaining much of the theoretical and methodological framing that was included in an earlier version of the present chapter (Kroskrity 1978b). The present version adds previously unpublished data on phonological and morphological variables and includes some clarifications and corrections not presented in the earlier study.

2. Among the other pragmatic factors that could be noted are lack of manpower, insufficient funds, unsympathetic speech communities, and so on. But perhaps the most important factor was simply the investigator's notion of problematicity. Most students of Native American languages have simply been more intrigued by problems of language structure.

3. A more complete discussion of the other variables can be found in Kroskrity 1977. In any event this list should not be construed as exhaustive: neither the Arizona Tewa account nor the analysis that constitutes the focus of this article adequately represents the full range of stylistic, or intrapersonal, variability that underlies members' interactional sociolinguistic competence. Since the phenomena under analysis here exhibit little stylistic variation within the speech of individual speakers, they can be best considered as manifestations of speakers' linguistic, not sociolinguistic, competence.

4. Though Randall H. and Anna Speirs have translated and published, through the Summer Institute of Linguistics, several introductory and missionary-related pamphlets in the Rio Grande Tewa dialect, these works had never reached the Arizona Tewa until I brought some representative samples with me in the

summer of 1975. No such popular publications have ever appeared in the Arizona dialect.

5. For example, the oldest word for "automotive vehicle" was *wá:-té:ge*—literally "wind wagon." This word has been replaced in the lexicons of all but the oldest (ninety years of age and older) speakers by /athu/, a phonemically retouched loan from English "auto." Today speakers up to thirty years of age simply use /kar/ when speaking in Tewa, despite the fact that [r] does not occur in Arizona Tewa at either the phonemic or phonetic level of analysis. Similarly, the native term for money—*kwɛk'u-c'ɛ́-'i* (metal-white-one) combined the concepts of "silver," "dollar," and "money"—has been replaced by /mani/ in the speech of younger members of the Arizona Tewa speech community.

6. For a discussion of gender-related variation, see Kroskrity (1983a), where gender-exclusive speech is discussed. Gender proved to be insignificant in all structural measures discussed here. The prominence of gender in folk accounts of variation is undoubtedly based on its salience in ceremonial speech.

7. My use of nonsyntactic/semantic criteria to rank speakers was, in part, an attempt to detail for the reader those linguistic manifestations that first suggested the relevance of age as an explanatory variable. In this regard this practice resembles David DeCamp's use of "scaling"—a practice which, as DeCamp (1971, 355) argues, permits the discovery of unanticipated social variables. This is accomplished by initially ranking isolects solely in accord with linguistic criteria and then interpreting whatever sociocultural patterns may be manifested by these rankings. All ages refer to age when first recorded in the initial four years of the project. Lexical replacement is measured by using the basic word list reproduced in appendix 1.

8. By "no fluency" in noncasual speech, I mean no generative capacity. In regard to song and narrative production I mean the ability to not only repeat and decode previously composed songs and oral texts but to also compose new songs and narratives in the traditional style. This kind of command is characteristically possessed solely by speakers fifty years of age and older. For the purpose of the present study knowledge of a person's command of the subcode was evidenced by two or more of the following: (1) actual public performance of self-composed songs (as in a secular dance like the *ya:niwɛ*) and chants, (2) the ability to spontaneously perform and explain songs/song texts to the analyst, (3) the ability to translate secular, hence exoteric, song and story texts, (4) reports on the behavior and linguistic knowledge of the ceremonial subcode of individuals by key consultants representing each of the two kiva groups, and (5) a person's self-report regarding his or her command of the ceremonial subcode.

9. For a discussion of this phenomenon consult Yegerlehner 1957, 14.

10. These samples consisted of data collected in the following ways: (1) hearing and later noting sentences containing the problematic phenomena that oc-

curred in conversations in which the analyst was either a participant or an audience member—this of course presupposed an unassisted understanding of the relevant Tewa utterance by the investigator. (2) Where such an understanding did not occur but an instance of the problematic phenomenon was noted by the analyst, the utterance was collectively reconstituted by participating native speaker consultants and the linguist shortly after the event occurred. (3) Several families recorded their own speech during various everyday situations while the analyst was entirely absent. Conditional use of these tapes was then granted to the analyst.

11. I offer the quantitative data in tables 4.2 and 4.5 more as a demonstration than as an attempt to approximate the rigorous statistical measures and probabilistic models of the "quantitative paradigm" within sociolinguistics (e.g., Sankoff 1974; Labov 1972b; 1980; Cedergren and Sankoff 1974). The nature of my field situation made the prerequisites of such analysis—a large and random sample—impossible to achieve. My sample is, in contrast, a small convenience sample carefully selected to best represent the age groups and genders. I follow Guy (1980) and Hill and Hill (1986, 71) in claiming the inapplicability of using large, random samples to collect the data in small face-to-face speech communities.

12. [ná] and [wá] are allomorphs of /-á-/, the focal emphatic, which are derived by morphophonemic rule. For further details see Kroskrity 1977.

13. There are other technical considerations that are often used to distinguish passives and inverses. In addition to the transitivity previously mentioned, inverses are typically obligatory when a speech act participant (first or second person) is affected by a third person agent. Also inverses do not typically suppress or reduce the topicality of agents, though they do semantically foreground the patient. Additional details about the inverse can also be found in my treatment of "functional-semantic" passives in Kroskrity 1985a.

14. Possessive verbs in Tewa are actually stative verb stems ("sit," "stand," "be," etc.) preceded by a possessive prefix. Recall discussion in chapter 3 and see Speirs 1974 for a treatment of this and related phenomena.

15. The actual measures presented here represent only a small portion of the potential linguistic indicators I investigated. In phonology, I briefly studied word final [n]/[ŋ] alternations and variation involving the alternation of [e] and [ɛ]. In morphology, I studied the nonsingular (either dual or plural) suffix, adverbial prefixes, and tense-aspect suffixes. In syntax-semantics I studied surface word order and postpositions. They are not reported here for a variety of reasons: the variation was either strictly idiosyncratic, insignificant, or insufficiently sampled.

16. As in other western pueblos, many Arizona Tewa offer a folk account of why some children grow up without significant exposure to the Tewa language by saying that "there aren't enough grandparents to go around." Neolocal resi-

dence, an increasingly prevalent pattern in Tewa Village and Polacca, certainly has had an impact in reducing this intergenerational contact. But modern pressures from the cash economy actually often reverse this impact. In many cases, as where both parents must work away from their home, children are usually deposited with the grandparents for adult supervision.

17. As Nagata (1971) has correctly observed, the choice really is not binary anymore. As his work at Moenkopi suggests, much of the Hopi Reservation and environs are undergoing a suburbanization. The Arizona Tewa of Tewa Village, Polacca, and Keams Canyon receive broadcasts, telecasts, and newspapers from such cities as Flagstaff, Winslow, Holbrook, Phoenix, and Gallup (New Mexico). As consumers they contribute significantly to the economy of the neighboring towns and have become dependent on them for the provision of various goods and services. There are three choices open to young people: urban migration, reservation residence and adoption of a traditional lifestyle, and reservation residence and adoption of a nontraditional lifestyle. This last alternative simply represents a continuation of trends initiated by the previous generations—trends that are consistently bringing to the First Mesa area, as well as to the entire Hopi Reservation, an unprecedented degree of cultural pluralism.

18. See Sherzer and Bauman 1972 for a discussion of areal linguistic research.

CHAPTER 5

1. The characterization as "deterministic" of any theory that views an idiolect as representative of the speech community's speech follows Milroy and Margrain's (1980, 43) summary of structuralist practice. For a similar criticism of the generativist position see Fillmore (1979, 86).

2. I say "partial" here for two reasons. One, many life histories perpetuate an uncritical preoccupation with "typical" cultural members, implicitly invoking an isomorphism between individuals and their cultures. Two, many life histories are not presented as analyzed anthropological documents but more as raw data in need of further investigation (Langness 1965; Frank 1978).

3. It would be wrong to suggest that the disinterest in the individual, on the part of sociolinguists, is either utterly unmotivated or complete. In Labov's (1972b) own work, for example, we find that the focal emphasis on language change and the diachronic interest that it implies does militate against a central preoccupation with the linguistic behavior of individuals. Even despite this alternative focus, Labov has devoted considerable peripheral attention to individual variation (as summarized in Labov 1979).

4. Intellectual similarities here are not accidental. Though a sociologist, Blumer did attend courses offered by Sapir at the University of Chicago (Hill 1988).

5. Here and later, in the conclusions, I mean the concept of the reference

group as expounded by the Chicago rather than the Iowa school of symbolic interactionism. The major difference between the two is that the former is phenomenological whereas the latter is positivist.

6. Certain notable exceptions can, however, be acknowledged (e.g., Friedrich and Redfield 1978; Hill 1985; 1988; and Hymes 1981). Alton Becker (personal communication) is currently undertaking another sort of lingual history (of Emerson).

7. This shortcoming of correlational sociolinguistics is well known (Bickerton 1973, 17; Gumperz 1982a, 29). It should be emphasized that this deficiency does not invalidate the detection of correlations or stable norms. Instead, such norms must be understood as a means rather than an end of sociolinguistic understanding. Certainly, insofar as using sociolinguistics as a means for understanding social as well as linguistic phenomena, no explanation can be considered comprehensive without appealing to the meanings that individuals assign to aspects of language use.

8. Though I applaud work in the "dialogical tradition" as described by Dennis Tedlock (1979), limitations of this approach make strict adherence to it unwise here. Though I agree that anthropologists would profit from research and publication strategies that emphasize the role of the interaction between anthropologists and native consultants in constituting the data and shaping the analysis, two limitations of dialogical work may be noted. First, the texts produced by such dialogical relations cannot provide a self-contained object of analysis. As Cicourel (1980, 117) has observed of the dangers of a discourse focus on texts: "A problem that all researchers must face when examining discourse materials in which the participant creates a history of past relationships is that each participant relies on the other's knowledge of their respective biographies." A second problem, one shared by other linguistic anthropological perspectives such as ethnoscience and its various reincarnations, is the relative exclusion of nonverbal communication. Between anthropologist and consultant, as between members of the same group, learning occurs not only through explicit verbal instruction but also by omnivorous inference.

9. In the brief lingual life histories that follow, the names of the three exceptional individuals have been fictionalized, in accord with their requests, to conceal their identities from those outside the community. Each individual read and edited his lingual life history, pruning any details he deemed too private.

10. This runs counter to the traditional norm of matrilocal residence but this type of flexibility, first noted in seasonal or temporary residences (Dozier 1954, 312), has become increasingly common for permanent residences as well.

11. These criteria, discussed in chapter 4, include code-switching, lexical replacement in conversation, knowledge of the ceremonial subcode, and observa-

tion of a morphophonemic rule that assimilates the vowel of the negative morpheme to the vowel of the following pronominal prefix.

12. Dan's words in the passages that follow are translations. Multivocal native terms are introduced parenthetically where concise translation is difficult. Underlined English terms were originally inserted by Dan in his otherwise Tewa response.

13. The reference is to his grandfather's afterlife as a kachina spirit. Elevated to the level of the supernatural, his grandfather can now view proceedings in Tewa Village in the form of a cloud. It is significant to note that the Arizona Tewa term is polysemous: *okhuwa* means both "cloud" and "kachina."

14. In the tightly ordered cosmos of the Arizona Tewa, like that of other Pueblo groups, misfortune must be meticulously accounted for as something other than mere coincidence. For some Arizona Tewa, especially older individuals, "witchcraft" still provides an explanation for illness, injury, and general misfortune (Dozier 1966a, 82).

15. The word translated as "police" is semantically extended from the native term for "scalp" or "war chief." This preference for native language encoding is characteristic of Dan's speech as it is of most older (e.g., group 3) speakers.

16. My use of "forceful" is borrowed from Geertz's (1968, 111) original application to Islamic religious adherence. Like him, I mean "the thoroughness with which such a pattern is intertwined in the personalities of the individuals who adopt it, its centrality or marginality in their lives," but I apply it to more secular emotions.

17. The Colorado River Reservation on the border of Arizona and California is home to a number of Arizona Tewa, Hopi, and Indians of other tribes. Another notable Arizona Tewa individual who also chose to retire there was Albert Yava, whose life history (Yava 1979; Kroskrity 1983b) is the only existing (partially) autobiographical account of any Arizona Tewa individual.

18. Here Ned simulates one of the formulaic beginnings of an Arizona Tewa personal or historical narrative of the *wowa:ci* genre. The key, or tone, is a mock parody.

19. By "kin" I mean both genealogical and fictive kinsmen.

20. In sociolinguistic practice, attention to the subjective factors has been inconsistent. Many have sought to avoid such considerations because of adherence to positivist canons of objectivity. Yet the importance of such factors cannot be minimized. Even Labov, hardly preoccupied with interpretive sociology, attributes evidence of reciprocal influence of black and white speech patterns to situations where there is daily contact and "the cultural values of the opposing groups are recognized and viewed as accessible" (Labov 1980, 264).

21. "Scope," like "force," is adapted from Geertz (1968, 111) and refers to the range of contexts in which some value or belief applies.

CHAPTER 6

1. Tedlock has noted this association of storytelling and agriculture for other Native American groups, including those of the Southwest.

2. The creation of an "authoritative" storytelling voice for traditional narrators in Tewa has some similarities to the "textualizing devices" used by Weyewa (Indonesia) and their function "to detach discourse from the immediate constraints of utterance and attach it to a shared, coherent, and authoritative tradition" (Kuipers 1990, 71). Of course the two traditions differ dramatically in the textual and contextual conventions that are culturally required. The most important contextual contrast is the fact that the Weyewa context is formal ritual whereas the Tewa is mundane and domestic.

3. Though native speakers judge isolated sentences consisting of only dependent clauses as less than maximally complete or well-formed, such sentences do occasionally occur in narrative texts of all types.

4. The Arizona Tewa notion of "carrying" the narrative hither resembles certain Zuni practices, mentioned by Tedlock (1983, 168–69) of both a frame-preserving and a frame-breaking nature. The importance of situating the stories in a culturally familiar landscape—one aspect of this principle—is also typical of Western Apache *'agodzaahi'* (Basso 1984) and traditional myths and stories of the Zuni (Tedlock 1983, 165) and the Eastern Pomo (McLendon 1977, 162).

5. In Sherzer's (1982) discussion of the Kuna line, he also finds a quotative to be a common line-final element. The resemblance, however, is somewhat superficial since the Kuna "say" verb—unlike Tewa *ba*, Hopi *yaw*, and Navajo *jini*—appears only in actual instances of quotation.

6. As mentioned in chapter 3, there is some evidence suggesting that Arizona Tewa *ba* has assumed some of the characteristics of Hopi *yaw* through linguistic diffusion. See also Kroskrity (1985c) for related discussion.

7. This association of "particle" and "pause" with the work of Hymes and Tedlock, respectively, is hardly novel here. It is suggested by Hymes's (1980) own analysis of the differences and Tedlock's somewhat ratifying rejoinder (1983, 56–61). My contention is that these metonyms focus undue attention on disparate principles of versification, obscuring the fundamentally different, even complementary, analytical objectives of these approaches to verbal art. The recognition of this complementarity and of other necessary levels of ethnopoetic analysis has become a generally accepted position by anthropological and linguistic students of verbal art. See, for example, the individual contributions of Sherzer and Woodbury 1987. Hymes (1992) himself has criticized such a simplistic interpretation of his work.

8. The use of *ba* as a segmental marker of the narrative voice may correspond

in function to the expressive use of intonation and vowel lengthening of Zuni narrators (Tedlock 1983, 41) in what I have referred to as marking the otherwise unmarked voice of the narrator. Arizona Tewa narrators very rarely use such prosodic devices except in the voice of a story character.

9. It is also noteworthy that this version omits the second "complaint," in which the younger sibling reciprocates consoling and encouraging words at a time when the older becomes discouraged.

10. The "older sister" is an especially important kin category for the Arizona Tewa. It is the only kinship term that represents a borrowed term (from Hopi), as discussed in chapter 3. See Dozier (1966a, 50) for extended discussion of the rights and duties associated with this kin category.

11. *'ó:wę́:hę:yámba* is the most typical introduction to stories in this genre. Its morphology, unlike that of most Arizona Tewa words, is not completely transparent. *'ó:wę́:* (away yonder) + *he:* [reduced form of *hęyę*] (long ago) + *yán* [*emphatic*] + *ba* [*evidential*]. As in the translation of a previous story (Kroskrity and Healing 1980), I am translating all constituents suffixed by the *emphatic* as loud or stressed in the English translation, indicating this through the use of upper case letters. Though these words do not receive a comparable prosodic treatment in the Tewa original, the emphatic particle provides the segmental functional equivalent of focal stress placement and contrastive stress in English. Scollon and Scollon (1981, 29) have noted the discourse significance of Athabaskan segments that are functionally equivalent to grammatical prosody in English, further lending support to this translation practice. See also Woodbury (1985) for a parallel acknowledgment that the effect of prosodic systems rather than mere reproduction of some overt features (like volume or stress) need to be attended to in matters of translation and ethnopoetic analysis. Another important aspect of *genre*, as Duranti (1983) has observed, is the range of variation found in performance within varied contexts.

12. This is the only line in which *ba* does not occur in narrative voice. It is pause-marked and in reviewing a recording of the story, the narrator—Dewey Healing—inserted one as he repeated the verse during the ancillary elicitations conducted while preparing the text. I leave it for the reader to decide whether this omission is dramatically motivated or merely represents a "performance error."

13. The song is sung in "modified" Hopi: "Birds, Birds; prepare yourselves; Fly! Fly! Fly! Fly!"

14. Both *némáhá* and *guba* (line 63) are among those terms usually described as *hęyę tų́* (archaic words).

15. Though these stories are often referred to as "coyote stories" (e.g., Bright 1978; Kendall 1980) the folk titles typically highlight the protagonists from the

Arizona Tewa point of view. As one who is extremely gullible especially in attempting to be something he is not, Old Man Coyote represents the antithesis of many Tewa values.

16. In this story my treatment of *ba* differs from translation practices adopted in Kroskrity and Healing 1980, where it is treated as a line marker but given no segmental translation. Here each occurrence of "so" in the English translation corresponds to Tewa *ba* in order to call attention to its role in the Tewa text—an appropriate objective given both the focus of the present chapter and the general ethnopoetic value on preserving, in translation, the structural parallelism of the original. Only in its initial appearance is the particle *ba* translated as "so they say"—a translation that captures its evidential meaning. Other occurrences of the more codable "so" are meant to be understood as an abbreviation of this expression. Since consistent translation of *ba* as "so they say" would be overly obtrusive, the present practice was adopted as a compromise between semantic fidelity and an attempt to capture its ethnopoetic function.

CHAPTER 7

1. The Pueblo conception of warfare and associated violence differs significantly from its Euro-American counterpart. See Ortiz (1972) for an attempt to unravel some of this cultural complexity.

2. The dichotomy between "social" and "sacred" dances is general to all southwestern Pueblos. In most, the latter involves the masked impersonation of kachinas, or spirit-beings, by initiated men.

3. The difference in advance notice depends on whether the "long" or "short" versions of the ritual will be performed. These take sixteen and eight days, respectively. In recent practice the shorter form has been preferred even when there are a sufficient number of boys to warrant initiation.

4. For examples of the scholarly tradition—largely summaries of ethnohistorical sources—see Spicer (1962, 162), Dozier (1961, 123ff.), and Schroeder (1979, 247–48).

5. Dozier (1951, 57) reports that at the time of his fieldwork the oldest Tewa Village residents used the term *Tano* as a self-designation in tracing their ancestry to New Mexico. The term itself was also adopted by the Spanish from Northern Rio Grande Tewa. *Tano* is simply an abbreviated form of *than-núge-'in t'owa*, literally "southern people," referring to the Southern Tewa. As Dozier (1951, 62) has observed, the term is currently devalued by the Arizona Tewa and applied to such non-Tewa groups as Sichomovi Hopi from the Mustard (*asa*) Clan and others who are considered to be relatively recent immigrants who had no part in the military defense of Hopi lands.

6. Approximately one-fourth of my code-switching data were self-recorded

by key consultants when I was not present. The remaining examples were either recorded and/or observed by me. Except for interviews with me, I was defined as a nonparticipant by the Arizona Tewa who were involved in these instances. None of the examples cited in this chapter derive from these semiformal interviews.

7. Excluded from what I am terming here as "code-switching" behavior are (1) use of loanwords that show phonological integration into Arizona Tewa and (2) direct quotes from non-Tewa-speaking others.

8. According to the Hopi constitution, traditional chiefs must approve councilmen elected from those villages over which the chiefs have authority.

9. I have observed this to be true of some *yani:we* songs performed in social dances since 1980.

10. This imitative joking is similar to Western Apache imitations of Euro-Americans in that both "contrast" and "distortion" principles (Basso 1979, 44–45) are analytically identifiable. Arizona Tewa imitations of Hopis often select the highly visible "traditionalists." As an element of "distortion," the speech of these impersonated Hopis is often delivered with exaggerated pitch elevation and movement as if in imitation of chanting styles. The disconnected phrases also exaggerate the perceived incoherence of these speakers, playing upon a stereotype of the Hopi as reluctant talkers who are ill-prepared for speech-making.

11. The appropriateness of the repertoire imagery that I am suggesting here is implied by Fischer's use of "interference" and "inter-reference" (Fischer 1986, 218–19).

12. As demonstrated in chapters 4 and 5, significant variation does exist in the speech community regarding code-switching behavior and the role of English. The patterns discussed here derive from group 2 and 3 speakers. Many younger speakers, especially those whose reference group consists of their peers, do not display metaphorical code-switching but only minimal situational code-switching.

13. This lack is somewhat surprising since Dozier's (1956) own study of differing patterns of linguistic acculturation among the Yaqui and the Rio Grande Tewa makes effective use of the notion of "compartmentalization" in explaining differential linguistic diffusion in these multilingual, contact situations. In retrospect it appears that he was not able to recognize analogous patterns in regard to processes of identification.

14. According to this evaluation metric, one can readily fault studies such as Giles et al. 1977, which fails to construct a theoretical framework capable of guiding future research into what they see as the neglected issues of ethnic "maintenance" versus "divergence" (p. 322).

15. It is appropriate to note that John Galaty (1982) has devised an alternative *linguistic* model in confronting the problem of ethnic identification among the Maasai. It is true that his analogy to "pragmatic shifters" that always involve "some aspect of the context in which the sign occurs" (Silverstein 1976, 11)

avoids the undesirable decontextualized and homogeneous imagery often associated with linguistic models. But his resulting notion of "ethnic shifters" is comparatively deficient in at least two ways. One, it does not address the issue of
ethnic versus other social identities, failing to provide a unified framework for
these related phenomena. Two, the imagery appeals more to a general context
than to the situated choice of the speaker, providing more of a focus on the
"when" than the "why" of identification than does the model I am proposing
here. A similar criticism can be leveled at other attempts to use semiotic imagery
as in Ochs's (1992) otherwise successful discussion about how socialization practices can be "indexed" to gender. While semiotic frameworks implicitly assume
the perspective of an "interpretant," they seem better suited to elucidate symbolic
systems than to capture the agency of social actors. This tendency for semiotic
models to neglect human agency in favor of a structural system has been noted
by Giddens (1984, 31).

CHAPTER 8

1. The views attributed to Wick Miller are those contained in the cited 1978
article and not those he currently holds. Partially as a result of our own discussions over the years, Wick Miller's current position closely approximates my
own as his most recent treatment of language attitudes clearly shows (Silver and
Miller MS).

2. Kenneth Hill is currently leading a team of investigators which will produce a definitive dictionary for Hopi. Unfortunately the lexicographical standards
for all other Pueblo Indian languages continue to lag far behind with many not
even documented by a word-list type dictionary. The only Tewa dictionary remains Esther Martinez's (1983) *San Juan Pueblo Dictionary.*

3. My use of "marked" language choice converges with a similar use by Scotton
(1988, 160).

. . .

BIBLIOGRAPHY

ABERLE, DAVID
1968   The Influence of Linguistics on Early Culture and Personality Theory.
        In *Theory in Anthropology*, ed. R. A. Manners and D. Kaplan, 303–17.
        Chicago: Aldine.

AGAR, MICHAEL
1980   Stories, Background Knowledge and Themes: Problems in the Analysis
        of Life History Narrative. *American Ethnologist* 7:223–39.

ALBERT, ROY, AND DAVID LEEDOM SHAUL
1985   *A Concise Hopi and English Lexicon*. Amsterdam: John Benjamins.

ANNAMALAI, E.
1989   The Linguistic and Social Dimensions of Purism. In *The Politics of
        Language Purism*, ed. B. H. Jernudd and M. Shapiro, 225–31. Berlin:
        Mouton.

ARNON, NANCY S., AND W. W. HILL
1979   Santa Clara Pueblo. In *Southwest*, volume 9, *Handbook of North Amer-
        ican Indians*, ed. A. Ortiz, 296–307. Washington, D.C.: Smithsonian.

BAILEY, CHARLES-JAMES N.
1974   *Variation in Linguistic Theory*. Arlington, Va.: Center for Applied Lin-
        guistics.

BAILEY, J. B.
1940   *Diego de Vargas and the Reconquest of New Mexico*. Albuquerque:
        University of New Mexico Press.

BAKHTIN, M. M.

1981   *The Dialogic Imagination,* tr. Caryl Emerson and Michael Holquist. Austin: University of Texas Press.

1986   *Speech Genres and Other Late Essays,* tr. Vern W. McGee. Austin: University of Texas Press.

BARNES, J. A.

1954   Class and Committees in a Norwegian Island Parish. *Human Relations* 7:24–47.

BARTH, FREDRIK

1969   *Ethnic Groups and Boundaries.* Boston: Little, Brown, and Company.

1972   Ethnic Processes on the Pathan-Baluch Boundary. In *Directions in Sociolinguistics,* ed. J. J. Gumperz and D. H. Hymes, 454–64. New York: Holt, Rinehart and Winston.

BASSO, KEITH H.

1979   *Portraits of "the Whiteman."* Cambridge: Cambridge University Press.

1984   "Stalking With Stories": Names, Places, and Moral Narratives Among the Western Apache. In *Text, Play, and Story: The Construction of Self and Society,* ed. E. M. Bruner, 19–55. (Proceedings of the American Ethnological Society). Washington, D.C.: The American Ethnological Society.

BATESON, GREGORY

1972   *Steps to an Ecology of Mind.* New York: Ballantine.

BAUMAN, RICHARD

1975   Verbal Art as Performance. *American Anthropologist* 77:290–311.

1986   *Story, Performance, and Event.* Cambridge University Press.

BAUMAN, RICHARD, AND CHARLES L. BRIGGS

1990   Poetics and Performance as Critical Perspectives on Language and Social Life. *Annual Review of Anthropology* 19:59–88.

BECKER, A. L.

1979   Text-building, Epistemology, and Aesthetics in Javanese Shadow Theatre. In *The Imagination of Reality,* ed. A. L. Becker and A. A. Yengoyan, 211–43. Norwood, N.J.: ABLEX.

1984   Biography of a Sentence: A Burmese Proverb. In *Text, Play, and Story: The Construction of Self and Society,* ed. E. M. Bruner, 135–55. Washington, D.C.: The American Ethnological Society.

1988   Attunement: An Essay on Philology and Logophilia. In *On the Ethnography of Communication: The Legacy of Sapir,* ed. P. V. Kroskrity, 109–46. Los Angeles: University of California, Los Angeles, Department of Anthropology.

BEN-AMOS, DAN
1976   Analytical Categories and Ethnic Genres. In *Folklore Genres*, ed. D. Ben-Amos, 215–42. Austin: University of Texas Press.

BERNSTEIN, BASIL
1971   *Class, Codes, and Control*. Volume 1. London: Routledge and Kegan Paul.

BICKERTON, DEREK
1973   The Structure of Polylectal Grammars. In *Georgetown University Round Table on Languages and Linguistics*, ed. R. Shuy, 17–42. Washington, D.C.: Georgetown University Press.

BLACK, ROBERT A.
1967   Hopi Grievance Chants: A Mechanism of Social Control. In *Studies in Southwestern Ethnolinguistics*, ed. D. Hymes and W. Bittle, 54–67. The Hague: Mouton.

BLOCH, BERNARD
1948   A Set of Postulates for Phonemic Analysis. *Language* 24:3–46.

BLOM, JAN-PETER, AND JOHN J. GUMPERZ
1972   Code-switching in Norway. In *Directions in Sociolinguistics*, ed. J. J. Gumperz and D. H. Hymes, 407–34. New York: Holt, Rinehart and Winston.

BLOOM, L. B.
1931   A Campaign Against the Moqui Pueblos. *New Mexico Historical Review*. 6:158–276.

BLOOMFIELD, LEONARD
1933   *Language*. New York: Holt, Rinehart and Winston.

BLU, KAREN I.
1980   *The Lumbee Problem: The Making of an American Indian People*. Cambridge: Cambridge University Press.

BLUMER, HERBERT
1962   Society as Symbolic Interaction. In *Human Behavior and Social Processes*, ed. A. M. Rose, 179–92. Boston: Houghton-Mifflin.
1969   *Symbolic Interactionism, Perspective and Method*. Englewood Cliffs, N.J.: Prentice-Hall.

BODINE, JOHN J.
1968   Taos Names: A Clue to Linguistic Acculturation. *Anthropological Linguistics* 10:23–27.

BOTT, ELIZABETH
1957   *Family and Social Network*. London: Tavistock.

BRANDT, ELIZABETH A.

1970a   Sandia Pueblo, New Mexico: A Linguistics and Ethnolinguistics Investigation. Unpublished Doctoral Dissertation, Southern Methodist University.

1970b   On the Origins of Linguistic Stratification. *Anthropological Linguistics* 12:46–51.

1980   On Secrecy and Control of Knowledge. In *Secrecy: A Cross-cultural Perspective*, ed. S. Teft, 123–46. New York: Human Science Press.

1981   Native American Attitudes Toward Literacy and Recording in the Southwest. *Journal of the Linguistics Association of the Southwest* 4:185–95.

1988   Applied Linguistic Anthropology and American Indian Language Renewal. *Human Organization* 47:322–29.

BRICKER, VICTORIA R.

1974   Some Cognitive Implications of Informant Variability in Zinacanteco Speech Classification. *Language in Society* 3:69–82.

BRIGGS, CHARLES L.

1988   *Competence in Performance: The Creativity of Tradition in Mexicano Verbal Art*. Philadelphia: University of Pennsylvania Press.

BRIGHT, WILLIAM.

1978   *Coyote Stories* (International Journal of American Linguistics Native American Texts Series, Monograph no. 1). Ann Arbor, Mich.: University Microfilms.

1979   A Karok Myth in "Measured Verse": The Translation of Performance. *Journal of California and Great Basin Anthropology, Papers in Linguistics* 1:117–23.

1980   Coyote Gives Salmon and Acorns to Humans (Karok). In *Coyote Stories II* (International Journal of American Linguistics Native American Texts Series, Monograph no. 6), ed. M. B. Kendall, 46–55. Ann Arbor, Mich.: University Microfilms.

BROWN, PENELOPE, AND STEPHEN L. LEVINSON

1978   Universals in Language Usage: Politeness Phenomena. In *Questions and Politeness*, ed. E. N. Goody, 56–289. Cambridge: Cambridge University Press.

BROWN, ROGER, AND ALBERT GILMAN

1960   The Pronouns of Power and Solidarity. In *Style in Language*, ed. T. A. Sebeok, 253–76. Cambridge: M.I.T. Press.

BIBLIOGRAPHY

BRUGGE, DAVID M.
1969   Pueblo Factionalism and External Relations. *Ethnohistory* 16:191–200.

BRUNER, EDWARD M.
1973   The Missing Tins of Chicken: A Symbolic Interactionist Approach to Culture Change. *Ethos* 1:219–38.

BURKE, KENNETH
1950   *A Rhetoric of Motives*. New York: Prentice-Hall.

CASAGRANDE, JOSEPH B.
1948   Comanche Baby Language. *International Journal of American Linguistics* 14:11–14.

CEDERGREN, HENRIETTA, AND DAVID SANKOFF
1974   Variable Rules: Performance as a Statistical Reflection of Competence. *Language* 50:333–55.

CHOMSKY, NOAM
1965   *Aspects of the Theory of Syntax*. Cambridge: M.I.T. Press.
1972   *Language and Mind*. New York: Harcourt Brace Jovanovich.

CICOUREL, AARON V.
1980   Three Models of Discourse Analysis: The Role of Social Structure. *Discourse Processes* 3:101–32.

CLIFFORD, JAMES A.
1983   On Ethnographic Authority. *Representations* 1:118–45.
1986a   Introduction: Partial Truths. In *Writing Culture*, ed. J. Clifford and G. E. Marcus, 1–26. Berkeley: University of California Press.
1986b   On Ethnographic Allegory. In *Writing Culture*, ed. J. Clifford and G. E. Marcus, 98–121. Berkeley: University of California Press.

CLIFFORD, JAMES A., AND GEORGE E. MARCUS
1986   *Writing Culture*. Berkeley: University of California Press.

COHEN, RONALD
1978   Ethnicity: Problem and Focus in Anthropology. *Annual Review of Anthropology* 7:379–403.

COLE, PETER
1976   The Interface of Theory and Description. *Language* 52:563–84.

COMRIE, BERNARD
1981   *Language Universals and Linguistic Typology*. Chicago: University of Chicago Press.

COOK, EUNG-DO
1991   Linguistic Divergence in Fort Chipewyan. *Language in Society* 20: 423–40.

CORDELL, LINDA S.
1979   Prehistory: Eastern Anasazi. In *Southwest*, volume 9, *Handbook of North American Indians*, ed. A. Ortiz, 131–51. Washington, D.C.: Smithsonian.

CRAWFORD, JAMES M.
1970   Cocopa Baby Talk. *International Journal of American Linguistics* 36: 9–13.

CREAMER, MARY HELEN
1974   Ranking in Navajo Nouns. *Diné Bizaad Nániljih/Navajo Language Review* 1:29–39.

CRYSTAL, DAVID
1971   Prosodic and Paralinguistic Correlates of Social Categories. In *Social Anthropology and Language*, ed. E. Ardener, 185–209. London: Tavistock.

CUSHING, FRANK HAMILTON
1979   *Zuni: Selected Writings of Frank Hamilton Cushing*. Lincoln: University of Nebraska Press.

DAVIS, IRVINE
1959   Linguistic Clues to Northern Rio Grande Prehistory. *El Palacio* 66: 73–84.
1979   The Kiowa-Tanoan, Keresan, and Zuni Languages. In *The Languages of Native America: Historical and Comparative Assessment*, ed. L. Campbell and M. Mithun, 390–443. Austin: University of Texas Press.

DECAMP, DAVID
1971   Toward a Generative Analysis of a Post-creole Speech Continuum. In *Pidginization and Creolization of Languages*, ed. D. H. Hymes, 349–70. Cambridge: Cambridge University Press.

DENISON, N.
1971   Some Observations on Language Variety and Plurilingualism. In *Social Anthropology and Language*, ed. E. Ardener, 157–85. London: Tavistock.

DORIAN, NANCY
1978   The Fate of Morphological Complexity in Language Death: Evidence from East Sutherland Gaelic. *Language* 54:590–609.
1981   *Language Death*. Philadelphia: University of Pennsylvania Press.
1989   *Investigating Obsolescence: Studies in Language Contraction and Death*. Cambridge: Cambridge University Press.

DOWNS, JAMES F.
1972   *The Navajo*. New York: Holt, Rinehart and Winston.

DOZIER, EDWARD P.
1951   Resistance to Acculturation and Assimilation in an Indian Pueblo. *American Anthropologist* 53:56–66.
1954   *The Hopi-Tewa of Arizona* (University of California Publications in American Archaeology and Ethnology, 44[3]:257–376). Berkeley: University of California Press.
1955   Kinship and Linguistic Change Among the Arizona Tewa. *International Journal of American Linguistics* 21:242–57.
1956   Two Examples of Linguistic Acculturation: The Yaqui of Sonora and the Tewa of New Mexico. *Language* 32:146–57.
1958   Cultural Matrix of Singing and Chanting in Tewa Pueblos. *International Journal of American Linguistics* 24:268–72.
1961   Rio Grande Pueblos. In *Perspectives in American Indian Culture Change*, ed. E. H. Spicer, 94–187. Chicago: University of Chicago Press.
1966a   *Hano, a Tewa Indian Community in Arizona*. New York: Holt, Rinehart and Winston.
1966b   Factionalism at Santa Clara Pueblo. *Ethnology* 5:172–85.
1970   *The Pueblo Indians of North America*. New York: Holt, Rinehart and Winston.

DUNDES, ALAN
1966   Metafolklore and Oral Literary Criticism. *The Monist* 50:505–16.

DURANTI, ALESSANDRO
1983   Samoan Speechmaking Across Social Events: One Genre In and Out of a *Fono*. *Language in Society* 12:1–22.
1985   Sociocultural Dimensions of Discourse. In *Handbook of Discourse Analysis*, volume 1, ed. T. A. Van Dijk, 193–230. London: Academic Press.

EDELMAN, SANDRA A.
1979   San Ildefonso Pueblo. In *Southwest*, volume 9, *Handbook of North American Indians*, ed. A. Ortiz, 308–16. Washington, D.C.: Smithsonian.

EDELMAN, SANDRA A., AND ALFONSO ORTIZ
1979   Tesuque Pueblo. In *Southwest*, volume 9, *Handbook of North American Indians*, ed. A. Ortiz, 330–35. Washington D.C.: Smithsonian.

EGGAN, FRED
1950   *Social Organization of the Western Pueblos*. Chicago: University of Chicago Press.

ELLEN, ROY F.

1979   Omniscience and Ignorance: Variation in Nualu Knowledge, Identification and Classification of Animals. *Language in Society* 8:337–64.

ELLIS, FLORENCE HAWLEY

1951   Patterns of Aggression and the War Cult in Southwestern Pueblos. *Southwest Journal of Anthropology* 7:177–201.

ESPINOSA, J. M.

1940   *First Expedition of Vargas into New Mexico, 1692.* (Coronado Historical Series, Volume 10.) Albuquerque: University of New Mexico.

FERGUSON, CHARLES A.

1959   Diglossia. *Word* 15:325–40.

FERGUSON, CHARLES A., AND JOHN J. GUMPERZ

1960   Introduction. In *Linguistic Diversity in South Asia,* ed. C. A. Ferguson and J. J. Gumperz, 1–8. Bloomington, Ind.: Indiana University Research Center in Anthropology, Folklore, and Linguistics.

FEWKES, JESSE WALTER

1894   The Kinship of a Tanoan-speaking Community in Tusayan. *American Anthropologist* 8:162–67.

1899   The Winter Solstice Altars at Hano Pueblo. *American Anthropologist* 1:251–76.

1900   Tusayan Migration Traditions. In *Nineteenth Annual Report of the Bureau of American Ethnology for the Years 1897–1898, Part 2,* 573–634. Washington, D.C.: Smithsonian.

1903   Hopi Katcinas Drawn by Native Artists. In *Twenty-first Annual Report of the Bureau of American Ethnology for the Years 1899–1900,* 13–126. Washington, D.C.: Smithsonian.

FILLMORE, CHARLES J.

1968   The Case for Case. In *Universals in Linguistic Theory,* ed. E. Bach and R. T. Harms, 1–88. New York: Holt, Rinehart and Winston.

1979   On Fluency. In *Individual Differences in Language Ability and Language Behavior,* ed. C. J. Fillmore, D. Kempler, and W. S.-Y. Wang, 85–101. New York: Academic Press.

FISCHER, MICHAEL M. J.

1986   Ethnicity and the Post-Modern Arts of Memory. In *Writing Culture: The Poetics and Politics of Ethnography,* ed. J. Clifford and G. E. Marcus, 194–233. Berkeley: University of California Press.

FISHMAN, JOSHUA

1972   Domains and the Relationship between Micro- and Macrosociolinguis-
        tics. In *Directions in Sociolinguistics,* ed. J. Gumperz and D. Hymes,
        435–53. New York: Holt, Rinehart and Winston.

1977   Language and Ethnicity. In *Language, Ethnicity and Intergroup Rela-
        tions,* ed. H. Giles, 15–57. London: Academic Press.

1989   *Language and Ethnicity in Minority Sociolinguistic Perspective.* Cleve-
        don: Multilingual Matters.

FORD, RICHARD I.

1972   Barter, Gift, or Violence: An Analysis of Tewa Intertribal Exchange. In
        *University of Michigan Museum of Anthropology, Anthropological Pa-
        pers,* ed. E. S. Wilmsen, 46:21–45.

FORD, RICHARD I., ALBERT H. SCHROEDER, AND STEWART L. PECKHAM

1972   Three Perspectives on Puebloan Prehistory. In *New Perspectives on the
        Pueblos,* ed. A. Ortiz, 19–40. Albuquerque: University of New Mexico
        Press.

FOX, J. R.

1959   A Note on Cochiti Linguistics. In *Cochiti, A New Mexican Pueblo,
        Past and Present* by C. H. Lange, 557–72. Carbondale: University of
        Southern Illinois Press.

FRANK, GELYA

1978   Finding the Common Denominator: A Phenomenological Critique of
        Life History Method. (Working Paper No. 2, Socio-Behavioral Group,
        Mental Retardation Research Center, School of Medicine, University of
        California, Los Angeles.)

FREIRE-MARRECO, BARBARA

1914   Tewa Kinship Terms from the Pueblo of Hano, Arizona. *American An-
        thropologist* 16:269–87.

FRIEDRICH, PAUL

1975   The Lexical Symbol and Its Relative Non-arbitrariness. In *Linguistics
        and Anthropology in Honor of C. F. Voegelin,* ed. M. D. Kinkade,
        K. Hale, and O. Werner, 199–294. Lisse, the Netherlands: Peter deRidder.

1979   *Language, Context, and the Imagination: Essays by Paul Friedrich,* ed.
        Answar S. Dil. Stanford, Calif.: Stanford University Press.

1986   *The Language Parallax.* Austin: University of Texas Press.

FRIEDRICH, PAUL, AND JAMES REDFIELD

1978   Speech as a Personality Symbol. *Language* 54:263–89.

FRIGOUT, ARLETTE

1979   Hopi Ceremonial Organization. In *Southwest,* volume 9, *Handbook of North American Indians*, ed. A. Ortiz, 564–76. Washington, D.C.: Smithsonian.

FROMKIN, VICTORIA
1973   *Speech Errors as Linguistic Evidence*. The Hague: Mouton.
1980   *Errors in Linguistic Performance: Slips of the Tongue, Ear, Pen, and Hand*. New York: Academic Press.

GAL, SUSAN
1979   *Language Shift, Social Determinants of Linguistic Change in Bilingual Austria*. New York: Academic Press.

GALATY, JOHN G.
1982   Being "Maasai"; Being "People-of-Cattle": Ethnic Shifters in East Africa. *American Ethnologist* 9:1–20.

GARDNER, PETER M.
1976   Birds, Words, and a Requiem for the Omniscient Informant. *American Ethnologist* 3:446–68.

GARDNER, PETER M., AND JANE CHRISTIAN
1977   *The Individual in Northern Dene Thought and Communication: A Study in Sharing and Diversity*. (Mercury Series, Canadian Ethnology Service Papers, 35). Ottawa: National Museum of Man.

GARFINKEL, HAROLD
1967   *Studies in Ethnomethodology*. Englewood Cliffs, N.J.: Prentice-Hall.

GEERTZ, ARMIN W.
1990   Hopi Hermeneutics: Ritual Person among the Hopi Indians of Arizona. In *Concepts of Person in Religion and Thought*, ed. H. G. Kippenberg, Y. B. Kuiper and A. F. Sanders, 309–35. Berlin: Mouton.

GEERTZ, CLIFFORD
1959   The Javanese Kijaji: The Changing Role of a Culture Broker. *Comparative Studies in Society and History* 2:228–49.
1968   *Islam Observed: Religious Developments in Morocco and Indonesia*. Chicago: University of Chicago Press.
1973   *The Interpretation of Cultures*. New York: Basic Books.

GIDDENS, ANTHONY
1973   *The Class Structure of Advanced Societies*. London: Hutchinson.
1979   *Central Problems in Social Theory*. Cambridge: Cambridge University Press.
1984   *The Constitution of Society*. Berkeley: University of California Press.

GILES, HOWARD, R. Y. BOURHIS, AND D. M. TAYLOR
1977   Toward a Theory of Language in Intergroup Relations. In *Language,*

Ethnicity and Intergroup Relations, ed. H. Giles, 307–48. London: Academic Press.

GODDARD, IVES

1976   Philological Approaches to the Study of North American Indian Languages. In *Native Languages of the Americas,* volume 1, ed. T. A. Sebeok, 73–92. New York: Plenum Press.

GODDARD, PLINY EARLE

1933   *Navajo Texts* (Anthropological Papers of the American Museum of Natural History, volume 34, part 1). New York: The American Museum of Natural History.

GOFFMAN, ERVING

1959   *The Presentation of Self in Everyday Life.* New York: Doubleday Anchor Books.

1974   *Frame Analysis.* New York: Harper.

GOLDSCHMIDT, WALTER

1972   An Ethnography of Encounters: A Methodology for Enquiry into the Relation Between the Individual and Society. *Current Anthropology* 13: 59–78.

GORBET, LARRY

1977   Headless Relatives in the Southwest: Are They Related? *Proceedings of the Berkeley Linguistics Society* 3: 270–78.

GUMPERZ, JOHN J.

1962   Types of Linguistic Communities. *Anthropological Linguistics* 4: 28–40.

1968   The Speech Community. *International Encyclopedia of the Social Sciences* 9: 381–86.

1971   *Language in Social Groups.* Stanford, Calif.: Stanford University Press.

1982   *Discourse Strategies.* (Studies in Interactional Sociolinguistics, 1). New York: Cambridge University Press.

GUMPERZ, JOHN J., AND JENNY COOK-GUMPERZ

1982   Introduction: Language and the Communication of Social Identity. In *Language and Social Identity,* ed. J. J. Gumperz, 1–21. Cambridge: Cambridge University Press.

GUMPERZ, JOHN J., AND DEBORAH TANNEN

1979   Individual and Social Differences in Language Use. In *Individual Differences in Language Ability and Language Behavior,* ed. C. J. Fillmore, D. Kempler, and W. S.-Y. Wang, 305–25. New York: Academic Press.

GUMPERZ, JOHN J., AND ROBERT WILSON
1971   Convergence and Creolization: A Case Study from the Indo-Aryan Dravidian Border. In *Pidginization and Creolization of Languages,* ed. D. H. Hymes, 157–68. London: Cambridge University Press.

GUY, GREGORY
1980   Variation in the Group and the Individual: The Case of Final Stop Deletion. In *Locating Language in Time and Space,* ed. William Labov, 1–36. New York: Academic Press.

HAAS, MARY
1944   Men's and Women's Speech in Koasati. *Language* 20:142–49.

HAILE, BERARD
1984   *Navajo Coyote Tales: The Curly To Aheedliinii Version.* Lincoln: University of Nebraska Press.

HALE, KENNETH
1965   On the Use of Informants in Field Work. *The Canadian Journal of Linguistics* 10:108–19.
1967   Toward a Reconstruction of Kiowa-Tanoan Phonology. *International Journal of American Linguistics* 33:112–21.
1973   A Note on Subject-Object Inversion in Navajo. In *Issues in Linguistics, Papers in Honor of Henry and Renee Kahane,* ed. B. B. Kachru. Urbana: University of Illinois Press.

HALE, KENNETH, AND DAVID HARRIS
1979   Historical Linguistics and Archeology. In *Southwest,* volume 9, *Handbook of North American Indians,* ed. A. Ortiz, 170–77. Washington, D.C.: Smithsonian.

HAMMOND, GEORGE P., AND AGAPITO REY
1940   *Narratives of the Coronado Expedition, 1540–1542.* Albuquerque: University of New Mexico Press.
1953   *Don Juan de Onate, Colonizer of New Mexico, 1598–1628.* Albuquerque: University of New Mexico Press.
1966   *The Rediscovery of New Mexico, 1580–1594.* Albuquerque: University of New Mexico Press.

HAMP, ERIC
1977   On Some Questions of Areal Linguistics. *Proceedings of the Berkeley Linguistics Society* 3:279–82.

HARRINGTON, JOHN PEABODY
1910   On Phonetic and Lexic Resemblances between Kiowan and Tanoan. *American Anthropologist* 12:119–23.

1928   *Vocabulary of the Kiowa Language.* Bureau of American Ethnology Bulletin 84. Washington, D.C.: GPO.

1947   Three Tewa Texts. *International Journal of American Linguistics* 13: 112–18.

HASAN, RUGAIYA

1973   Code, Register, and Social Dialect. In *Class, Codes, and Control,* volume 2, ed. B. Bernstein, 253–93. London: Kegan Paul.

HAUGEN, EINAR

1956   *Bilingualism in the Americas: A Bibliography and Research Guide.* Publications of the American Dialect Society, volume 26.

HEATH, JEFFREY

1989   *From Code-Switching to Borrowing: Foreign and Diglossic Mixing in Moroccan Arabic.* London: Kegan Paul International.

HELLER, MONICA

1988a   Introduction. In *Codeswitching,* ed. Monica Heller, 1–24. Berlin: Mouton.

1988b   Where Do We Go from Here? In *Codeswitching,* ed. Monica Heller, 265–72. Berlin: Mouton.

HENNINGSEN, MANFRED

1989   The Politics of Purity and Exclusion. In *The Politics of Language Purism,* ed. B. Jernudd and M. Shapiro, 31–52. Berlin: Mouton.

HERZOG, GEORGE

1941   Culture Change and Language: Shifts in the Pima Vocabulary. In *Language, Culture and Personality,* ed. L. Spier, A. I. Hallowell, and S. Newman, 66–74. Menasha, Wis.: Sapir Memorial Fund.

HILL, JANE H.

1985   The Grammar of Consciousness and the Consciousness of Grammar. *American Ethnologist* 12:725–37.

1988   Language, Genuine and Spurious? In *On the Ethnography of Communication: The Legacy of Sapir,* ed. P. V. Kroskrity, 9–53. Los Angeles: University of California, Los Angeles, Department of Anthropology.

HILL, JANE H., AND KENNETH C. HILL

1980   Metaphorical Switching in Modern Nahuatl: Change and Contradiction. *Papers from the Chicago Linguistics Society* 16:121–33.

1986   *Speaking Mexicano, Dynamics of Syncretic Language in Central Mexico.* Tucson: University of Arizona Press.

HINTON, LEANNE

1980   When Sounds Go Wild. *Language* 56:320–44.

HOCKETT, C. F.
1958   *A Course in Modern Linguistics.* New York: Macmillan.

HODGE, FREDERICK W., GEORGE P. HAMMOND, AND AGAPITO REY
1945   *Fray Alonso de Benavides' Revised Memorial of 1634.* Albuquerque: University of New Mexico Press.

HODGE, WILLIAM H.
1971   Navajo Urban Migration: An Analysis from the Perspective of the Family. In *The American Indian in Urban Society,* ed. J. O. Waddell and O. M. Watson, 346–91. Boston: Little, Brown, and Company.

HOENIGSWALD, HENRY M.
1960   *Language Change and Linguistic Reconstruction.* Chicago: University of Chicago Press.

HOIJER, HARRY
1946   Chiracahua Apache. In *Linguistic Structures of Native North America,* ed. H. Hoijer, 55–84. New York: Viking Fund Publications in Anthropology, no. 6.

HOIJER, HARRY, AND EDWARD P. DOZIER
1949   The Phonemes of Tewa, Santa Clara Dialect. *International Journal of American Linguistics* 15 : 139–45.

HOMANS, GEORGE C.
1950   *The Human Group.* New York: Harcourt, Brace, and World, Inc.

HOUSEHOLDER, FRED W.
1973   On Arguments from Asterisks. *Foundations of Language* 10 : 365–76.

HOUSER, NICHOLAS P.
1979   Tigua Pueblo. In *Southwest,* volume 9, *Handbook of North American Indians,* ed. A. Ortiz, 336–42. Washington, D.C.: Smithsonian.

HUDSON, R. A.
1980   *Sociolinguistics.* London: Cambridge University Press.

HYMES, DELL H.
1962   The Ethnography of Speaking. In *Anthropology and Human Behavior,* ed. T. Gladwin and W. C. Sturtevant, 13–54. Washington, D.C.: The Anthropological Society of Washington.
1970   Linguistic Method in Ethnography: Its Development in the United States. In *Method and Theory in Linguistics,* ed. P. Garvin, 249–325. The Hague: Mouton.
1971   Sociolinguistics and the Ethnography of Speaking. In *Social Anthropology and Language,* ed. E. Ardener, 47–93. London: Tavistock.
1972   Models of the Interaction of Language and Social Life. In *Directions*

in Sociolinguistics, ed. J. J. Gumperz and D. H. Hymes, 35–71. New York: Holt, Rinehart and Winston.

1974   Ways of Speaking. In *Explorations in the Ethnography of Speaking,* ed. R. Bauman and J. Sherzer, 433–51. London: Cambridge University Press.

1979   Sapir, Competence, Voices. In *Individual Differences in Language Ability and Behavior,* ed. C. J. Fillmore, D. Kempler, and W. S.-Y. Wang, 33–46. New York: Academic Press.

1980   Particle, Pause, and Pattern in American Indian Narrative Verse. *American Indian Culture and Research Journal* 4:7–51.

1981   *"In Vain I Tried to Tell You": Essays in Native American Ethnopoetics.* Philadelphia: University of Pennsylvania Press.

1983   *Essays in the History of Linguistic Anthropology.* (Amsterdam Studies in Theory and History of Linguistic Science, volume 25). Amsterdam: John Benjamins.

1992   Use All There Is To Use. In *On the Translation of Native American Literatures,* ed. B. Swann, 83–124. Washington, D.C.: Smithsonian.

IRVINE, JUDITH

1979   Formality and Informality in Communicative Events. *American Anthropologist* 81:773–90.

JACKSON, JEAN

1974   Language Identity of the Colombian Vaupes Indians. In *Explorations in the Ethnography of Communication,* ed. R. Bauman and J. Sherzer, 50–64. Cambridge: Cambridge University Press.

JACOBS, MELVILLE

1959   *The Content and Style of An Oral Literature.* Chicago: University of Chicago Press.

JERNUDD, BJORN

1973   Language Planning as a Type of Language Treatment. In *Language Planning: Current Issues and Trends,* ed. J. Rubin and R. Shuy, 11–23. Washington, D.C.: Georgetown University Press.

JERNUDD, BJORN, AND MICHAEL SHAPIRO

1989   *The Politics of Language Purism.* Berlin: Mouton.

JORGENSON, JOSEPH

1971   Indians and the Metropolis. In *The American Indian in Urban Society,* ed. J. Waddell and O. M. Watson, 66–113. Boston: Little, Brown, and Company.

KALECTACA, MILO

1978   *Lessons in Hopi.* Tucson: University of Arizona.

KAMMER, JERRY

1980   *The Second Long Walk: The Navajo-Hopi Land Dispute.* Albuquerque: University of New Mexico.

KAPLAN, ABRAHAM

1964   *The Conduct of Inquiry.* Scranton, Pa.: Chandler.

KAY, PAUL, AND CHAD MCDANIEL

1979   On the Logic of Variable Rules. *Language in Society* 8:151–87.

KEALIINOHOMOKU, JOANN W.

1980   The Drama of the Hopi Ogres. In *Southwestern Indian Ritual Drama,* ed. C. Frisbie, 37–69. Albuquerque: University of New Mexico Press.

KEESING, ROGER

1972   "Paradigms Lost," The New Ethnography and the New Linguistics. *Southwestern Journal of Anthropology* 28:299–332.

1974   Theories of Culture. *Annual Review of Anthropology* 3:73–97.

KENDALL, MARTHA B., ED.

1980   *Coyote Stories II* (International Journal of American Linguistics Native American Texts Series, Monograph No. 6). Ann Arbor, Mich.: University Microfilms.

KEYES, CHARLES F.

1976   Towards a New Formulation of the Concept of Ethnic Group. *Ethnicity* 3:202–13.

KROCH, ANTHONY, AND CATHY SMALL

1978   Grammatical Ideology and Its Effect on Speech. In *Linguistic Variation, Models and Methods,* ed. D. Sankoff, 45–56. New York: Academic Press.

KROSKRITY, PAUL V.

1976   The Ethnohistorical Significance of Arizona Tewa *Hen Khi khaw.* Paper presented at the Annual Meeting of the American Anthropological Association, Washington, D.C.

1977   Aspects of Arizona Tewa Language Structure and Language Use. Unpublished Doctoral Dissertation, Indiana University.

1978a   On the Lexical Integrity of Arizona Tewa /-di/: A Principled Choice between Homophony and Polysemy. *International Journal of American Linguistics* 44:24–30.

1978b   Aspects of Syntactic and Semantic Variation in the Arizona Tewa Speech Community. *Anthropological Linguistics* 20:235–58.

1978c   Inferences from Spanish Loanwords in Arizona Tewa. *Anthropological Linguistics* 20:340–50.

1982   Language Contact and Linguistic Diffusion: The Arizona Tewa Speech

Community. In *Bilingualism and Language Contact: Spanish, English, and Native American Languages,* ed. Florence Barkin, Elizabeth A. Brandt, and Jacob Ornstein-Galicia, 51–72. New York: Teachers College Press.

1983a   Male and Female Speech in the Pueblo Southwest. *International Journal of American Linguistics* 49:75–79.

1983b   Review of *Big Falling Snow* by Albert Yava. *American Indian Quarterly* 7:96–98.

1984   Negation and Subordination in Arizona Tewa, Discourse-Pragmatics Influencing Syntax. *International Journal of American Linguistics* 50: 94–104.

1985a   A Holistic Understanding of Arizona Tewa Passives. *Language* 61: 306–28.

1985b   Areal-historical Influences on Tewa Possession. *International Journal of American Linguistics* 51:486–91.

1985c   Growing With Stories: Line, Verse, and Genre in an Arizona Tewa Text. *Journal of Anthropological Research* 41:183–99.

1986   Ethnolinguistics and American Indian Education: Native American Languages and Cultures as a Means of Teaching. In *American Indian Policy and Cultural Values: Conflict and Accommodation,* ed. J. R. Joe, 99–110. Los Angeles: University of California, Los Angeles, American Indian Studies Center.

1990   Arizona Tewa Public Announcements: Form, Function, and Linguistic Ideology. Paper presented to the Annual Meeting of the American Anthropological Association, New Orleans.

1992   Arizona Tewa Kiva Speech as a Manifestation of Linguistic Ideology. *Pragmatics* 2:297–309.

MS   Arizona Tewa and Rio Grande Tewa: An Assessment of Their Linguistic Distance. *Anthropological Linguistics.* (Manuscript in press)

KROSKRITY, PAUL V., AND DEWEY HEALING

1978   Coyote and Bullsnake (Arizona Tewa). In *Coyote Stories* (International Journal of American Linguistics, Native American Texts Series, Monograph No. 1), ed. W. Bright, 162–70. Ann Arbor, Mich.: University Microfilms.

1980   Coyote Woman and the Deer Children (Arizona Tewa). In *Coyote Stories II* (International Journal of American Linguistics, Native American Texts Series, Monograph No. 6), ed. M. B. Kendall, 119–28. Ann Arbor, Mich.: University Microfilms.

KROSKRITY, PAUL V., AND GREGORY A. REINHARDT
1984   Spanish and English Loanwords in Western Mono. *Journal of California Anthropology, Papers in Linguistics* 4:107–38.

KUIPERS, JOEL C.
1990   *Power in Performance.* Philadelphia: University of Pennsylvania Press.

KUNITZ, STEPHEN J.
1974   Factors Influencing Recent Navajo and Hopi Population Changes. *Human Organization* 33:7–16.

LABOV, WILLIAM
1963   The Social Motivation of a Sound Change. *Word* 19:273–309.

1966   *The Social Stratification of English in New York City.* Washington, D.C.: Center for Applied Linguistics.

1971   Methodology. In *A Survey of Linguistic Science,* ed. W. O. Dingwall. College Park: University of Maryland Press.

1972a   Some Principles of Linguistic Methodology. *Language in Society* 1:97–120.

1972b   *Sociolinguistic Patterns.* Philadelphia: University of Pennsylvania Press.

1973   Where Do Grammars Stop? In *Report of the Twenty-third Annual Roundtable Meeting on Linguistics and Language Studies,* ed. R. Shuy, 43–88. Washington, D.C.: Georgetown University Press.

1979   Locating the Frontier Between Social and Psychological Factors in Linguistic Variation. In *Individual Difference in Language Ability and Language Behavior,* ed. C. J. Fillmore, D. Kempler, and W. S.-Y. Wang, 327–40. New York: Academic Press.

1980   The Social Origins of Sound Change. In *Locating Language in Time and Space,* ed. W. Labov, 251–65. New York: Academic Press.

LABOV, WILLIAM, AND JOSHUA WALETZKY
1967   Narrative Analysis. In *Essays on the Verbal and Visual Arts: Proceedings of the 1966 Annual Spring Meeting of the American Ethnological Society,* ed. June Helm, 12–44. Seattle: American Ethnological Society.

LAMBERT, MARJORIE F.
1979   Pojoaque Pueblo. In *Southwest,* volume 9, *Handbook of North American Indians,* ed. A. Ortiz, 324–29. Washington, D.C.: Smithsonian.

LANGE, CHARLES H., CARROLL L. RILEY AND ELIZABETH M. LANGE
1975   *The Southwestern Journals of Adolph F. Bandelier 1885–1888.* Albuquerque: University of New Mexico Press.

LANGNESS, L. L.
1965   *The Life History in Anthropological Science.* New York: Holt, Rinehart and Winston.

LANGNESS, L. L., AND GELYA FRANK
1981   Lives: An Anthropological Approach to Biography. Novato, Calif.:
        Chandler and Sharp.

LEAP, WILLIAM L.
1981   American Indian Language Maintenance. Annual Review of Anthro-
        pology 10:209–36.
1988   Applied Linguistics and American Indian Language Renewal. Human
        Organization 47:283–91.

LEPAGE, R. B., AND ANDREE TABOURET-KELLER
1985   Acts of Identity: Creole-based Approaches to Language and Ethnicity.
        Cambridge: Cambridge University Press.

LEVY, ROBERT I.
1983   Introduction: Self and Emotion. Ethos 11:128–34.

MCLENDON, SALLY
1977   Cultural Presuppositions and Discourse Analysis: Patterns of Presup-
        position and Assertion of Information in Eastern Pomo and Russian
        Narratives. In Georgetown University Round Table on Languages and
        Linguistics, 1977, ed. M. Saville-Troike, 153–89. Washington, D.C.:
        Georgetown University Press.

MALOTKI, EKKEHART
1978   Hopitutuwutsi, Hopi Tales. Flagstaff, Ariz.: Museum of Northern Ari-
        zona Press.

MALOTKI, EKKEHART, AND MICHAEL LOMATUWAY'MA
1984   Hopi Coyote Tales: Istutuwutsi. Lincoln: University of Nebraska Press.

MARCUS, GEORGE E., AND MICHAEL M. J. FISCHER
1986   Anthropology as Cultural Critique. Chicago: University of Chicago
        Press.

MARING, JOEL
1975   Speech Variation in Acoma Keresan. In Linguistics and Anthropology
        in Honor of C. F. Voegelin, ed. M. D. Kinkade, K. Hale and O. Werner,
        473–86. Lisse: Peter deRidder.

MARTINEZ, ESTHER
1983   San Juan Pueblo Dictionary. Portales, N.M.: Bishop Publishing
        Company.

MASON, LYNN D.
1965   Hopi Domestic Animals: Past and Present. Unpublished Manuscript,
        Museum of Northern Arizona, Flagstaff, Ariz.

MEAD, GEORGE HERBERT
1934   Mind, Self, and Society. Chicago: University of Chicago.

MILLER, WICK R.
1959   A Note on Kiowa Linguistic Affiliations. *American Anthropologist* 61:
        102–5.
1965   *Acoma Grammar and Texts*. University of California Publications in
        Linguistics, 40. Berkeley: University of California Press.
1978   Multilingualism in its Social Context in Aboriginal North America. *Pro-
        ceedings of the Annual Meeting of the Berkeley Linguistics Society* 4:
        610–16.

MILROY, LESLEY, AND SUE MARGRAIN
1980   Vernacular Language Loyalty and Social Network. *Language in Society*
        9:43–70.

MINDELEFF, VICTOR
1891   A Study of Pueblo Architecture, Tusayan and Cibola. In *Eighth Annual
        Report of the Bureau of American Ethnology*, 13–234. Washington,
        D.C.: GPO.

MITCHELL, J. CLYDE
1969   *Social Network in Urban Situations*. Manchester: Manchester Univer-
        sity Press.

MOERMAN, MICHAEL
1965   Ethnic Identification in a Complex Civilization: Who Are the Lue? *Amer-
        ican Anthropologist* 67:1215–30.
1974   Accomplishing Ethnicity. In *Ethnomethodology*, ed. R. Turner, 54–68.
        London: Penguin.
1988   *Talking Culture: Ethnography and Conversation Analysis*. Philadelphia:
        University of Pennsylvania Press.
1990   Studying Gestures in Social Context. In *Culture Embodied*, ed. M. Moer-
        man and M. Nomura, 5–52. Osaka, Japan: National Museum of
        Ethnology.

NAGATA, JUDITH A.
1974   What Is a Malay? Situational Selection of Ethnic Identity in a Plural
        Society. *American Ethnologist* 1:331–50.

NAGATA, SHUICI
1971   The Reservation Community and the Urban Community: Hopi Indians
        of Moenkopi. In *The American Indian in Urban Society*, ed. O. M. Wat-
        son and J. Waddell, 114–59. Boston: Houghton-Mifflin.

NARO, ANTHONY J.
1981   The Social and Structural Dimensions of a Syntactic Change. *Language*
        57:63–98.

NELSON, NELS C.

1914   Pueblo Ruins of the Galisteo Basin, New Mexico. *Anthropological Papers of the American Museum of Natural History* 15(1). New York: American Museum of Natural History.

NEWMAN, STANLEY

1955   Vocabulary Levels: Zuni Sacred and Slang Usage. Southwestern Journal of Anthropology 11:345–54.

1958   *Zuni Dictionary.* Bloomington: Indiana University Research Center in Anthropology, Folklore, and Linguistics.

OCHS, ELINOR

1979a   Planned and Unplanned Discourse. In *Discourse and Syntax.* Volume 12, *Syntax and Semantics,* ed. T. Givon, 51–88. New York: Academic Press.

1979b   Social Foundations of Language. In *New Directions in Discourse Processing,* ed. R. O. Freedle, 207–21. Norwood, N.J.

1990   *Culture and Language Development.* Cambridge: Cambridge University Press.

1992   Indexing Gender. In *Rethinking Context,* ed. A. Duranti and C. Goodwin, 335–58. Cambridge: Cambridge University Press.

OPLER, MORRIS, AND HARRY HOIJER

1940   The Raid and War-path Language of the Chiracahua Apache. *American Anthropologist* 42:617–34.

ORTIZ, ALFONSO

1969   *The Tewa World.* Chicago: University of Chicago Press.

1972   Ritual Drama in the Pueblo World View. In *New Perspectives on the Pueblos,* ed. A. Ortiz, 135–61. Albuquerque: University of New Mexico Press.

1979   San Juan Pueblo. In *Southwest,* volume 9, *Handbook of North American Indians,* ed. A. Ortiz, 278–95. Washington, D.C.: Smithsonian.

ORTNER, SHERRY

1984   Theory in Anthropology since the Sixties. *Comparative Studies in Society and History* 26:126–66.

PAHONA, DUKE

1977   Clansman Speaks His Mind. *Qua' Toqti* (New Oraibi, Ariz.) 3(49): 1–6.

PARSONS, ELSIE CLEWS

1925   A Pueblo Indian Journal 1920–1921. *Memoirs of the American Anthropological Association,* 32. Menasha, Wis.: Collegiate Press.

1926   The Ceremonial Calendar of the Tewa of Arizona. *American Anthropologist* 28:208–29.

1929   The Social Organization of the Tewa of New Mexico. *Memoirs of the American Anthropological Association* 36. Menasha, Wis.: Collegiate Press.

1939   *Pueblo Indian Religion.* 2 vols. Chicago: University of Chicago Press.

PATTISON, ROBERT

1982   *On Literacy: The Politics of the Word from Homer to the Age of Rock.* Oxford: Oxford University Press.

PELTO, PERTTI, AND GRETEL H. PELTO

1975   Intra-cultural Diversity: Some Theoretical Issues. *American Ethnologist* 2:1–18.

PHILIPS, SUSAN U.

1972   Participant Structures and Communicative Competence: Warm Springs Children in Community and Classroom. In *Functions of Language in the Classroom,* ed. C. B. Cazden, V. P. John, and D. H. Hymes, 370–94. New York: Teachers College Press.

1976   Some Sources of Cultural Variability in the Regulation of Talk. *Language in Society* 5:81–95.

1983   *The Invisible Culture.* New York: Longman.

PLOG, FRED T.

1979   Prehistory: Western Anasazi. In *Southwest,* volume 9, *Handbook of North American Indians,* ed. A. Ortiz, 108–30. Washington, D.C.: Smithsonian.

POPLACK, SHANA

1980   Sometimes I'll Start a Sentence in Spanish y Termino en Español: Toward a Typology of Code-switching. *Linguistics* 18:581–618.

PRESS, IRWIN

1969   Ambiguity and Innovation: Implications for the Genesis of the Culture Broker. *American Anthropologist* 71:205–17.

REED, ERIK K.

1943   The Origins of Hano Pueblo. *El Palacio* 50:73–76.

1954   Transition to History in the Pueblo Southwest. *American Anthropologist* 56:592–604.

REEVE, FRANK D.

1957   Seventeenth Century Navaho-Spanish Relations. *New Mexico Historical Review* 32:36–52.

ROSALDO, MICHELLE
1972   "I Have Nothing to Hide": The Language of Ilongot Oratory. *Language in Society* 2:193–223.

ROSALDO, RENATO I.
1984   Grief and a Headhunter's Rage: On the Cultural Force of Emotions. In *Text, Play, and Story* (1983 Proceedings of the American Ethnological Society), ed. E. M. Bruner, 178–95. Washington, D.C.: The American Ethnological Society.

ROUSSEAU, PASCALE, AND DAVID SANKOFF
1978   Advances in Variable Rule Methodology. In *Linguistic Variation,* ed. D. Sankoff, 57–70. New York: Academic Press.

ROYCE, ANYA PETERSON
1982   *Ethnic Identity.* Bloomington: Indiana University Press.

SAMARIN, WILLIAM
1967   *Field Linguistics.* New York City: Holt, Rinehart and Winston.

SANKOFF, DAVID, AND SUZANNE LABERGE
1978   Statistical Dependence Among Successive Occurrences of a Variable in Discourse. In *Linguistic Variation,* ed. D. Sankoff, 119–26. New York: Academic Press.

———, AND WILLIAM LABOV
1979   On the Uses of Variable Rules. *Language in Society* 8:189–222.

SANKOFF, GILLIAN
1974   A Quantitative Paradigm for the Study of Communicative Competence. In *Explorations in the Ethnography of Speaking,* ed. R. Bauman and J. Sherzer, 18–49. London: Cambridge University Press.

SAPIR, EDWARD
1916   *Time Perspective in Aboriginal American Culture: A Study in Method.* Anthropological Series 13, Memoirs of the Canadian Geological Survey 90. Ottawa.
1929   The Status of Linguistics as a Science. *Language* 5:207–14.
1932   Cultural Anthropology and Psychiatry. *Journal of Abnormal and Social Psychology* 27:229–42. (Reprinted in *Selected Writings of Edward Sapir* [*1951*], ed. D. G. Mandelbaum, 509–21. Berkeley: University of California Press.)
1934   The Emergence of a Concept of Personality in a Study of Cultures. *Journal of Social Psychology* 5:408–15. (Reprinted in *Selected Writings of Edward Sapir* [1951] ed. D. G. Mandelbaum, 590–97. Berkeley: University of California Press.)

1938   Why Cultural Anthropology Needs the Psychiatrist. *Psychiatry* 1:7–12. (Reprinted in *Selected Writings of Edward Sapir* [1951], ed. D. G. Mandelbaum, 569–77. Berkeley: University of California Press.)

1949   Male and Female Forms of Speech in Yana. In *Selected Writings of Edward Sapir* [1951], ed. D. G. Mandelbaum, 206–12. Berkeley: University of California Press.

SCHMIDT, ANNETTE
1985   *Young People's Dyirbal.* Cambridge: Cambridge University Press.

SCHNEIDER, DAVID
1968   *American Kinship, A Cultural Account.* Englewood Cliffs, N.J.: Prentice-Hall.

SCHOLES, FRANCE V.
1938   Notes on the Jemez Missions of the Seventeenth Century. *El Palacio* 44(1–2):61–102.

SCHROEDER, ALBERT H.
1972   Rio Grande Ethnohistory. In *New Perspectives on the Pueblos,* ed. A. Ortiz, 180–203. Albuquerque: University of New Mexico Press.

1979   Pueblos Abandoned in Historic Times. In *Southwest,* volume 9, *Handbook of North American Indians,* ed. A. Ortiz, 236–54. Washington, D.C.: Smithsonian.

SCHROEDER, ALBERT H., AND DAN S. MATSON
1965   *A Colony on the Move: Gaspar Castano de Sosa's Journal.* Santa Fe: School of American Research.

SCHUTZ, ALFRED
1932   *Der Sinnhafte Aufbau der Sozialen Welt.* Vienna: Julius Springer.

1955   Symbol, Reality, and Society. In *Symbols and Society,* ed. L. Finkelstein, H. Hoagland, and R. M. MacIver, 135–203. New York: Harper and Row.

1962   *Collected Papers I: The Problem of a Social Reality.* Ed. M. Natanson. The Hague: Martinus Nijhoff.

1964   *Collected Papers II: Studies in Social Theory.* Ed. M. Natanson. The Hague: Martinus Nijhoff.

SCOLLON, RONALD
1979   Variable Data and Linguistic Convergence: Texts and Contexts in Chipewyan. *Language in Society* 8:223–42.

SCOLLON, RONALD, AND SUZANNE B. K. SCOLLON
1979   *Linguistic Convergence: An Ethnography of Communication at Fort Chipewyan, Alberta.* New York: Academic Press.

1981   *Narrative, Literacy and Face in Interethnic Interaction.* Norwood, N.J.: ABLEX.

SCOTTON, CAROL MYERS

1988   Codeswitching as Indexical of Social Negotiations. In *Codeswitching,* ed. Monica Heller, 151–86. Berlin: Mouton.

SCRIBNER, SYLVIA, AND MICHAEL COLE

1973   Cognitive Consequences of Formal and Informal Education. *Science* 182:553–59.

1981   *The Psychology of Literacy.* Cambridge, Mass.: Harvard University Press.

SEAMAN, P. DAVID

1985   *Hopi Dictionary.* Northern Arizona University Anthropological Paper No. 2. Flagstaff: Northern Arizona University.

SEUMPTEWA, EVELYN, C. F. VOEGELIN, AND F. M. VOEGELIN

1980   Wren and Coyote (Hopi). In *Coyote Stories II* (International Journal of American Linguistics Native American Texts Series, Monograph No. 6), ed. M. B. Kendall, 104–10. Ann Arbor, Mich.: University Microfilms.

SHERZER, JOEL

1976   *An Areal-Typological Study of American Indian Languages North of Mexico.* Amsterdam: North-Holland Publishing Company.

1982   Poetic Structuring in Kuna Discourse: The Line. *Language in Society* 11:371–90.

1983   *Kuna Ways of Speaking, An Ethnographic Perspective.* Austin: University of Texas Press.

SHERZER, JOEL, AND RICHARD BAUMAN

1972   Areal Studies and Culture History. *Southwest Journal of Anthropology* 28:131–53.

SHERZER, JOEL, AND ANTHONY WOODBURY, EDS.

1987   *Native American Discourse: Poetics and Rhetoric.* Cambridge: Cambridge University Press.

SHIBUTANI, TAMOTSU

1962   Reference Groups and Social Control. In *Human Behavior and Social Processes,* ed. A. M. Rose, 128–47. Boston: Houghton-Mifflin.

SHOPEN, TIM

1972   Logical Equivalence is Not Semantic Equivalence. *Papers of the Chicago Linguistics Society* 8:340–50.

SILVER, SHIRLEY, AND WICK R. MILLER

American Indian Languages in Their Social and Cultural Context. (Manuscript submitted)

SILVERMAN, CAROL
1988   Negotiating "Gypsiness": Strategy in Context. *Journal of American Folklore* 101:261–75.

SILVERSTEIN, MICHAEL
1976   Shifters, Linguistic Categories, and Cultural Description. In *Meaning in Anthropology,* ed. K. Basso and H. Selby, 11–55. Albuquerque: University of New Mexico Press.
1977   Cultural Prerequisites to Grammatical Analysis. In *Georgetown University Round Table on Languages and Linguistics,* ed. M. Saville-Troike, 139–51. Washington, D.C.: Georgetown University Press.
1979   Language Structure and Linguistic Ideology. In *The Elements: A Parasession on Linguistic Units and Levels,* ed. P. R. Clyne, 193–247. Chicago: Chicago Linguistics Society.

SIMMONS, MARC
1979   History of Pueblo-Spanish Relations to 1821. In *Southwest,* volume 9, *Handbook of North American Indians,* ed. A. Ortiz, 178–93. Washington, D.C.: Smithsonian.

SOUTHWORTH, FRANKLIN C.
1971   Detecting Prior Creolization: An Analysis of the Historical Origins of Marathi. In *Pidginization and Creolization of Languages,* ed. D. Hymes, 255–74. Cambridge: Cambridge University Press.

SPEIRS, ANNA
1974   Classificatory Verb Stems in Tewa. *Studies in Linguistics* 24:45–64.

SPEIRS, RANDALL H.
1966   Some Aspects of the Structure of Rio Grande Tewa. Unpublished Doctoral Dissertation, State University of New York at Buffalo.
1979   Nambe Pueblo. In *Southwest,* volume 9, *Handbook of North American Indians,* ed. A. Ortiz, 317–23. Washington, D.C.: Smithsonian.

SPEIRS, RANDALL H., AND ANNA SPEIRS
1981   The Rio Grande Tewa Prefix System. Paper presented at the Annual Meeting of the Kiowa-Tanoan Language Conference, Albuquerque.

SPICER, EDWARD H.
1962   *Cycles of Conquest: The Impact of Spain, Mexico, and the United States on the Indians of the Southwest.* Tucson: University of Arizona Press.

STANISLAWSKI, MICHAEL B.
1979   Hopi-Tewa. In *Southwest,* volume 9, *Handbook of North American Indians,* ed. A. Ortiz, 587–602. Washington, D.C.: Smithsonian.

STOCKING, GEORGE W.

1968   *Race, Culture, and Evolution.* New York: Free Press.

STOUT, S. O.

1979   Sociolinguistic Analysis of English Diversity Among Elementary-aged Students from Laguna Pueblo. Unpublished Doctoral Dissertation, American University.

STURTEVANT, WILLIAM C.

1966   Anthropology, History, and Ethnohistory. *Ethnohistory* 13:1–51.

TANNEN, DEBORAH

1989   *Talking Voices: Repetition, Dialogue, and Imagery in Conversational Discourse.* Cambridge: Cambridge University Press.

TEDLOCK, DENNIS

1972   *Finding the Center.* New York: Dial.

1979   The Analogical Tradition and the Emergence of a Dialogical Anthropology. *Journal of Anthropological Research* 35:387–400.

1983   *The Spoken Word and the Work of Interpretation.* Philadelphia: University of Pennsylvania Press.

IN PRESS. Verbal Art. In *Introduction,* volume 1, *Handbook of North American Indians,* ed. William C. Sturtevant. Washington, D.C.: Smithsonian.

THOMPSON, LAURA

1950   *Culture in Crisis.* New York: Harper.

TIMM, LENORE A.

1975   Spanish-English Code-switching: El Porque y How-not-to. *Romance Philology* 28:473–82.

TODOROV, TZVETAN

1984   *Mikhail Bakhtin: The Dialogical Principle.* Minneapolis: University of Minnesota Press.

TOELKEN, BARRE

1969   The "Pretty Languages" of Yellowman: Genre, Mode, and Texture in Navaho Coyote Narratives. *Genre* 2:211–35.

TOELKEN, BARRE, AND TACHEENI SCOTT

1981   Poetic Retranslation and the "Pretty Languages" of Yellowman. In *Traditional Literatures of the American Indian,* ed. K. Kroeber, 65–116. Lincoln: University of Nebraska Press.

TRAGER, GEORGE L.

1944   Spanish and English Loanwords in Taos. *International Journal of American Linguistics* 10:144–58.

1946   An Outline of Taos Grammar. In *Linguistic Structures of Native America,* ed. H. Hoijer, 184–221. Viking Fund Publications in Anthropology.

1967   The Tanoan Settlement of the Rio Grande Area: A Possible Chronology. In *Studies in Southwestern Ethnolinguistics,* ed. D. H. Hymes and W. E. Bittle, 335–49. The Hague: Mouton.

TRAGER, GEORGE L., AND EDITH CROWELL TRAGER
1959   Kiowa and Tanoan. *American Anthropologist* 61:1078–83.

TYLER, STEPHEN A.
1969   *Cognitive Anthropology.* New York: Holt, Rinehart and Winston.
1978   *The Said and the Unsaid.* New York: Academic Press.

VANSINA, JAN
1965   *Oral Tradition: A Study in Historical Methodology,* tr. H. M. Wright. London: Routledge and Kegan Paul.

VINCENT, JOAN
1974   The Structuring of Ethnicity. *Human Organization* 33:375–79.

VOEGELIN, C. F.
1960   Casual and Non-casual Utterances Within Unified Structure. In *Style in Language,* ed. T. A. Sebeok, 57–68. Cambridge, Mass.: M.I.T. Press.

VOEGELIN, C. F., AND F. M. VOEGELIN
1957   Hopi Domains, A Lexical Approach to the Problem of Selection. *International Journal of American Linguistics* 23 (2, part 2): 1–82.

VOLOŠINOV, V. N.
1973   [1930] *Marxism and the Philosophy of Language,* tr. L. Matejka and I. R. Titunik. New York: Seminar Press.

WALLACE, ANTHONY F. C.
1961   *Culture and Personality.* New York: Random House.

WATKINS, LAUREL J.
1984   *A Grammar of Kiowa.* Lincoln: University of Nebraska.

WEINREICH, URIEL
1953   *Languages in Contact.* New York: Linguistic Circle of New York.

WHITE, LESLIE
1942   The Pueblo of Santa Ana, New Mexico. Memoirs of the American Anthropological Association 60. Menasha, Wis.: Collegiate Press.
1944   A Ceremonial Vocabulary Among the Pueblos. *International Journal of American Linguistics* 10:161–67.

WILCOX, DAVID R.
1981   The Entry of the Athapaskans into the American Southwest: The Problem Today. In *The Protohistoric Period in the American Southwest, A.D. 1450–1700,* ed. by D. R. Wilcox and W. Masse, 213–56. Arizona State University, Anthropological Research Paper 24. Tempe: Arizona State University Press.

WILSON, THOMAS P.

1970   Normative and Interpretive Paradigms in Sociology. In *Understanding Everyday Life: Toward the Reconstruction of Sociological Knowledge*, ed. J. D. Douglas, 57–79. Chicago: Aldine.

WITHERSPOON, GARY

1977   *Language and Art in the Navajo Universe*. Ann Arbor: University of Michigan Press.

WOLF, ERIC

1956   Aspects of Group Relations in a Complex Society. *American Anthropologist* 58 : 1065–78.

WOLFSON, NESSA

1976   Speech Events and Natural Speech: Some Implications for Sociolinguistic Methodology. *Language in Society* 5 : 189–209.

WOODBURY, ANTHONY

1985   The Functions of Rhetorical Structure: A Case Study of Central Alaskan Yupik Eskimo Discourse. *Language in Society* 14 : 153–90.

WOOLARD, KATHRYN A.

1988   Codeswitching and Comedy in Catalonia. In *Codeswitching*, ed. Monica Heller, 53–76. Berlin: Mouton.

1989   *Double Talk: Bilingualism and the Politics of Ethnicity in Catalonia*. Stanford, Calif.: Stanford University Press.

WORCESTER, DONALD E.

1951   The Navajo During the Spanish Regime in New Mexico. *New Mexico Historical Review* 26 : 101–18.

WRONG, DENNIS

1961   The Oversocialized Conception of Man in Modern Sociology. *American Sociological Review* 26 : 183–93.

1976   *Skeptical Sociology*. New York: Columbia University Press.

YAVA, ALBERT

1979   *Big Falling Snow*, ed. H. Courlander. New York: Crown.

YEGERLEHNER, JOHN F.

1957   Phonology and Morphology of Hopi-Tewa. Unpublished Doctoral Dissertation, Indiana University.

YOUNG, ROBERT W., AND WILLIAM MORGAN

1980   *The Navajo Language: A Grammar and Colloquial Dictionary*. Albuquerque: University of New Mexico.

■ ■ ■

INDEX

■ ■ ■

ABOUT THE AUTHOR

Paul V. Kroskrity earned an A.B. in comparative literature, oriental studies, and religion in 1971 from Columbia College, Columbia University. He pursued graduate training in anthropology and linguistics at Indiana University, leading to a Ph.D. in anthropology in 1978. Since then he has been a professor of anthropology at the University of California, Los Angeles, and is currently associate professor of anthropology. Dr. Kroskrity has served as the chairperson of American Indian Studies since 1985. His research interests include such topics as language contact, language and identity, verbal art, ethnography of communication, historical linguistics, voice constructions, and linguistic ideology. He has conducted extensive research on these topics in two Native American communities: the Arizona Tewa of First Mesa on the Hopi Reservation in northeastern Arizona and the Western Mono of east central California.